The Corn Woman

World Folklore Series

Heather McNeil, Series Editor

The Corn Woman

Stories and Legends
of the Hispanic Southwest

*(La Mujer del Maíz:
Cuentos y Leyendas del Sudoeste Hispano)*

Retold by Angel Vigil

Translated by
Jennifer Audrey Lowell and Juan Francisco Marín

1994

Libraries Unlimited Inc.
Englewood, Colorado

I dedicate this book to my father and mother.
They gave me my culture and a deep love of family.

Libraries Unlimited, Inc.
P.O. Box 6633
Englewood, CO 80155-6633
1-800-237-6124

Project Editor: Kevin W. Perizzolo
Copy Editor: Connie Hardesty
English Proof Reader: Eileen Bartlett
Spanish Proof Reader: Pat Dubrava Keuning
Interior Book Design and Typesetting: Judy Gay Matthews
Interior Graphic Elements: Al Cardenas

Library of Congress Cataloging-in-Publication Data

Vigil, Angel.
   The corn woman : stories and legends of the Hispanic Southwest : La mujer del maiz : cuentos y leyendas del sudoeste hispano / retold by Angel Vigil ; translated by Jennifer Audrey Lowell and Juan Francisco Marin.
   xxxi, 234 p. 19x26 cm.
   Includes bibliographical references.
   ISBN 1-56308-194-6
   1. Hispanic Americans--Folklore. 2. Indians of North America--Southwest, New--Legends. 3. Southwest, New--Folklore. I. Title.
GR111.H57V54 1994
398.2'089'68079--dc20
                                    94-2091
                                       CIP

Contents

1
In the Beginning: Stories from the Spirit of the Aztecs

2
The Traditional Cuentos

3
Contemporary *Cuentos*

4
Finale

Preface: The Cuento of This Book

Beginning with Memory

My earliest memory is of going to a pond with my Grandpa Martínez at his farm outside Springer, New Mexico. It was a hot, dusty day, and the walk seemed to take forever for my little legs. When we arrived at the pond, we sat down and spent a few minutes talking. Flies buzzed around us. Dust and heat covered us. Suddenly a snake appeared, long, thin, and green with yellowish markings. The snake's red tongue flickered in and out in a menacing rhythm. I remember being very scared. Without a word my grandfather grabbed the snake and held it close to my face. Then I was really scared! My grandfather told me not to be afraid, it was just a harmless water snake.

I remember he then told me a story about a snake, a man, and an amazing power, but I lost the memory of it in the passing of childhood. Years later, when I rediscovered the story, I found it sparked my memory of a day at the pond with my long-dead Grandpa Martínez.

My second-earliest memory is of pigs being slaughtered. Again I was at the Martínez farm. The men of the family were busy cleaning the pigs. To my awe and surprise, one of the men took a pig's stomach and blew it up like a balloon. This singular image stayed in my memory for years. Eventually I recalled the incident as a bit of personal folklore, a story from a distant time that I remembered with fondness, probably not even true.

Other memories from childhood are filled with images of family gatherings. I was raised in a large, traditional Hispanic extended family, with loving grandparents and plenty of aunts, uncles, and cousins. At the farmhouse we children would often gather at the periphery of the adult circle. The adults would talk late into the night, telling stories, exchanging jokes, and sharing memories. The beauty of family life in this time before television was that it often centered around nothing more than people sitting around and passing the time talking to each other for hours.

A few years ago, a cousin sent me a picture he had found in a collection of family photos. The photo showed a group of men at the Martínez farm standing around three butchered pigs that were hanging from a wooden frame. There was Grandpa Martínez in his overalls; my father; my mother's uncle, Tio Joe; cousin Simon; and me. I must have been about five years old. One of the men was holding a butcher knife in his hand. On a bench nearby was a flask.

In my excitement I called my daughters over to tell them about the picture. I pointed out my father and Grandpa Martínez. I also told them about my memory of the pig's stomach being blown up like a balloon, and I told them that this picture was proof of that memory. After explaining the picture to my daughters I then told them about my other earliest memory—my grandfather and the snake by the pond and the story he had told me. I told them how, just like the picture, I had found a story that had confirmed one of my earliest personal memories.

In the months that followed the arrival of this powerful picture, I spent endless hours quizzing my mother and aunts about "the old days," especially the oral traditions I remembered from my childhood as I sat listening to the adults talking.

It was as much fun for them to remember as it was for me to hear. With their memories came stories about *La Llorona, brujas,* the evil eye, and *alabados.* My aunts, in particular, enjoyed having an audience of children when they started talking about their own childhood. My mother made a special point to tell me many stories about *primo* Amarante and in my mind he assumed mythic proportions as the family raconteur. "The first hippie" was how my mother described him. Late into the night my mother and aunts would sit around the kitchen table, laughing and remembering *chistes, dichos,* and *adivinanzas,* always with an apology for the English they used and with a reminder that "it is so much better in Spanish." Always these sessions ended with heartfelt sighs expressing their sadness that the old stories were being lost. My mother often lamented that my own children would never know the richness of the *cuentos* from her own childhood on a farm in northern New Mexico.

For me there was no greater joy than to hear my mother or aunts tell a *cuento* or say a *dicho* that I had found in a folklore text or heard from another person. As I shared my work with them, they would recall some long-forgotten tale. Quite unexpectedly they became a way to confirm stories and legends I was collecting from other sources.

As I was reconnecting with my own oral traditions from my mother's side of the family, an aunt and uncle on my father's side were writing their memories of growing up in Barelas, Albuquerque, New Mexico. I felt overwhelmed by the powerful confluence of generations and felt strongly the importance of the oral tradition in my parents' generation. I began to remember and recognize stories I had heard as a child that had since been displaced by the stories of

Preface: The *Cuento* of This Book

movies and television. I was amazed to discover that my living relatives were sources of folklore. Suddenly I recognized the truth that oral tradition is passed from generation to generation and that the passing depends on close contact between the generations.

I imagined a folklorist of the past interviewing some distant relative of mine. My grandparents were alive when most of the important activity in recording folklore took place, and they lived in the regions of prime interest to folklorists. My grandparents were of the culture that was being recorded, and my parents were the children of that culture.

Unfortunately, my generation may be the first gap in this generations-old flow of oral tradition and heritage. The changes in Hispanic culture in just one generation and the effects these changes have had on family life have ended the rich context of oral traditions within family experiences. Urbanization, the loss of Spanish as a primary language, the decrease of extended family living situations, and of course television—all have contributed to my generation's decreased access to the oral traditions of my parents' generation.

I had a telling experience when I traveled through New Mexico and Colorado collecting stories: In every house I had to ask for the television to be turned down so that I could record without background interference. When I asked if anyone was interested in hearing the old stories, I was frequently told, "No one. The young ones are too busy to be interested." One person told me in a sad but accepting voice, "No one. The only people interested are the white people from the university."

Fortunately I am still connected to the last generation—my parents' generation—that grew up with the Hispanic oral tradition. Part of the *cuento* of my own journey was to reconnect with that earlier wisdom before it was gone forever.

Pieces of the Puzzle

It was from these beginnings that this book eventually took shape. I felt a calling to do what I could to make sure that the rich oral tradition of my childhood would continue through my generation. I continued to spend time with my relatives, collecting stories and family memories from them and remembering the stories I had heard so many times as a child in New Mexico. I received grants and fellowships to support research and field trips to collect stories from *los ancianos,* the old ones. This financial support allowed me to travel throughout southern Colorado and northern New Mexico with my tape recorder, interviewing elderly Hispanic men and women. I researched the collections of Hispanic *cuentos* from the early part of the twentieth century. I cowrote a play based on the *cuentos*; the play successfully toured throughout

Preface: The *Cuento* of This Book

schools in Colorado. More importantly, I continued to tell the stories to any audience willing to have me as a storyteller.

The more I study the *cuentos,* the more I appreciate that they existed within the context of a larger oral tradition made up of many forms and fulfilling many cultural needs for Hispanic families. The stories themselves were used to pass cultural and family memories from one generation to the next. They were also used to provide entertainment or to admonish children about how to live the good and moral life. Accompanying these stories were *dichos,* or proverbs, and *adivinanzas,* or riddles. *Cuentos, dichos,* and *adivinanzas*—stories, proverbs, and riddles—a triumvirate of oral tradition containing the cultural memory and wisdom of my people.

As I collected and studied the *cuentos,* I realized they were part of a large cultural tableau extending from the distant past, through a classic, traditional period, to the immediate future. My understanding of them came to me like pieces of a puzzle; each discovery was a new piece of the puzzle, and I began to see the complete picture of the development of the *cuentos.* I found the first puzzle piece, the connection to the past, in a quite unexpected place: not in Spain but in ancient Mexico.

Growing to adulthood in the 1960s, I was greatly influenced by the work that Chicano artists and political leaders did in developing a philosophy of *Chicanismo,* or Chicano pride. This cultural movement brought to many Hispanics the awareness that the indigenous cultures of Mexico were important strands in the fabric of Hispanic culture. Although members of my own family refer to themselves as Spanish, as do most families in New Mexico, I came to recognize that my family's traditions incorporate the cultural traditions of Mexico as well as Spain. For example, two of the most important Hispanic legends, *La Llorona* and the Virgin of Guadalupe, have their roots in Mexico four centuries ago. In addition, I especially liked the idea that the American Southwest was *Aztlan,* the mythic homeland of the Aztec culture and people.

While performing a storytelling show based upon the Aztec creation myths for the Denver Museum of Natural History's Aztec exhibit, I witnessed people discovering a cultural past that many Hispanics knew little about. Time after time I listened to Hispanic adults, teenagers, and children talk about how revealing it was to learn about the glory of the Aztec indigenous culture. Especially important was the acceptance that Hispanic culture in America was influenced not only by its Spanish roots but also by its indigenous past. The legacy of *my family's cuentos* were only enhanced by the inclusion of the stories of the ancient culture that came from *Aztlan,* the Aztec people's mythic homeland to the north.

I found the second piece of the puzzle in the memories of my family, my own memories, and the collections published by pioneering researchers in the early part of the twentieth century. These memories and collections feature stories from the traditional, or classic period, that is, the period of Spanish colonization of New Mexico and southern Colorado. While many of these stories form a common and shared heritage of this region, passed down for generations within families like my own, their original sources are often Spain and medieval Europe. These traditional stories were the subject of the intensive field collections that took place in the first half of this century. It is usually stories from this category that appear in *cuento* collections.

I found the final piece of my storytelling puzzle, the piece of the immediate future, in my work with other Latino storytellers. Often I had been told that Hispanic storytelling is a dying art because the cultural context of the *cuentos* no longer exists. The rural, agricultural, extended-family society that provided experienced storytellers ample time for storytelling is in decline as children move to cities to find work. And television has forever ended the experience of extended conversation among generations in the home. As soon as the last of *los ancianos* died, I was told, the *cuentos* would be of interest only to academicians and folklorists. The *cuentos* would never again be as vibrant or central to the culture as are the work of Hispanic *santeros, muralistas*, musicians, or visual artists.

Instead I found a small but committed group of Latino storytellers who loved the old *cuentos*, enjoyed telling them, and even created new stories in the tradition of the old *cuentos*. These storytellers enjoy the beauty of literature and the pleasures of storytelling. They appreciate the power and magic of a good story well told. Most of all they are committed to keeping their culture and its traditions alive and growing through artistic expression. The only concession they make to the passage of time and changing realities is that they work primarily in English.

In many ways it seemed to me that these storytellers were working in a living art form, not a dying one. The Latino storytellers of today are living repositories of the stories of the past even as they are doing the work of storytellers of all cultures in all ages. They are taking the stories of the past, internalizing and personalizing them, and creating their own stories for audiences of their own time at schools, museums, festivals, art centers, theaters, and in their own families.

I also found an active Latino visual art community creating art influenced by the *cuentos*. These artists are developing personal artistic styles that contribute to the continuing beauty of Latino culture. They recognize the *cuentos* as an important part of the effort to keep their culture alive. These visual artists are often inspired by the *cuentos*. I have used this art to illustrate the stories in this book to show how the vibrant tradition of the *cuentos* can be joined with another art form to give expression to a culture.

The puzzle of my storytelling search is now complete. From the ancient past of myth and legend to the living traditions of modern storytellers, the *cuentos* have formed a narrative arc of truth and beauty of a people and their continuing culture.

And Here Begins the Story

Because of the variety and scope of experiences I had as I collected, studied, and told the *cuentos* of my culture, this book has a larger scope than most books on the *cuentos*. The introduction is historical. In short summary I have tried to answer the journalistic questions—who, what, why, where, and when—about the development of the *cuentos*. I have also added a short introduction to *dichos* and *adivinanzas* to create the larger context of oral traditions within which the *cuentos* flourished.

The first group of *cuentos* covers the earliest stories. These include the creation myths of the Aztec people and two stories that show the effect of the momentous collision of cultures that occurred when the indigenous culture of Mexico mixed with the emergent Spanish culture in the New World—the legends of the Virgin of Guadalupe and *La Llorona*, the Weeping Woman.

The second and largest group of *cuentos* contains the traditional stories of the Hispanic culture of the American Southwest. These stories represent many well-known tales, and they are the stories that people usually think of when they hear the word *cuentos*. About this section many people have given me advice, usually something like, "How can you even think of writing a book on the *cuentos* and not include . . . !" their suggestion invariably a personal childhood favorite. Included are several stories that appear in other collections of *cuentos*, but because they have become "standards," they could not be left out of any survey of *cuentos*. Also included are many traditional stories that seldom appear in anthologies. I chose these stories because they are my favorites and because my audiences have enjoyed them.

The final group of *cuentos* holds the most promise for the continuing life of the *cuentos*. The stories in this section are original stories told by modern Latino storytellers. This eclectic collection presents the wide range of work by these storytellers.

The versions of the stories presented here are my own. I have told these stories countless times to audiences of all ages. I confess to taking narrative license because my interest is not in the academic preservation of museum pieces but in the breathing of life into a contemporary, evolving, art. I have respected the integrity of the traditional tale but like any good storyteller, I have allowed audiences to influence the telling of the stories. I have found the stories richer as I have incorporated elements based on audience reaction.

I am thankful to all those before me who recognized the beauty and strength of these *cuentos*. Family members, folklorists, and storytellers have contributed to the preservation and continuation of this rich oral tradition. It is due to their efforts in the remembering, collecting, and telling of these stories that I have the living heritage of the *cuentos* to pass on to my children.

But these stories, while they come from the Hispanic culture, are really part of the larger culture of the world. They contain the cultural memory and wisdom of a people. The stories reveal who these people were and what they thought was important in life. The stories express deep respect for the love of family, the joys of childhood, and what it means to lead the good life here on earth. Religious yearnings are contained in stories warning how to prepare for life in the hereafter. And in their deepest sense, the stories preserve the memory of those who passed here before us.

So I give these stories to you with a saying I remember from my own childhood: *Buenos Cuentos, Buenos Amigos,* Good Stories, Good Friends.

Introduction

The *cuentos* developed in a geographic area that includes portions of northern New Mexico and south-central Colorado. Santa Fe, New Mexico, marks the southern edge of the area, and the San Luis Valley in Colorado marks the northern edge. The area is a high plateau that forms a broad, level valley surrounded by mountains—the Sangre de Cristo range on the east and the San Juan and Jemez mountains on the west. Today this rugged, arid landscape is divided by a political boundary, the state line between New Mexico and Colorado. Despite this arbitrary boundary, the area has remained culturally unified for the generations who have lived there, joined by language, religion, and custom.

The Origins and Development
of the *Cuentos*

Any consideration of the *cuentos* must also consider the land in which the people lived and the conditions under which they made a life. For centuries adventurers, artists, and travelers have been drawn to the Southwest because of its endless vistas, its incredible light, and its magical mix of desert, mountains, and sky. They were impressed with the region's romantic, stark beauty, the solitude of the desert landscape, and the strong presence of an *Indio-Hispano* culture.

For the descendants of the first Spanish *conquistadores*, however, the relationship with the land has not been quite so poetically realized. The arid climate made it difficult to sustain agriculture. People had to be wise in the uses of water and land. Families often had to struggle to establish a meager living. The land contributed to the development of a hardy, self-sufficient character.

Geographically isolated, far from centers of political, religious, and cultural life both within Mexico and later the United States, the people sustained their Hispanic way of life for generations. Struggling in a difficult climate and a sparse landscape, the people took strength and support from the comforts of family, church, and the rhythms of daily life. The *cuentos*, in a way unimaginable today, contributed to a sense of place for the people in the region and played a central part in helping them persevere under sometimes difficult conditions.

Historical Context

"In 1492 Columbus sailed the ocean blue." This children's rhyme pinpoints the birth of the traditional Hispanic *cuentos* in the New World. These stories, which date from the Spanish colonial period, began to be circulated when the first Spanish *conquistadores* set foot in the New World. The history of the early *cuentos* is one of centuries of blending the European culture of the *conquistadores* with the indigenous cultures that existed when the *conquistadores* arrived.

When the *conquistadores* landed, long-established cultures flourished in all parts of the New World. Of particular interest is the Aztec culture, the dominant culture of Mexico at the time of Spanish arrival. The Aztecs had a profound oral tradition and a complex story structure representing their cosmology. As the *Indio-Hispano* culture evolved, its members spread throughout the New World, taking their stories with them. As the centuries passed, this *Indio-Hispano* culture would affect *the cuentos* that the Spanish brought to the New World.

In 1539 explorer Francisco Vásquez de Coronado, under orders from the Viceroys of New Spain, entered the northern frontier of New Spain to search for the legendary Seven Cities of Gold. His search was futile, but his explorations established the northern frontiers of New Spain for colonizing expeditions.

In 1598 Don Juan de Oñate established the first permanent colony in New Mexico, along the Upper Rio Grande Valley. The clergy and military soon followed, further colonizing the northern frontier of New Spain. These early settlers founded the first Spanish communities in northern New Mexico and southern Colorado, in the Upper Rio Grande Valley and the San Luis Valley. In 1610 Santa Fe was established as the administrative outpost of this area. Still, these communities were far from the centers of culture, population, and political power of New Spain, which was 1,000 miles to the south across a vast and barren frontier.

Throughout the seventeenth century colonists came into the region, bringing with them the Hispanic cultural elements of Mexican colonial society. The colonists represented the various groups present in Mexico at the time, including Spaniards who had settled in Mexico, children of these Spaniards, *mestizos* of Spanish and Indian parentage, and Indians from various ethnic groups in Mexico.

For generations these communities developed in relative isolation, adhering to a primarily Hispanic way of life. The early settlers brought with them the language, religion, and customs of Spain. They also brought with them the stories of Spain. Joined by common cultural bonds, they forged a strong sense of community. Geographically and politically isolated, they developed a culture that maintained its Spanish roots while adapting to the new land.

In 1848 the treaty of Guadalupe Hidalgo ended the Mexican-American war. The treaty ceded the northern portion of Mexico to the United States. Although the Hispanic communities of the northern Mexican frontier suddenly came under the jurisdiction of the United States government, life in the remote villages remained relatively unchanged. The traditional way of life in these Hispanic communities continued to unfold as it had for generations.

Stanley Robe expresses this idea in his introduction to *Hispanic Folktales from New Mexico*:

> Of all those people who came under the jurisdiction of the United States under the terms of the treaty of Guadalupe Hidalgo of 1848, those who live in the Rio Grande Valley of northern New Mexico have been the most successful in defending their language, oral traditions, and their Hispanic way of life. To a greater extent than other Mexicans who lived in the ceded territories, their cultural roots were deeper. (1977, 1)

Cultural Development

The traditional way of life in these Hispanic communities is most easily imagined by detailing the images that first come to mind as we consider the area. High-walled adobe churches; children playing along village streams, chasing snakes and lizards; black-veiled women on a pilgrimage to the village church; men toiling in the field, tending to crops and sheep; a wedding procession winding through the village, led by musicians playing violin and guitar; the *Entrega de Novios* after the wedding; graves piled high with flowers, mourners paying their last respects; summer rainstorms, flooding dusty roads, creating ankle-deep mud; winter snowstorms isolating homes and travelers; praying church members, lit by votive candles, kneeling before painted wooden statues depicting the passion of Jesus Christ; *santeros* carving the holy statues for the church; the *mayordomo* leading a group of men in the annual cleaning of the *acequia*; the religious brotherhood singing *alabados* during Holy Week services; family members gathering after a successful harvest to celebrate and feast; fathers and sons going up into the mountains to gather wood for the long winter ahead; parents blessing their kneeling children before a long journey; mothers and daughters peeling chilies and cooking tortillas for the evening meal; family groups going into the mountain forests to gather *piñon* nuts; the *curandero* curing the sick with the dirt of the earth, the plants of the mountainside, and the water of the river; the *cuentista*, or storyteller, casting a spell on a willing audience of family members.

These images portray the daily rhythms of a culture steeped in ritual and centered in the land, family, and religion. They suggest a culture with the values and family structure to support a strong oral tradition. Songs, proverbs, riddles, conversation, and stories were part of the daily experience of this pastoral people.

Because of the geographic and cultural isolation of the areas, the elements of traditional storytelling have been carefully preserved. These remote valleys and mountains were the ideal place to preserve the stories almost unchanged well into the twentieth century. Since the early part of the twentieth century, Hispanic folklorists have concentrated on collecting and categorizing the oral narratives of this region. Few cultures have provided folklorists such a large body of narrative for study.

The *cuentos* flourished in this culture because they served an important function for the people. The shared experience of listening to the stories bound family members together. The religious nature of many of the *cuentos* provided ongoing strength to the religious life in communities seldom visited by priests. The stories allowed older generations to pass on their wisdom and values to succeeding generations. They provided a way for people to make sense of their world and to explain the mysterious events that accompany human life.

The storytellers of that distant time were not professional entertainers as so many are today. They were members of the community and would have described themselves as farmers, weavers, shepherds, laborers, fathers, aunts, and uncles. They were family members who, probably because of a gift for narration or a special reputation as a *cuentista,* were called on to tell stories at family gatherings. Often the stories evolved out of common conversation to make a special point or to illustrate some event for children.

Nothing so artificial as a storytelling performance would have occurred to these storytellers. The stories' natural context was family gatherings: weddings, funerals, birthdays, harvests, or just sitting around the fire on a winter evening.

Stories were passed from one generation to the next. Storytellers told the stories they had heard when they were children. Sometimes, they "made up" new stories, and these stories joined the oral tradition. The stories were alive within the context of a family's oral tradition. It is only through the efforts of folklorists of this century that systematic written versions of these oral narratives have become available.

The stories did not exist in a vacuum; they existed within a larger context of oral and musical traditions consisting of songs, *cuentos, dichos,* and *adivinanzas.* The study of Hispanic music and its contribution to the Hispanic way of life in this region is a book in itself. Here it will suffice to say that any family gathering included the playing of a traditional folk tune on violin or guitar, often accompanied by singing or dancing.

Each of these art forms complemented the others to form a rich tradition that helped to sustain the Hispanic way of life for centuries. In many respects the *cuentos* comprised the literary heritage of these Hispanic families. Often the only book in the house was the Bible, and many members of a family were unable to read. The *cuentos* were the literature of the people—stories of the eternal human struggle and its constant affirmation of life.

The Larger Oral Tradition: Proverbs and Riddles

Along with *cuentos*, *dichos* and *adivinanzas*, or proverbs and riddles, were part of a powerful oral tradition in Hispanic communities. In many instances *dichos* and *adivinanzas* worked their way into *cuentos*.

Dichos

Dichos, or proverbs, were part of everyday conversation. Often they served as a final comment. Uttered with finality, many an elder closed a discussion with words of wisdom and experience. The *dichos* reflect a kind of philosophy and proverbial folk wisdom. They were often used to reveal to young people the unseen qualities in another person or to give insight into a particular situation. The proverbs also provided guidelines for moral values and social behavior. *Dichos* existed alongside *cuentos* as part of the Hispanic heritage.

The following examples of the *dichos*, in Spanish followed by English translation, illustrate this rich oral tradition. There are literally hundreds of recorded *dichos*. Many have an idiomatic, untranslatable quality. The best one can do is provide an English proverb with similar meaning.

Un gato viejo, ratón tierno
An old cat, a young mouse.
(He is an old man who likes young girls.)

Andar por las ramas
Walking through the branches.
(He is wasting his time. He is beating around the bush.)

Cada oveja con su pareja
Each sheep with its flock.
(To each his own.)

En boca cerrada, no entra mosca.
Into a closed mouth no fly enters.
(Keep quiet and you will not make trouble for yourself. Keep your own
counsel.)

De tal palo salta la estilla.
From such a log comes the splinter.
(A chip off the old block; like father, like son.)

Dieron calabasas.
They gave squash.
(When a man asks a woman to marry him and she or her family say no,
this *dicho* represents a refusal.)

Un gato llorón no caza ratón.
A crying cat does not hunt a mouse.
(A complaining person gets nothing.)

Entra por aquí y sale por allá.
It comes in here and goes out there.
(In one ear and out the other.)

Las canas no quitan ganas.
Gray hair does not end desires.
(You are as old as you feel.)

No hay rosa sin espinas.
There is no rose without thorns.
(Nothing comes easily.)

Cada oveja con su pareja
Each sheep with his partner.
(Birds of a feather flock together.)

Más vale andar solo que mal acompañado.
It is better to walk alone than with bad companions.

El tiempo causa olvido.
Time causes forgetfulness.
(Out of sight, out of mind.)

Aunque la mona se vista de seda mona se queda.
Although the monkey is seen in silk, it remains a monkey.
(You can't make a silk purse out of a sow's ear.)

Adivinanzas

Adivinanzas were riddles often used to entertain children. They were a common social pastime. In many traditional *cuentos,* the plot revolved around a riddle. Often the hero had to solve a riddle to accomplish a task or goal. As with *dichos,* there are literally hundreds of recorded *adivinanzas.* The following riddles, given in English, are a few examples of this entertaining oral tradition.

Which *santo* (saint) has the most bones? (*El camposanto,* the cemetery) (In Spanish, this riddle is a wonderful play on words.)

What is full of meat by day but full of air by night? (A shoe)

What is black as coal, is in every book, speaks every language? (Ink)

Who is the most fragrant saint? (*Santa Rosa,* Saint Rose)

He who makes it doesn't use it. He who sells it doesn't use it. But he who uses it doesn't see it. What is it? (A coffin)

I am a little box that opens and closes but never wears out. What am I? (Your eye)

I am a little old woman with just one tooth, and I call all my people. What am I? (A bell)

Your mother stutters. Your father is a good singer. You have white clothes and your heart is yellow. What are you? (An egg)

Hard on top. Hard below. Head of a snake. Legs like poles. What are you? (A turtle)

I am a beautiful royal chest, but no carpenter is able to build me. Only God in his great power can build me. What am I? (The soul)

I am in a box full of bones and I am worth more than 100 *pesos*. What am I? (Your teeth)

I am draped in red. I make the strong cry and the eyes flash with lightning. What am I? (Chile)

From morning to night I am as bald as your grandpa. What am I? (An onion)

What has a mouth and is not able to eat? (A river)

I have neither color nor flavor, but you cannot live without me. What am I? (Air)

I am not a bird but I can fly to great heights. I can go many places without walking. What am I? (A thought)

What walks all day and all night but is always in the same place? (A clock)

What burns but is not on fire? (A mouth after eating chile)

Many *adivinanzas* are stated as a poem rather than a question, as in the following examples:

An old man with 12 sons,
Each son with 30 grandsons,
Half white, half black.
(A year, 12 months, days and nights)

A corral all round, cows in the back,
A violent bull, and a solo pastor.
(The earth, the people of the earth, the devil, and God)

This final *adivinanza* contains a riddle about the four basic math functions.

A banker
A thief
A woman
A butcher.
(A banker adds, a thief subtracts, a woman multiplies, a butcher divides)

Types of *Cuentos*

For the *cuentista* telling stories around the fire on a winter evening in Spanish colonial New Mexico, the origins of the *cuentos* were lost in cultural memory. This cultural memory was carried in the rich oral tradition the colonists of New Spain brought with them to the New World. In *The Folklore of Spain in the American Southwest*, Aurelio Espinosa reports that 90 percent of the folk literature of this region can be traced to Spain.

Folklorists have traced the roots of the traditional *cuentos* as far back as the magical tales of the *Thousand and One Arabian Nights* and the fables of medieval Europe. The folktales that the settlers of the northern frontier of New Spain brought with them were of European origin. During the age of colonization, Spanish culture was influenced by the Greek, Roman, Arab, and Jewish people who had lived on the Iberian peninsula. Oriental and Indian folktales also existed in the Spanish oral tradition. The Spanish culture of the *conquistadores* blended these diverse influences with the powerful influence of the Catholic church. The prominence of religion during the time of the Inquisition was central to the Iberian culture in which Spanish *cuentos* developed.

Juan B. Real, in the introduction to his two-volume collection *Cuentos Españoles Colorado y Nuevo Méjico*, describes similarities among the *cuentos* that he collected and the fabliaux of medieval French literature as well as Boccaccio and Marguerite de Navarre.

Although most *cuentos* are of European origin, some traditional *cuentos* reflect the *conquistadores'* and colonists' encounters with the native cultures of the New World, which had their own myths and legends. The story of *La Llorona*, the Weeping Woman, is one example of this cultural cross-fertilization. This story is perhaps the most common and best-known legend in southwestern Hispanic culture. The origins of the story, while contested and lost in antiquity, can be traced to Aztec legends.

Many folklorists consider the Hispanic tales of this region to be the richest store of folktales in the United States. In the introduction to *Hispanic Folktales from New Mexico*, Stanley Robe describes the significance of the *cuentos*:

> Folklorists have long been aware of the wealth of oral narratives that is available among the New Mexican Hispanic population. They have cultivated carefully the northern section of the Rio Grande Valley and the adjacent San Luis Valley of southern Colorado. . . . It is doubtful that any comparable area in the United States has contributed as many narrative texts for study. (1977, 5)

More than 800 texts of these tales have been collected and published in Spanish. Much work has been done by folklorists to categorize the stories according to the conventions of academic research and tale type classification. In an overview like this, it is impossible to fully represent all the types of Hispanic folktales. However, the major types of *cuentos* are similar to the major types of all common folktales: stories of magic, transformation stories, animal stories, moral tales, tales containing riddles, stories about death, religious tales, picturesque tales, and tales of enchantment. In substance the stories cover the long human journey from birth to death.

Cuentos in This Book

In this book, the traditional stories have been gathered by theme:

- Moral and religious stories have God, the devil, or death as major characters. The human characters encounter the religious figures and must make choices that affect their lives. Each story contains a moral, which may be obvious or subtle. These stories reflect the strong influence of the Catholic church and its teachings.

- *Los dos compadres* stories contrast opposite character types for dramatic effect and moral teaching.

- *Chistes* are short, anecdotal tales, usually with a comic twist at the end. Over time the *cuentos* tradition has changed from favoring long, fully detailed stories to favoring shorter stories, mainly legends and *chistes*.

- Tales of transformation, magic, and wisdom share the motif of the fantastic event, the "once upon a time" fairy tale, or the journey to gain wisdom. In traditional folktale categorization, many of these stories are considered "ordinary folktales." This type of story is what people usually consider folktales—fairy tales of witches, ghosts, royalty, devils, giants, dwarfs, magic, and enchanted objects.

- Animal stories feature animals as primary characters. Often appearing to be children's stories, these stories frequently reflect profound values concerning morality.

Legend Versus Folktale

Scholars and folklorists use various definitions to describe the difference between legends and folktales. One of the simplest is that legends are stories about things that actually happened and folktales are stories about things that did not actually happen.

The Hispanic oral tradition of legends is as rich and full as that of folktales. In many instances the line between legend and folktale is blurred, depending on the beliefs of the storyteller and his or her community. The clearest example of this is the story of *La Llorona*. While it exists as a folktale in its own right, there are innumerable accounts of actual appearances of the legendary Weeping Woman in communities throughout the Southwest.

The wonder of these folktales is that, while they developed under very specific historical, geographic, and cultural circumstances, they are universal in appeal and content. Stith Thompson, one of the foremost scholars of folktales, confirms this. In *The Folktale*, he discusses the fact that stories of all cultures contain similar elements.

> The limitations of human life and the similarity of its basic situations necessarily produce tales everywhere that are much alike in all important structural respects. Stories may differ in subject from place to place, the conditions and purposes of taletelling may change as we move from land to land or from century to century, and yet everywhere it ministers to the same basic social and individual needs. (1946, 5, 7)

Most important to understanding the *cuentos* is the realization that they are as diverse as the human spirit itself. They contain the roots of many world cultures, and they are as significant as the folktales of all world cultures. For centuries they served the Hispanic culture as it evolved according to the needs of a strong people. They are as old as the human impulse for storytelling. Their power comes from the fact that they existed at the center of traditional family life for generations and they continue to attract and fascinate through our own modern age.

Acknowledgments

In writing this book I came to appreciate how much a writer needs the help of others to realize his or her literary vision. The *cuento* of this book is a long one filled with acts of kindness and generosity.

I wish to thank my editor, Suzanne Barchers, for giving me the opportunity to write this book.

I want to recognize the storytellers and visual artists who so willingly shared their great artistry to enhance the beauty of this book. Storytellers Geraldina Lawson, Abelardo Delgado, George Rivera, and Pat Mendoza each provided original stories. Visual artists Arlette Lucero, Stevon Lucero, Carlota Espinoza, Meggan DeAnza Rodriquez, Carlos Santistevan, Tony Ortega, Carlos Martinez, Al Cardenas, and Daniel Luna provided the wonderul artwork for the book. I am deeply indebted to all these generous artists.

I want to thank two friends, Anne Strobridge and Suzanne Kolsun-Jackson, for their critical reading of the manuscript.

I also want to thank Geraldina Lawson for sharing her great love of *cuentos* with me.

Special thanks go to Jennifer Audrey Lowell and Juan Francisco Marín for their wonderful translations.

And most of all I want to thank my wife, Sheila, for her constant support and encouragement.

Map

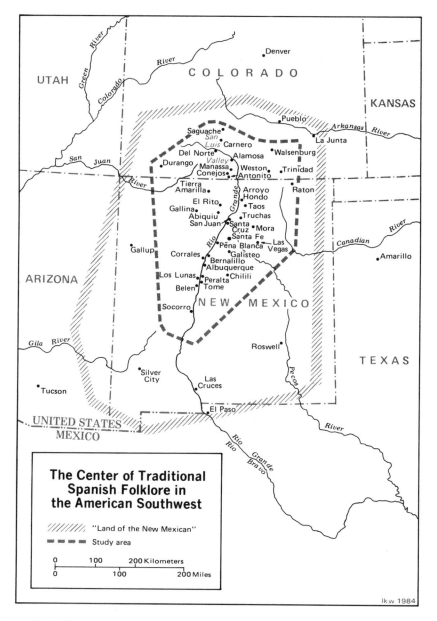

UTAH

COLORADO

•Denver

KANSAS

Green River

Colorado River

•Pueblo

Arkansas River

•La Junta

San Juan

Saguache•

San Luis Carnero

•Walsenburg

Del Norte•

Alamosa•

•Durango

Manassa•

Weston•

•Trinidad

Valley Conejos•

Antonito•

Tierra Amarilla•

Arroyo Hondo

•Raton

El Rito•

•Taos

Gallina•

Truchas•

Abiquiu•

Santa Cruz•

San Juan•

•Mora

Santa Fe•

Canadian River

Peña Blanca•

Las Vegas•

•Gallup

Corrales•

•Galisteo

Bernalillo•

•Amarillo

Albuquerque•

•Chilili

Los Lunas•

Peralta•

Belen•

Tome•

Socorro•

NEW MEXICO

•Roswell

TEXAS

Gila River

Pecos

•Silver City

Las Cruces•

•Tucson

UNITED STATES
MEXICO

•El Paso

River

Rio Grande / Rio Bravo

The Center of Traditional Spanish Folklore in the American Southwest

////// "Land of the New Mexican"

▬ ▬ ▬ Study area

| 0 | 100 | 200 Kilometers |
| 0 | 100 | 200 Miles |

lkw 1984

From *The Folklore of Spain in the American Southwest: Traditional Spanish Folk Literature in Northern New Mexico and Southern Colorado* by Aurelio M. Espinosa. Copyright © 1985 by the University of Oklahoma Press.

1

In the Beginning: Stories from the Spirit of the Aztecs

The Aztec Creation Legend

THE FIVE SUNS

According to Aztec cosmology the earth has had five incarnations. (See fig. 7.) The Aztecs marked each of these incarnations with the creation of the sun. In the Aztec creation legend, which describes the events that determined their great and tragic fate, the earth is destroyed four times before the present and final age of the sun. The creation story explains several natural phenomena as well as the origins of many aspects of Aztec life. But the creation legend goes beyond the usual "How It Came to Be" and "Why It Is So" features of most creation legends. The Aztec creation legend is especially powerful because it places the Aztecs at the center of a complex cosmos; the Aztecs are a chosen people called on to give life to the sun.

As a result of their special status, the Aztec people led a life proscribed by religious ritual, that is, all aspects of life were governed by the requirements of their position as the chosen people of the sun. Their relationship to their gods was unusual in that all their gods depended upon them for sustenance. According to the Aztecs' cosmic vision, they and their gods relied on each other for continued life.

This creation legend has a critical corollary legend about the god Quetzalcoatl. Quetzalcoatl was described as a fair-skinned god with a beard. Some time after the fifth creation, Quetzalcoatl and Tezcatlipoca, his brother and the Supreme Deity of the Aztec people, were battling for supremacy. Tezcatlipoca tricked Quetzalcoatl into committing a vile act against the morals of his people. Because of his act, the people banished Quetzalcoatl. Quetzalcoatl left in a ship traveling to the East. He prophesied to his people that one day he would return to reclaim his divine right. It was foretold by the Aztec people that Quetzalcoatl would return to them in the year One Reed. (See figs. 1 and 2.)

It was in 1519 when the Aztec emperor Moctezuma received reports of a bearded, fair-skinned person coming from the East. According to the Aztec calendar, it was the year One Reed, and the Aztecs believed that Cortez was the god Quetzalcoatl returning as had been prophesied. This belief, rooted in legend, was a significant contributing factor to the Spanish conquest of the Aztecs.

Thus the legend of Quetzalcoatl contributed to the beginning of the Hispanic era in the New World. Just as the Spaniards brought stories and legends from Europe, the indigenous people had their own powerful stories. Like Tezcatlipoca and Quetzalcoatl, the Spaniards and Aztecs fought a great battle for supremacy. History records the victory of the Spanish over the Aztecs. And with that victory was laid the foundation for the eventual supremacy of the oral traditions of the Spanish in this part of the New World.

THE FIVE SUNS

In the beginning, time and space were created at the same instant. During this time of creation, The Ometeotl, or The Creator Pair, or The Lord and Lady of Duality, gave birth to two gods, Tezcatlipoca and Quetzalcoatl.

The first god born of the Creator Pair was Tezcatlipoca. He was the supreme divinity of the Aztec people. He was called Smoking Mirror, god of darkness and light. This dark god of the night was the god of fate, both beneficial and destructive. The Aztec emperors prayed to Tezcatlipoca to bless their reign.

The second god born of the Creator Pair was Quetzalcoatl, the Plumed Serpent. This wise and benevolent god was the creator god, the god of civilization and learning.

The eternal struggle between these two gods, Tezcatlipoca and Quetzalcoatl, for ascendancy is the history of the Aztec people. According to Aztec cosmology, the competition of these two gods for the honor of bearing the sun caused the destruction of the heavens and earth four times. Each time their battle destroyed the earth. But after each battle the earth was created anew. Our present time is the time of the fifth sun.

In the time of the first sun, the earth was ruled by giants who lived on acorns and roots. It was a time of power for Tezcatlipoca. He declared that it was his right to lead the sun through the sky on its daily journey of lighting the heavens above and the earth below. Each day with great pride he would harness the sun and lead it on its fiery path to the end of the day.

Quetzalcoatl felt that it was not right for Tezcatlipoca to have the glory of carrying the sun. He knew that he was the god destined for that honor. One day he followed Tezcatlipoca into the sky and struck him with one mighty blow, knocking Tezcatlipoca from the sky.

As Tezcatlipoca fell, in his anguish he turned into a jaguar. As he landed in the form of a jaguar, he devoured all living things on the earth, and the earth was covered in darkness. In this way the time of the first sun came to an end with the destruction of the earth. The Aztecs marked this day of destruction with the name 4 Jaguar.

Now it was Quetzalcoatl's turn to carry the sun on its daily journey. As the plumed serpent he proudly brought light to the dark earth. The earth was created anew, and it was the time of the second sun. During this time the earth was ruled by monkeys who lived on pine nuts.

From his fallen state Tezcatlipoca could see Quetzalcoatl in his glory as the carrier of the sun. Now it was Tezcatlipoca's turn to destroy the earth. He rose into the sky and delivered a fierce blow to Quetzalcoatl. Quetzalcoatl fell to the earth with such force that a great windstorm destroyed all living creatures. For the second time the age of the sun had ended with the destruction of the earth. The Aztecs called this day 4 Wind.

By this time the gods had grown weary of the battle between Tezcatlipoca and Quetzalcoatl. They decided to give another god the honor of carrying the sun. They selected Tlaloc, the god of rain.

As Tlaloc began his fiery journey with the sun high upon his back, both Tezcatlipoca and Quetzalcoatl plotted against him. They attacked Tlaloc and Tlaloc fell, causing a celestial rain of fire that scorched the earth. Once again the earth and its sun were destroyed. The Aztecs marked the end of this third age of the sun with the day 4 Rain.

Now the gods were even more angered by the actions of the two battling brothers, Tezcatlipoca and Quetzalcoatl. Once more the gods selected another to carry the sun. This time they selected the sister of Tlaloc. She was Chalchiuhtlicue, the goddess of corn.

In their great jealousy that any other god should carry the sun, Tezcatlipoca and Quetzalcoatl once again struck down the appointed carrier. As Chalchiuhtlicue fell to the earth, the sky opened up with heavenly waters. A great flood covered the earth, and for a fourth time the earth and all living creatures on it were destroyed. The Aztecs called this day 4 Water.

It is the time between the fourth and fifth sun that was most important to the Aztec people. For it was during this time that their world, our world, was created.

During this time of darkness between the fourth and fifth suns, the world was flooded and there was not a living creature on the earth. The sky had fallen onto the earth, and there was no heaven above. Tezcatlipoca and Quetzalcoatl looked down on the earth and knew that battle must come to an end if there was to be another sun. Both descended to the earth and went to the two ends of the fallen sky. They stood firm and using their godly powers, they became towering trees growing forever. They lifted the sky back into the heavens. When the sky was back in its place, they walked across the sky and met at the center to gaze on the world below.

To this day the celestial path they walked is marked by a trail of stars. On a clear night you can see the long white trail that marks their footsteps. The people of our time call this path the Milky Way.

Next Tezcatlipoca and Quetzalcoatl descended into the depths of the floodwaters and found a crocodilian creature, Cipactli. They raised her to the surface of the water. Transforming themselves into snakes, they wrapped themselves around her and tore her asunder.

The gods were angered by this cruel act. They decided that they would take the remains of Cipactli and create a new earth. The gods took half the remains to create a new sky above. They then used the other half to create a new earth below. They took her hair and made forests, trees, and herbs. They made pools and springs from her eyes. From her mouth they made flow the waters that sustain life on our earth. Her shoulders became mountains, and her nose became valleys. Finally they used her skin to make the grass and the small flowers of the valleys.

Now there was once again earth and sky. But there were still no people on the earth. Quetzalcoatl decided that he would bring living people back to the earth. To do this he descended into the land of the dead. There he met the Lord God of the Dead and the Underworld, Mictlantecuhtli. He asked the Lord God of the Dead if he could have the bones of all the people who had lived on the earth in the previous four suns. (See figs. 4 and 5.)

Before he answered, Mictlantecuhtli, the Lord God of the Dead, gave Quetzalcoatl a challenge. He gave Quetzalcoatl a solid wooden horn and insisted that he play music on it. Immediately Quetzalcoatl called upon the worms from the land of the dead to help him. The worms burrowed inside the solid wood and ate it until it was as hollow as a flute. Quetzalcoatl played a haunting melody on the wooden flute, and the Lord God of the Dead knew that Quetzalcoatl had outsmarted him.

Finally the Lord God of the Dead said that Quetzalcoatl could take the bones of the dead on one condition: When the people made from those bones died, they must return to the land of the dead. Quetzalcoatl agreed to this condition, but in his heart he knew that he was lying to the Lord God of the Dead. Quetzalcoatl wanted his people to live forever and never return to the land of the dead.

As Quetzalcoatl was leaving with the bones, the Lord God of the Dead realized that Quetzalcoatl was lying and sent the quail birds to capture him before he escaped with the bones. As he was running Quetzalcoatl tripped and fell, breaking all the bones he was carrying. As he collected them he noticed that the broken pieces were all different sizes. We are made from these bones, and that is why to this day the people of this earth are of all different sizes.

The quail birds caught up with Quetzal-coatl and began to peck at the broken bones. As the birds pecked the bones became weaker and weaker. It is because of the damage the quail birds did to the bones that the people who came from the bones are too weak to live forever. In this way the request of the Lord God of the Dead holds true. One day we must all return to the land of the dead.

The Aztec Creation Legend

Quetzalcoatl took the bones to the gods. They put the bones into a sacred vessel and ground them into a fine powder. They then sliced their skin and shed their blood into the vessel. In four days the first man emerged from the vessel, and in four more days the first woman emerged. The people of the earth had been created once more. The gods declared that because they had shed their blood to create the people of the earth, the people of the earth must shed their blood to give life to the gods.

As he returned from the heavens, Quetzalcoatl noticed an ant going into a mountain called the Hill of Sustenance. Quickly changing himself into an ant, he followed it into the mountain. Once inside he saw that the mountain was filled with maize—a full, rich, yellow corn. Quetzalcoatl used his powers to cause lightning to split open the Hill of Sustenance. As the hill opened up, the corn spilled out onto the land. Quetzalcoatl stole a piece of the corn and brought it to the people of the earth. The people ate the corn and realized that it was food from the gods and that it would sustain life for them. That is why to this day corn is the staple of life for the descendants of the Aztec people.

First sky, then earth. Now people and food. The earth was created for the fifth time. But still it was a time of darkness because the sun did not rise in the sky.

The gods gathered to find a god who would sacrifice himself to give life to the sun. All of the gods were willing, but when the sacrificial fire was built, no god was brave enough to fling himself into the fire. Finally two gods said that they would sacrifice themselves to give life to the sun. One was a rich and proud god. The other was a poor, humble god named Nanahuatzin.

The two gods prayed for four days and four nights. At the end of the time of prayer, the rich and proud god approached the fire. When he felt its great heat, his courage faltered and he stepped back from the flames. At the end of his time of prayer, Nanahuatzin approached the flames, and in one brave and bold moment, he leapt into the fire. Immediately the flames roared up and he was transformed into the sun. By his noble sacrifice life came to the sun.

In the excitement of the fierce fire, the jaguar jumped into the flames. The fire was too hot for the jaguar, and as he came out of the fire, he was covered with spots of ash. To this day the jaguar is covered with black spots as a reminder to the world of his courage in jumping into the fire.

The moon, seeing that the sun was coming alive, tried to rise before the sun. To punish this audacity the gods took a rabbit and slapped the moon in the face. That is why to this day, as you look at the full moon, you can see the mark of a rabbit on its face. (See fig. 6.)

Finally the sun, which was reborn by the sacrifice of Nanahuatzin, was ready to rise again. The gods declared that because the sun was born out of sacrifice, it would be necessary for the people of the sun to continue to provide sacrifices in order to give life to the sun on its daily journey across the sky.

But there was no one to carry the sun into the sky. The gods selected one of the strongest of all the gods, Huitzilopochtli, for the important job of carrying the sun into the sky to mark the beginning of the age of the fifth sun.

Huitzilopochtli, the Aztec god of war, had been born in a fierce battle. His mother, Coatlique, had given birth to 400 sons and 1 daughter before him. The sons became the first stars, and the daughter, who was called Coyolxauhqui, became the moon.

After giving birth to these celestial children, Coatlique had retired to the temple for a life of chastity, work, and prayer. One day as she was cleaning the temple, she noticed a bundle of down feathers falling from the sky. She gathered the down feathers and placed them under her smock. Later, when she looked for the bundle of down, she discovered that it was gone but that she was pregnant.

The 400 sons and the daughter were incensed that their mother was once again pregnant. They plotted to kill the unborn child. As they approached their unsuspecting mother, the unborn child, Huitzilopochtli, was suddenly born fully armed for battle. He killed the 400 sons and dismembered the daughter. For this fearless and bold act of vengeance the Aztecs made Huitzilopochtli their god of war.

The gods then selected the warrior god Huitzilopochtli to do daily battle against the forces of darkness. Each day Huitzilopochtli carries the sun on his back as it vanquishes the darkness of the night. As he did in his epic battle of birth, each day he sends the stars and the moon back to the darkness and lets the sun rule supreme. The light of the sun had finally returned to a new earth and its people. (See fig. 3.)

The Aztec people placed this eternal, daily battle between the forces of light and the forces of darkness at the center of Aztec cosmology. The Aztecs' sacred and chosen calling was to provide the precious nectar that gave daily life to the sun in its battle against the forces of darkness.

The earth had finally been created for a fifth time. The earth from Cipactli. The people from the bones from the land of the dead. Food, sacred maize, from the Hill of Sustenance. And the sun itself from noble sacrifice.

It was the age of the fifth sun. Our own age. The final age of the Aztec people.

Stories from the Merging of Two Cultures

THE WEEPING WOMAN (LA LLORONA)

The story of *La Llorona* is the best-known of all Hispanic folktales. She has often been called "The Mexican Medea." (See fig. 9.)

The origins of *La Llorona* have been traced to the time of the Aztecs, who had stories about Cihuacoatl, a pre-Columbian goddess who ruled childbirth and death. This powerful goddess, also known as Snake Skirt, was the virgin mother of a god or son who killed his own siblings. The Aztecs told of hearing each night the screams of Cihuacoatl as her children were being killed.

Another possible origin of *La Llorona* is the story of *La Malinche,* the Aztec woman who was Cortez's mistress and interpreter. In this story Cortez wanted to keep their son because the son had Spanish blood, but he abandoned *La Malinche* because she was only a mistress and an Indian. In despair she killed the son and, as the spirit left his body, she cried out, "Ay, mi hijo." (Alas, my son.)

The *La Llorona* story appears in many forms, and villages throughout the Spanish-speaking world claim the *La Llorona* legend as their own. This story has been elevated to the category of legend because of personal narratives that describe actual encounters with *La Llorona*. Reported encounters with *La Llorona* range from being chased by her on a dark country road to actually being captured by her and barely escaping with one's life.

There are many versions of the *La Llorona* story. The story changes according to the storyteller and the folklore of the region. In some versions the children die accidentally. In others she has many illegitimate children whom she kills, and her divine punishment is to look throughout the world for children to replace her own. In others she loses the children instead of killing them. The version told here is the one most often told in the Southwest.

The legend of *La Llorona* was often used to frighten children into proper behavior. For generations parents have admonished their children to correct their ways or *"La Llorona* will get you!"

THE WEEPING WOMAN (LA LLORONA)

Once in a poor Indian village there lived a young woman. Hers was the greatest beauty of all the maidens in the village, and all the young men of the village asked for her hand in marriage. But she was a very proud young woman, and no man in the village was to her liking. She told all of them no, and she remained firm in her resolve to wait for the right man to marry.

One day a Spanish soldier, an officer, came to the village. He was the commander of a group of soldiers sent from Mexico City to assist the settlers in that region. As he rode into the village, sitting high upon his shiny, black horse, he appeared like a god to the people. He was a man of the world and easily commanded the respect of all the people in the village. To the young women in the village, he was the handsomest and most noble man they had ever seen.

The Spanish officer was immediately drawn to the young Indian woman. Her beauty and proud manners intrigued him. He made it clear to all the maidens in the village that she was the one for him. He courted her, and over time, the Indian maiden and the Spanish soldier fell in love. They were soon blessed with two children. The children were the most precious thing in the world to the Indian woman.

The soldier often was away for long periods. While he was away his children would long for his return. Their mother would reassure them, saying their father was away doing important work for the people of their village and he would soon return to them. He would always return with stories of his great adventures.

One day, after an especially long journey, he returned to the village in a carriage. In the carriage beside him was a Spanish *señorita,* a young Spanish woman. His Indian wife ran up to the carriage and asked who was the woman by his side. The Spanish soldier said she was the woman he was soon to marry.

The Indian woman asked how he could marry another when he was already married to her. The Spanish soldier said that a marriage between an Indian woman and a Spanish soldier was not a true marriage. When the Indian woman asked how he could do this to his children, he told her that they were illegitimate and that no child of an Indian woman could ever be the heir of a Spanish gentleman.

The Indian woman was overcome with anger and grief. She thought of the cruelest way that she could get back at the Spanish soldier. In a moment of rage and madness, she took the two children of the Spanish soldier and blindly hurled them into the river.

As soon as she had thrown them into the river, she realized her terrible mistake. She jumped into the river and tried to save them, but it was too late. Both children had drowned in the river.

Overwhelmed with sadness she began to cry and wail for her two lost children. For days and nights she walked along the banks of the river, crying for her children to return to her. Her mournful and anguished wailing could be heard throughout the village. The people of the village took their own children into their houses when they heard the cries of *La Llorona,* the crying woman, because they feared that she would take their children to replace her two tragically drowned children. (See fig. 8.)

For all eternity she is doomed to walk by the banks of the river, searching for her children. On many a cold and dark night you can hear her crying and calling for her children. Her long, loud, mourning cry of grief often comes disguised as the sound of the wind by the river.

So all of you children who hear this story, take care. Mind your parents and be good boys and girls. Because if you are not careful, *La Llorona,* the weeping woman, will take you to replace her two beloved, lost children.

Stories from the Merging of Two Cultures

LA LLORONA (THE WEEPING WOMAN)

Hace mucho tiempo en un pobre pueblo indio vivía una joven. Su belleza era la más grande de todas las doncellas del pueblo, y todos los jovenes pedían su mano para casarse con ella. Pero ella era muy orgullosa y no le gustaba ningún hombre en todo el pueblo. Les dijo a todos que no se casaría, y permaneció firme en su decisión de esperar al hombre ideal para casarse.

Un día un soldado español, un oficial, llegó al pueblo. Era el comandante de un grupo de soldados enviados desde la ciudad de Méjico para ayudar a los colonos de la región. Cuando entró en el pueblo, montado a lomos de su lustroso caballo negro, pareció a la gente como un dios. Era un hombre de mundo y consiguió fácilmente el respeto de todos los del pueblo. Para las mujeres jovenes, era el hombre más guapo e ilustre que jamás habían visto.

El oficial español se fijó inmediatamente en la joven india. Su belleza y sus maneras orgullosas le intrigaron. El hizo saber a todas las doncellas del pueblo que ella era la que él quería. La cortejó, y con el tiempo, la doncella india y el soldado español se enamoraron. Pronto fueron bendecidos con dos hijos. Estos eran lo más precioso del mundo para la india.

A menudo el soldado estaba ausente largas temporadas. Cuando estaba lejos sus hijos añoraban su retorno. La madre los consolaba diciendo que su padre estaba haciendo un trabajo importante para la gente de su pueblo y que pronto volvería a ellos. El siempre volvía con historias de sus grandes aventuras.

Un día, después de un viaje especialmente largo, volvió al pueblo en un carruaje. Dentro del carruaje, a su lado, venía una señorita española. La esposa india corrió hacia el carruaje y preguntó quién era la mujer sentada a su lado. El soldado español le dijo que era la mujer con quien pronto se iba a casar.

La mujer india preguntó cómo podía casarse con otra cuando ya estaba casado con ella. El soldado dijo que un matrimonio entre una mujer india y un soldado español no era un matrimonio verdadero. Cuando la india preguntó cómo podía hacer esto a sus hijos, él le contestó que eran hijos ilegítimos y que ningún hijo de mujer india podría nunca ser heredero de un caballero español.

La india estaba vencida por la rabia y la pena. Pensó en la manera más cruel de vengarse del soldado español. En un momento de ira y locura cogió a los dos hijos del soldado y ciegamente los arrojó al río.

En cuanto los arrojó se dió cuenta de su terrible error. Se lanzó al río e intentó salvarlos, pero ya era demasiado tarde. Ambos hijos se habían ahogado.

Abrumada por la tristeza empezó a llorar y a lamentarse por sus dos hijos desaparecidos. Durante días y noches anduvo por las orillas del río, llorando y llamándolos. Su llanto penoso y angustiado se escuchaba por todo el pueblo. La gente del pueblo recogía a sus hijos en sus casas cuando escuchaba a La Llorona, porque temía que ella se los llevara para sustituir a sus dos hijos trágicamente ahogados.

Por toda la eternidad está condenada a andar por las orillas del río buscando a sus hijos. En muchas noches oscuras y frías se puede escuchar su llanto y su voz llamándolos. Su largo y fuerte llanto de pena a menudo viene disfrazado como el sonido del viento por el río.

Así que todos los niños que escuchen este cuento, que tengan cuidado. Que obedezcan a sus padres y sean buenos niños y niñas. Porque si así no lo hacen, La Llorona se los llevará para sustituir a sus dos queridos y perdidos hijitos.

OUR LADY OF GUADALUPE
(NUESTRA SEÑORA DE GUADALUPE)

The clearest example of the merging of Aztec Indian and Hispanic heritage is the story of the apparition of the Virgin of Guadalupe. The Virgin of Guadalupe is a religious figure well known throughout Mexico and the southwestern United States. She is the patron saint of Mexico. (See fig. 10.)

After the conquest of the Aztecs by Cortez in 1521, Mexico was making the transition from an Aztec society to a Hispanic culture. The Spanish missionaries were charged with converting the Aztec Indians from their religion to Catholicism. The legend of the Virgin of Guadalupe is an example of how Catholic beliefs were combined with the sites and ceremonies of the indigenous culture to facilitate the Aztecs' conversion to Catholicism. The legend of the Virgin quickly became very powerful in Mexico and spread throughout the territory of New Spain. Today the legend is a Hispanic truth representing the possibility of apparitions and miracles for true believers of the Catholic faith.

The story of the Virgin of Guadalupe takes place on a hill named Tepeyac. The hill of Tepeyac was the site of the shrine of an Aztec goddess, Tonantzin, the protector of earth and corn. Before the conquest by Cortez, the Aztecs had come to the shrine of Tonantzin to pray and seek cures. After the Spaniards built a shrine to the Virgin on the same spot, the Aztecs continued to come to the site as they had before the conquest. The Spanish eased the Indians' religious transition to the Virgin by

creating paintings in which the Virgin looked like an Aztec princess and by saying she spoke Nahuatl, the Aztec language. Through this legend the Spanish missionaries were successful in fusing the Aztec goddess with the Christian Virgin Mary.

Through the following centuries the legend of the Virgin of Guadalupe was widely dispersed and believed among all levels of Hispanic culture. Today the image of the Virgin, surrounded by a wreath of roses and enveloped by the sun's rays, is a powerful icon in Hispanic culture.

OUR LADY OF GUADALUPE
(NUESTRA SEÑORA DE GUADALUPE)

On one cold winter morning in December 1531, a poor Indian man named Juan Diego was walking to church. It had been 10 years since the mighty battles with the men of Cortez had ended. The soldiers and warriors had put down their weapons, and peace had returned to his land. Juan himself had recently converted to Christianity. It was his habit to go to the church for religious instruction.

His church was not in his village but in Tlatelolco, a village just outside Mexico City. His usual path took him by the houses in the village, but this morning for some reason he decided to walk over the hill of Tepeyac.

As he neared the top of the hill, he heard voices singing. Now, he had heard the voices of people singing the holy praises to the Lord in church, but he had never heard such beautiful music as this in all his life. He heard the tinkling of bells, and the voices moved around him like the wind itself. He thought that this must be what the voices of heavenly angels sound like.

As he reached the top of the hill, the beautiful singing voices and music stopped. Everything became very still, and Juan no longer even felt the cold. He heard his name being called, "Juan, Juan."

Suddenly he saw a bright cloud with the shafts of a colorful rainbow coming out of it. The cloud came to a stop before him, and when the cloud split in two, there was a woman standing there. The woman looked like a beautiful Aztec princess. Her clothes shone like the sun, and she was surrounded by the heavenly light. When she spoke Juan heard the heavenly music he had heard before. He knew it was a miracle, so he fell to his knees to pray.

"Juan," the heavenly woman said, "I have chosen you to deliver a message to the bishop at the cathedral."

"But beautiful woman," answered Juan, "I am a poor Indian. I am not worthy to deliver a message to the bishop. Why have I been chosen?"

With soothing kindness the woman answered, "I am the Blessed Virgin Mary, the mother of the Lord Jesus Christ. Just know that I have chosen you to be my messenger on this earth. Go to the bishop and tell him that he is to build a church for me here on the top of this hill. The church is to be a shrine that will show my love for all my people. Go, give the bishop my message."

Juan ran faster than he ever had to the cathedral to give the Virgin's message to the bishop. When he arrived at the cathedral, he knocked on the door to the bishop's quarters. The bishop's helpers opened the door and asked Juan what he wanted. He told them, "I have a message for the bishop from the Virgin Mary, the Mother of God."

The bishop's helpers could not help but laugh to hear a poor Indian tell such a story. But Juan was persistent, and eventually they let him in to see the bishop. The bishop listened to Juan's story but did not believe him. He told him, "Juan, your story is incredible. Imagine the Virgin appearing to you on a hill with a message for me to build a church! Go for now, and I will think about it."

Juan left feeling like a failure. He knew the bishop's helpers had laughed at him and that the bishop had not believed his story. He felt that he had let the Blessed Virgin down. When he returned to Tepeyac he once again saw the Virgin. She floated on air, as if nothing were holding her up except her heavenly powers.

"O Holy Mother. I have failed you. The bishop did not believe me. I knew I was not worthy."

"Juan, do you not know that you are within my graces? I have chosen you, and I will make this happen as it should. Go back to the bishop and give him my message again. A church must be built on this hill in my name."

Juan returned to the bishop a second time. Again the bishop did not believe Juan. He said, "Juan, if you have truly seen the Blessed Virgin Mary, bring me a sign that the miracle is real. If not, then never come to me with this story again."

On his way back to tell the Virgin that he needed a sign, Juan received the news that his uncle was dying of typhoid fever. Juan rushed to his uncle's side, but when he arrived it was almost too late. His uncle asked him to bring the priest because he knew he would not live another day.

Juan rushed to the Virgin to tell her what the bishop had said and to ask forgiveness for not coming right back to her. "Oh, Blessed Virgin, I was late because my uncle is dying and is not expected to last another day. Also, the bishop requires a sign that my vision of you is a real miracle. Please help me, Blessed Mother."

"Juan, do you not know that I am here to help you? I have already cured your uncle. He will live. Now go to the top of the hill, where only the cactus grows. There you will find a rosebush in bloom. Take those roses to the bishop and he will believe."

Juan went to the top of the hill, and there was a beautiful rosebush in full bloom. When Juan saw the roses blooming on that cold winter day, he knew that this was the miracle he had asked for, and he kneeled down to pray. Juan knew that when the bishop saw the roses that had bloomed in the middle of winter and smelled their beautiful fragrance, he would believe the miracle. Juan gathered the roses in his *tilma*, which is a kind of poncho. He showed the roses to the Virgin, and she said, "Now take these to the bishop and tell him to build the church in my honor."

When Juan arrived at the cathedral for the third time, the bishop's helpers refused to let him in. Juan told them that he had the sign the bishop had asked for. They said, "If you have the sign, let us see it. Let us see the sign of a miracle. Then you will see the bishop."

Juan opened his *tilma* and showed the roses to the bishop's helpers. In their astonishment they reached out to touch the roses. But each time they tried to touch a rose, it faded back into the fabric of the *tilma*. They knew that it was indeed a miracle.

When Juan showed the bishop the roses, the bishop also saw that they were a holy sign from heaven. Even more miraculously, inside Juan's *tilma* was the image of the Holy Mother as Juan had seen her on the hill of Tepeyac. At the sight of the holy image, the bishop and his helpers fell to their knees and prayed to the Virgin. (See fig. 11.)

The bishop built a church on the site that Juan showed him on the hill of Tepeyac. Now the site is called Guadalupe. To this day Juan's *tilma* with the image of the Holy Mother is kept inside the shrine to the Blessed Virgin. Prayerful worshipers can look at the *tilma* and be reminded of the love the Holy Mother has for her people. For all eternity the shrine of Our Lady of Guadalupe is a reminder of the miraculous apparition that appeared to Juan Diego many years ago.

NUESTRA SEÑORA DE GUADALUPE
(OUR LADY OF GUADALUPE)

Una mañana fría de invierno en diciembre de 1531, un pobre indio llamado Juan Diego caminaba hacia la iglesia. Habían pasado diez años desde que las grandes batallas con los hombres de Cortéz se habían acabado. Los soldados y guerreros habían depuesto sus armas, y la paz había vuelto a su tierra. Juan mismo se había convertido al cristianismo. Era su costumbre ir a la iglesia para instruirse en religión.

La iglesia no estaba en su pueblo sino en Tlatelolco, un pueblo en las afueras de la ciudad de Méjico. Su camino usual lo llevaba por las casas del pueblo, pero esta mañana por alguna razón decidió cruzar la colina de Tepeyac.

Conforme se acercaba a la cima de la colina, escuchó voces que cantaban. El había oído las voces de la gente cantando las santas alabanzas al Señor en la iglesia, pero nunca había oído una música tan bella en toda su vida. Escuchó el sonido de campanas, y las voces le rodearon como el viento mismo. Pensó que esto debía ser como sonaban las voces de los ángeles del cielo.

Al llegar a la cima de la colina, las voces preciosas que cantaban y la música se pararon. Todo quedó en silencio, y Juan ni siquiera sentía el frío. Escuchó que lo llamaban, "Juan, Juan."

De repente vió una nube brillante de la cual salían los rayos de un arco iris. La nube se paró delante de él, y cuando se dividió en dos, apareció una mujer allí de pie. La mujer parecía una hermosa princesa azteca. Su ropa brillaba como el sol, y le rodeaba una luz celestial. Cuando ella habló Juan escuchó aquella música del cielo que había oído antes. El sabía que era un milagro, y se postró de rodillas para rezar.

"Juan," dijo la mujer del cielo, "te he escogido para dar un mensaje al obispo en la catedral."

"Pero, bella mujer," contestó Juan, "Soy un pobre indio. No merezco el privilegio de dar un mensaje al obispo. ¿Por qué he sido escogido?"

Con bondad consoladora, la mujer le contestó, "Yo soy la Bendita Virgen María, la madre del Señor Jesucristo. Sabe que yo te he escogido para ser mi mensajero en la tierra. Ve al obispo y dile que tiene que construir una iglesia para mí en lo alto de esta colina. La iglesia debe ser un templo que mostrará mi amor para toda mi gente. Ve, dale mi mensaje al obispo."

Juan corrió más rápido que nunca a la catedral para dar el mensaje de la Virgen al obispo. Cuando llegó a la catedral, llamó a la puerta de los aposentos del obispo. Los ayudantes del obispo abrieron la puerta y preguntaron a Juan qué quería. El les dijo, "Tengo un mensaje para el obispo de la Virgen María, la Madre de Dios."

Los ayudantes del obispo no pudieron evitar la risa al escuchar a un pobre indio contar tal historia. Pero, Juan fué persistente, y al final lo dejaron ver al obispo. El obispo escuchó la historia de Juan pero no lo creyó. Le dijo, "Juan, tu historia es increíble. ¡Imaginar que la Virgen se te aparece en una colina con un mensaje para que yo construya una iglesia! Vete por ahora, que ya lo pensaré."

Juan se fué sintiéndose fracasado. Sabía que los ayudantes del obispo se habían reído de él y que el mismo obispo no había creído su historia. Sintió que había decepcionado a la Virgen Bendita. Cuando volvió a Tepeyac vió otra vez a la Virgen. Ella flotaba en el aire, como si nada la sostuviera salvo sus poderes celestiales.

"Oh Santa Madre, te he decepcionado. El obispo no me creyó. Yo sabía que no valgo nada."

"¿Juan, no sabes que estás en gracia conmigo? Te he escogido, y yo haré que esto suceda como debe ser. Vuelve al obispo y dale mi mensaje otra vez. Una iglesia debe ser construida en mi nombre en esta colina."

Juan volvió al obispo por segunda vez. Otra vez el obispo no lo creyó. Pero le dijo, "Juan, si de verdad has visto a la Bendita Virgen María, tráeme una señal de que el milagro es real. Si no, nunca más vuelvas con esta historia."

En su camino de vuelta para decirle a la Virgen que necesitaba una señal, Juan recibió la noticia de que su tío se estaba muriendo de la fiebre tifoidea. Corrió al lado de su tío, pero cuando llegó era ya casi demasiado tarde. Su tío le pidió que trajera al cura porque sabía que no viviría hasta el siguiente día.

Juan se fue rápidamente a la Virgen para contarle lo que le había dicho el obispo y para pedirle perdón por no haber vuelto en seguida. "Oh, Virgen Bendita, llego tarde porque mi tío se está muriendo y no parece que va a durar otro día más. Además el obispo quiere una señal de que mi visión de ti es un milagro de verdad. Por favor, ayúdame, Madre Bendita."

"¿Juan, no sabes que estoy aquí para ayudarte? Ya he curado a tu tío. El vivirá. Ahora, vete a la cima de la colina, donde solamente crece el cactus. Allí encontrarás un rosal florecido. Lleva esas rosas al obispo y él creerá."

Juan fué a la cima de la colina, y allí había un rosal en plena flor. Cuando Juan vió el rosal florecido ese día frío de invierno, supo que esto era el milagro que había pedido, y se arrodilló para rezar. Juan sabía que cuando el obispo viera las rosas que habían florecido en pleno invierno y oliera su hermosa fragancia creería en el milagro. Recogió las rosas en su "tilma" que es un tipo de poncho. Las enseñó a la Virgen, y ella dijo, "Ahora, lleva estas flores al obispo y dile que construya la iglesia en mi honor."

Cuando Juan llegó a la catedral por tercera vez, los ayudantes del obispo le negaron la entrada. Juan les dijo que tenía la señal que el obispo había pedido. Ellos dijeron, "Si tienes la señal, déjanos verla. Déjanos ver la señal del milagro. Entonces verás al obispo."

Juan abrió su tilma y enseñó las rosas a los ayudantes del obispo. Ellos en su asombro alargaron la mano para tocar las rosas. Pero cada vez que intentaban tocar una rosa, ésta se desvanecía en la tela de la tilma. Entonces, supieron que era de verdad un milagro.

Cuando Juan enseñó las rosas al obispo, éste también vió que eran una señal sagrada del cielo. Y un milagro mayor era que dentro de la tilma de Juan estaba la imagen de la Santa Madre tal como Juan la había visto en la colina de Tepeyac. Al ver la santa imagen, el obispo y sus ayudantes se arrodillaron y rezaron a la Virgen.

El obispo construyó una iglesia en el lugar que Juan le indicó en la colina de Tepeyac. Ahora el sitio se llama Guadalupe. Hasta este día se guarda la tilma de Juan con la imagen de la Santa Madre dentro del santuario de la Virgen Bendita. Los devotos adoradores pueden ver la tilma y recordar el amor que tiene la Santa Madre a su gente. Para toda la eternidad el santuario de Nuestra Señora de Guadalupe es un recuerdo de la aparición milagrosa que tuvo Juan Diego hace tantos años.

2

The
Traditional
Cuentos

Moral and Religious Stories

DOÑA SEBASTIANA

The fascinating story of Doña Sebastiana has been well documented in New Mexico and Colorado. The carved wooden figure of Doña Sebastiana, riding her death cart and drawing her bow and arrow, is very common throughout the region. (See fig. 12.) Often the figure was pulled in religious processions during Holy Week as a reminder of the power of death. An exceptionally fine example of this wooden sculpture is on display at the Denver Museum of Art's Spanish Colonial section.

In *Favorite Folktales from around the World,* Jane Yolen presents two versions of this story. One of these, "Godfather Death," appears in collections of Grimm's fairy tales and had been reported in Europe since 1300. The second version Yolen presents, "The Hungry Peasant, God, and Death," is from a collection of Mexican folktales. In his pioneering collection of Hispanic folktales, *Cuentos Españoles de Colorado y Nuevo Méjico,* recorded in New Mexico and Colorado in the 1930s and 1940s, Juan B. Rael presents three versions of *La Comadre Sebastiana.* These versions are similar to those derived from Germany and

Mexico and retold by Jane Yolen in *Favorite Folktales.* In his collection from the 1950s, R. D. Jameson presents two much shorter versions of the story collected in northeastern New Mexico. In 1987 I recorded a version of the story as told by New Mexico National Heritage Storyteller Cleofes Vigil. His version was remarkably similar to the others, although there was the embellishment and change of detail that marked the story as his individual version. As with many *cuentos* in this book, this is a story I remember from my childhood in New Mexico.

DOÑA SEBASTIANA

Once in the high mountains of northern New Mexico, there lived a poor farmer with his family. Those of us who have lived in this area know that in a year when the rain is plentiful, the ground gives forth its abundance and there is food for everyone. In a year of drought, however, the ground is barren and the people struggle to make their living. It just so happened that this year had been a year of drought. The ground was rocky and barren, and there was little food.

As the farmer tucked his children into bed, he looked into their eyes and saw that they were hungry. They tried to be brave little girls and boys and said they weren't hungry, but he knew the truth. They had not eaten for days. The thought of his children going hungry gave him great pain.

Finally he made up his mind to do something that was not in his character but that was in his will. He would be a man of action. He decided to become a thief. That night he would steal food, and tomorrow his children would eat.

In the still darkness of the night, he crept to his neighbor's chicken coop. Carefully stepping around the sleeping guard dog, who was doing a better job of sleeping than guarding, he stepped into the chicken coop. He grabbed one chicken.

"If I am a thief once, I might as well be a thief twice," he said as he grabbed a second chicken. He carefully crept out of the chicken coop, past the sleeping guard dog, and began the long walk back to his farm.

As he walked home he was happy that his children would eat tomorrow. He held up one chicken and said, "Tomorrow my children will eat!" But then he remembered that he, too, had not eaten for several days. Looking at the second chicken, he said, "And tonight I will eat!" He took out his pocketknife and cut off the chicken's head. He then plucked it, and after making a fire with stone sparks and dry grass, he began to cook it on a makeshift wooden spit he constructed from sticks on the ground.

Suddenly a man came out of the darkness. The farmer was very afraid that he had been discovered as a thief and that he had brought shame to his family name.

The man approached the farmer and said, "Often on my travels through the world, people share their food with me. Will you share your food with me?"

The farmer looked at the man and knew he was a stranger in those parts. The farmer replied, "You are a stranger here. Please tell me who you are, and we shall share the chicken."

The stranger replied, "I am the Lord Jesus Christ, and I am on my nightly journey, tending to the welfare of the people of this earth."

After thinking for a moment, the farmer told the Lord Jesus Christ that he would not share his chicken with him. He told the Lord Jesus Christ, "You have created an unjust and unfair world. You created a world with two kinds of people. On one side are those who are rich and wealthy beyond all worth and justice, and on the other are the poor and miserable beyond all compassion and understanding. And since I am one of the poor and miserable, I do not think that you have created a fair and just world. For this reason I will not share my food with you."

The Lord Jesus Christ said thank you and left. As the farmer continued to cook his chicken, he saw another person coming out of the darkness of the forest. This time it was a woman. Again the farmer thought he had been discovered as a thief, and quickly he tried to put out the fire over which he was cooking the chicken. But as the woman approached the farmer, she said, "I am weary from traveling the world this night. Will you share your food with me?"

Again the farmer asked who the stranger was. She said, "I am Maria Santissima, Holy Mary, the Virgin Mary, the Holy Mother of God."

The farmer thought for a while and said, "No. I will not share my chicken with you tonight. Your son, the Lord Jesus Christ, created an unjust and unfair world. He has created a world with two kinds of people. On one side are those who are rich and wealthy beyond all worth and justice, and on the other are the poor and miserable beyond all compassion and understanding. And since I am one of the poor and miserable, I do not think that the Lord Jesus Christ created a fair and just world. And since you are his mother, you should have been a better influence on him! For this reason I will not share my chicken with you."

The Holy Mother said thank you and left. Once more the farmer continued to cook his chicken. Then from the darkness he heard a sound that he had never heard before. He heard the sound of someone pulling a heavy wooden cart across the barren and rocky ground of northern New Mexico. As a person came out of the darkness into the light of the moon, the farmer felt a chill go down his spine. He was frightened by the strange, dark figure. As the light of the moon shone beneath her hood, he could see the skeleton shape of an old woman.

In a raspy voice the woman said, "Good evening. I am tired from my long nightly journey. Will you share your meal with me?"

In a shaking, frightened voice the farmer asked, "Who are you?"

The woman answered, "You know who I am. I am Doña Sebastiana, La Muerte, Death herself. I am on my nightly journey collecting souls in my *carreta de la muerte* for their long journey into eternity. But do not worry, farmer. Tonight is not your night. Will you share your meal with me?"

The farmer thought for a moment and said, "Yes, I will share my meal with you. You above all people treat all people equally. At the moment of your touch all people—rich, poor, young, old, beautiful, ugly—all people must answer your call. For this reason I will share my meal with you."

Doña Sebastiana was pleased with the farmer's words. After they had eaten the chicken, to reward his generosity and courage, she offered him a reward. She said, "Because you have been brave and wise, I will give you a reward. Ask and you shall receive."

The farmer, still frightened, answered, "Doña Sebastiana, I am but a poor and humble farmer. I am not worthy to ask for a gift from you. Give and I shall receive."

"Farmer," she said, "tonight I will give you the power over life and death. I will give you the power of the *curandero*. You shall enter a house of sickness, and you shall take the dirt of the earth, the plants of the mountainside, and the water of the river, and with the power I give you tonight, you shall lay your hands on that sick and dying person, and life will return to that person. However, *curandero*, remember the agreement we make tonight. If you ever enter a house of sickness and see me at the head of the bed, you are to tell that person there is nothing you can do, and he is to say his prayers and prepare his soul for the long journey into eternity. If, however, you enter that room and see me at the foot of the bed, then know that I am but passing through, and you may use the powers I give you tonight to heal

that sick and dying person. Remember this agreement, *curandero*. Your own life depends on it."

As the years passed the healing powers of the farmer became known throughout the valley. Indeed he became very wealthy because of them. Many times he had entered a house of sickness and had seen Doña Sebastiana at the foot of the bed, and he had used his powers to save the sick person. On the few occasions he had seen Doña Sebastiana at the head of the bed, he had said there was nothing to be done, for the soul of the sick person now belonged to Doña Sebastiana.

One night he was called to the house of the richest rancher in the valley. The rancher lay with the sickness of death. As the *curandero* entered the house of sickness, the rancher called to him with the eternal human cry, "*Curandero*, save me. Give me one more day to live. I am too young to die. Save me, *curandero!*"

As the farmer entered the sick rancher's room, he saw Doña Sebastiana at the head of the bed. He told the rancher, "There is nothing I can do. Say your prayers and prepare your soul for the long journey into eternity."

The rancher struggled to raise himself and desperately told the farmer, "*Curandero*, save me. I know it is within your powers. If you bring life back to me, I will give you all my wealth. Give me one more day to live!"

At the thought of all that wealth and in a moment of human weakness, the farmer was overcome with greed and the promise of the rancher's great wealth. For the second time in his life, he decided to be a man of action. He picked up *Doña Sebastiana* and carried her to the foot of the bed. He then healed the rancher of his sickness.

As he was returning home that night, the farmer heard a sound he had not heard for many years. It was the sound of someone dragging a heavy wooden cart across the barren and rocky ground of northern New Mexico.

Out of the darkness of the forest came the skeletal figure of Doña Sebastiana. She said, "*Curandero*, tonight you made a grave mistake." She pointed to her *carreta de la muerte*. On her death cart were two candles. One was tall, burning brightly, with hours left to burn. The other was short, with a weak, flickering flame, about to be extinguished by the slightest breeze.

"*Curandero,* but a few moments ago the tall candle was your soul, brightly burning with a long life ahead. The short candle was the soul of the rancher, about to lose the bright energy of life. But now the tall candle is the soul of the rancher, with many more years to burn. And the short candle is your own weak and fragile soul." She took out one of her arrows and shot it through the flame of the short candle, extinguishing it. (See fig. 13.)

At the moment the flame went out, the soul of the farmer left his body to join the other souls that Doña Sebastiana had gathered that night in her *carreta de la muerte* for their long journey into eternity.

DOÑA SEBASTIANA

Hace mucho tiempo en las altas montañas del norte de Nuevo Méjico, vivía un pobre granjero y su familia. Los que hemos vivido en esa zona, sabemos que en los años de mucha lluvia la tierra produce en abundancia, y hay comida suficiente para todos. Sin embargo en años de sequía la tierra es árida, y la gente trabaja mucho para ganarse la vida. Ocurrió que este año había sido de sequía. La tierra estaba dura y seca, y había poca comida.

Una noche cuando el granjero estaba acostando a sus hijos, los miró a los ojos, y vió que estaban hambrientos. Ellos, intentando ser valientes, dijeron que no tenían hambre, pero él sabía la verdad. No habían comido durante días, y el pensar en sus hijos pasando hambre le causó mucho dolor.

Por último, determinó hacer algo que, aunque no le gustaba, sí estaba decidido a llevar a cabo. Sería un hombre de acción. Decidió convertirse en ladrón. Aquella noche robaría comida, y al día siguiente comerían sus hijos.

En la oscuridad silenciosa de la noche, se arrastró hasta el gallinero de su vecino. Sigilosamente pasó junto al perro guardián, el cual dormía mejor que guardaba, entró en el gallinero, y cogió un pollo.

"Si soy ladrón una vez, igual da que lo sea dos veces," se dijo mientras cogía un segundo pollo. Con cuidado salió del gallinero, pasó de nuevo junto al perro dormido, y empezó el largo camino de vuelta a su casa.

Mientras caminaba se sentía feliz al pensar que sus hijos comerían al día siguiente. Sosteniendo un pollo en la mano, dijo, "¡Mañana mis hijos comerán!" Pero entonces recordó que él tampoco había comido en varios días. Mirando al segundo pollo, dijo, "¡Y esta noche yo también comeré!" Sacó su navaja y cortó la cabeza del pollo. Lo desplumó, y después de hacer un fuego con chispas de piedra y hierba seca, empezó a asarlo en un asador de madera que hizo con algunos palos que había por el suelo.

De repente salió un hombre de la oscuridad. El granjero temió haber sido descubierto como ladrón y haber manchado el nombre de su familia.

El hombre se acercó al granjero y le dijo, "A menudo en mis viajes por el mundo la gente comparte su comida conmigo. ¿Compartirás tu comida conmigo?"

El granjero miró al hombre y vió que era extranjero en aquellas tierras. El granjero contestó, "Ud. es extranjero aquí. Por favor dígame quién es, y compartiremos el pollo."

El extranjero contestó, "Soy el Señor Jesucristo, y estoy haciendo mi ronda nocturna, comprobando el bienestar de la gente de la tierra."

Después de pensar un momento, el granjero dijo al Señor Jesucristo que no compartiría su pollo con él. Le dijo, "Ud. ha creado un mundo injusto. Ha creado un mundo con dos tipos de personas. Por un lado están los que son ricos más allá de todo merecimiento y justicia, y por otro lado están los que son pobres y miserables más allá de toda compasión y entendimiento. Y como yo soy uno de los pobres y miserables, no creo que haya creado un mundo imparcial y justo. Por esta razón no compartiré mi comida con Ud."

El Señor Jesucristo le dió las gracias y se fué. El granjero continuó asando su pollo cuando vió a otra persona salir de la oscuridad del bosque. Esta vez era una mujer. Otra vez pensó el granjero que había sido descubierto, y rápidamente intentó apagar el fuego donde estaba asando el pollo. Pero cuando la mujer se le acercó, le dijo, "Estoy cansada de viajar por todo el mundo esta noche. ¿Compartirás tu comida conmigo?"

El granjero preguntó quién era la extranjera. Ella dijo, "Yo soy María Santísima, María la Santa, la Virgen María, la Santa Madre de Dios."

El granjero pensó un momento y dijo, "No. No compartiré mi pollo con Ud. esta noche. Su hijo, el Señor Jesucristo, creó un mundo injusto. El ha creado un mundo con dos tipos de personas. Por un lado están los que son ricos más allá de todo merecimiento y justicia, y por otro lado están los que son pobres y miserables más allá de toda compasión y entendimiento. Y como yo soy uno de los pobres y miserables, no creo que el Señor Jesucristo creó un mundo justo. ¡Y como Ud. es su madre, debió haber sido de mejor influencia para él! Por esta razón, no compartiré mi pollo con Ud."

La Santa Madre le dió las gracias y se fué. Una vez más el granjero continuó asando su pollo. Entonces desde la oscuridad escuchó un sonido que nunca había oído antes. Escuchó a alguien tirando de un carro pesado de madera por la tierra seca y dura del norte de Nuevo

Méjico. Entonces una persona salió desde la oscuridad a la luz de la luna, y el granjero sintió que un escalofrío recorría su espalda. Estaba asustado por la figura extraña y oscura. Cuando la luz de la luna brilló debajo de la capucha, pudo ver el esqueleto de una vieja.

En una voz ronca la mujer le dijo, "Buenas noches. Estoy cansada de mi larga jornada nocturna. ¿Compartirás tu comida conmigo?"

Con voz temblorosa y asustada, el granjero preguntó, "¿Quién es Ud.?"

La mujer le contestó, "Tú sabes quien soy. Soy Doña Sebastiana, La Muerte misma. Estoy en mi jornada nocturna recolectando almas en mi carreta de la muerte para su largo viaje hacia la eternidad. Pero no te preocupes, granjero. Esta no es tu noche. ¿Compartirás tu comida conmigo?"

El granjero pensó un momento y dijo, "Sí, compartiré mi comida con Ud., porque Ud. más que nadie, trata a la gente con igualdad. En el momento en que Ud. toca a cualquiera - ricos, pobres, jovenes, viejos, hermosos, feos - todos deben responder a su llamada. Por esta razón compartiré mi comida con Ud."

Doña Sebastiana estaba contenta con las palabras del granjero. Después de que habían comido el pollo, para premiar su generosidad y valor, le ofreció una recompensa. Le dijo, "Porque has sido valiente y sabio, te daré un premio. Pide y recibirás lo que quieras."

El granjero, todavía asustado, contestó, "Doña Sebastiana, sólo soy un granjero pobre y humilde. No merezco pedirle nada. Deme lo que Ud. quiera."

"Granjero," dijo ella, "esta noche te daré el poder sobre la vida y la muerte. Te daré poderes de curandero. Entrarás en una casa donde haya enfermedad, cogerás tierra del suelo, plantas de la ladera de la montaña, y agua del río, y con el poder que te doy esta noche, pondrás tus manos sobre los enfermos y moribundos, y la vida retornará a ellos. Sin embargo, curandero, recuerda el trato que hacemos esta noche. Si alguna vez entras en una casa y me ves a la cabecera de la cama, debes decir a esa persona que no puedes hacer nada, y que debe rezar y preparar su alma para el largo viaje hacia la eternidad. Pero, si entras en esa habitación y me ves al pie de la cama, sabe entonces que estoy de paso, y que puedes utilizar los poderes que te doy esta noche para curar a esa persona enferma y moribunda. Recuerda este trato, curandero. Tu propia vida depende de ello."

Conforme pasaron los años, los poderes del granjero llegaron a conocerse en todo el valle. En verdad se hizo bastante rico gracias a ellos. Muchas veces cuando había entrado en casas donde había visto a Doña Sebastiana al pie de la cama, había usado sus poderes para salvar a los enfermos. En las pocas ocasiones en las cuales había visto a Doña Sebastiana a la cabecera de la cama, había dicho que no podía hacer nada, porque el alma del enfermo ya pertenecía a Doña Sebastiana.

Una noche fué llamado a la casa del ganadero más rico del valle. El ganadero tenía la enfermedad de la muerte. Cuando el curandero entró en la casa, el ganadero lo llamó con el eterno grito humano, "¡Curandero, sálvame. Dame un día más para vivir. Soy demasiado joven para morir. Sálvame, curandero!"

Cuando el granjero entró en la habitación, y vió a Doña Sebastiana a la cabecera de la cama, dijo al ganadero, "No puedo hacer nada. Rece y prepare su alma para el largo viaje hacia la eternidad."

El ganadero se esforzó para incorporarse y le dijo desesperadamente, "Curandero, sálvame. Sé que está en tu poder. Si me devuelves la vida, te daré todas mis riquezas. ¡Dame un día más de vida!"

Al pensar en tanta riqueza y en un momento de debilidad humana, el granjero fué cegado por la codicia y la promesa del ganadero. Por segunda vez en su vida, decidió ser un hombre de acción. Cogió a Doña Sebastiana en brazos, y la llevó al pie de la cama. Entonces curó al ganadero de su enfermedad.

Cuando volvía a su casa esa noche, el granjero escuchó un sonido que no había escuchado en muchos años. Era el sonido de alguien arrastrando un carro de madera pesado por la tierra seca y dura del norte de Nuevo Méjico.

De la oscuridad del bosque salió la figura de esqueleto de Doña Sebastiana, que le dijo, "Curandero, esta noche has cometido un grave error." Señaló a su carreta de la muerte en la que había dos velas. Una era alta, y ardía brillantemente con muchas horas todavía para quemar. La otra era corta, con una llama débil y parpadeante, a punto de ser extinguida por la más mínima brisa.

"Curandero, hace sólo unos minutos, la vela alta era tu alma, ardiendo fuertemente con una larga vida por delante. La vela corta era el alma del ganadero, a punto de perder la energía vital de su vida. Pero ahora, la vela alta es el alma del ganadero, con muchos años más para quemar. Y la vela corta es tu propia alma, débil y frágil." Y diciendo esto, sacó una de sus flechas y la disparó a la llama de la vela corta, extinguiéndola.

En el momento en que la llama se apagó, el alma del granjero dejó su cuerpo para unirse con las otras almas que Doña Sebastiana había recolectado esa noche en su carreta de la muerte para su largo viaje hacia la eternidad.

EL SANTO NIÑO

Once in a village not too far from here, there were three brothers. The brothers were very close; they had grown up as playmates and best friends. Their parents had raised them to follow the ways of the Lord, the teachings of the church, and to respect, obey, and honor their elders. Every Sunday they went to church as a family and prayed for the souls of the dearly departed.

The two older brothers were the leaders. They protected the youngest brother and tried to teach him the ways of the world. One day, however, it was time for the oldest brother to go into the world to seek his fortune.

The oldest brother went to his parents and asked for their blessing as he was about to go into the world. He received their blessing and prepared his belongings for the journey. The two younger brothers were very sad that the older brother was leaving them. But he assured them, saying, "One day it will be your turn to go into the world. By that time I will have found my place in the world, and you will be able to come and join me. For now you must stay home and take care of our parents. They will need your help now that I am gone."

Soon after he left his home, the oldest brother was traveling along the road and came to a farmhouse. Standing in the doorway was a small child. The oldest brother thought that this might as well be the first place to look for work.

He approached the child and said, "Good morning. Are your parents at home, and may I please speak to them?"

The child looked at him with eyes that seemed older and wiser than his years, but the older brother told himself that he was imagining things. The child said, "My parents are in a city far away from here. I do have a job for you, though, if you are looking for work."

The older brother was overjoyed at what the child said. Imagine, a job already, and he had just left on his journey! He excitedly told the child, "Yes, I am looking for work. You will find that I am a very hard worker, and you will be pleased with my work."

The child looked at him with his wise eyes and answered, "Many people have told me the same thing, but few have completed the job I ask of them."

"You can count on me. I will finish the job."

"We will see. Take this letter to my mother. She is in a city on a hill many miles from here. You will see many strange things on the journey, but do not be afraid. I will always be by your side, and I will give you strength to finish the journey. There is but one rule you must follow: You will pass a house of temptation, and many people will try to persuade you to come into the house. You are not to go into the house. You are to complete the journey. Give the letter to my mother, and I will join you at the end of the journey."

The older brother had never imagined that his first job would be so easy and yet so strange. He thanked the child for the job, took the letter, and began the journey.

As he began the journey, he thought of his family and brothers. He wished that they were well and said a prayer for them.

When he had gone over the first hill beyond the child's house, he came to a house set off from the road. Many beautiful women called to him and asked him to come into the house. The music coming from the house was loud and raucous, and he knew that this must be the house of temptation the child had told him about. The women were beautiful and he was curious, but he remembered his job and continued on his way.

Soon he came to a river. At first it seemed as if the river would be easy to cross, but as he began to wade, the water began to rush by him faster and faster. Suddenly he was in a very deep part of the river, and he thought he was going to drown. He used all his strength to get to the bank of the river and then fell exhausted on the ground.

He began to wonder if this job really was any good at all. After all, the house of temptation didn't seem that bad, and what good is a job if it gets you killed? But he decided to give the job one more chance, and he continued on his way.

Immediately he came upon another river. This time the river was a river of blood. As he approached the river, some of the blood splashed on him. Never in his life had he imagined a river of blood, and he thought that it must be the blood of all the travelers who had drowned in the river. He was so afraid that he started shaking, and he turned around to head back to the child's house. This job was too small to risk so much.

On the way back he passed the house of temptation again. This time he was cold, wet, and tired. The women calling to him made it seem as if resting in the house would be a wonderful thing to do. He thought to himself, "I will just rest for the night. The little child is too young to know if I do or not."

The next morning he arrived at the little child's house. Just as before the child was standing at the door as if he were expecting him. As the oldest brother approached the door, the child said, "You have not completed the journey as I asked you. I know that you stayed at the house of temptation, and that was forbidden. Because of this you must be punished." He took the older brother to the back of the house and put him in a barrel of boiling oil.

Back at the parents' house, the other two brothers often wondered what was happening to the oldest brother on his journey. Another year passed, and now it was time for the second brother to leave home to seek his fortune in the world. As he left the home of his parents, he told his parents that he would find his older brother and bring back news of him. They wished him well and gave him their blessing.

Soon the second brother came upon the same house that his older brother had come upon. The child was waiting at the door. The second brother had the same conversation with the child as the older brother had, and soon he was on his way to deliver the letter to the child's mother. When the second brother passed the house of temptation, he was attracted to the house and did not see much wrong with it. But he continued on his way.

When he came to the river of water, he almost drowned but was able to pull himself out of the water just in time. He sat on the bank of the river and rested while he thought about what a strange job this was.

When he came to the river of blood, he was frightened more than he had ever been in his life. As he waded into the water, he closed his eyes and lunged to the other side. When he climbed onto the bank, he looked back and saw that all the blood had turned to water. He thought to himself, "That child must have very strong powers. Perhaps he is in league with *El Diablo*. I must be very careful for the rest of the journey."

The next river he came to was calm and peaceful. The second brother was glad that this river would be no danger or challenge. The first two rivers had made him wonder whether the job was worth it. After all, it was only a letter.

As he waded into the river, all of a sudden sharp knives jutted out of the water. The knives surprised him, and he fell on one, cutting himself. Now he knew that the journey had an evil spell on it, and he immediately decided to return the letter to the child.

The Traditional *Cuentos*

On the way back, just as his brother had, he stayed in the house of temptation for the night.

The next morning he gave the letter back to the little child and told him that the job was too dangerous. The child reminded the second brother that he, the child, had promised to be with the brother on the journey and keep him safe. The brother had lost faith, and that was why the journey had seemed dangerous. Also, the brother had spent the night in the house of temptation, and that was forbidden. The child then took the second brother to the back of the house and put him in a barrel of boiling oil.

Time passed, and the youngest brother finally was ready to leave home to seek his fortune in the world. He asked his parents for their blessing. His parents told him, "We are worried about what has become of your brothers. We have a feeling that their journeys came to a bad end. You are our youngest child, and we do not want you to go into the world where harm might come to you."

"But I am a grown man now. It is time I leave home. May I have your blessing?"

The parents relented, and with grief in their voices, they told the youngest brother, "Take our blessing, and if ever you are in trouble, remember that you carry the protection of your parents' blessing and no harm will come to you."

The youngest brother left the home of his parents, and just as his brothers had, he soon saw the child standing at the doorway of the house. As his brothers before him, the youngest brother agreed to take the letter to the child's mother.

As he left the child told him, "Remember, do not stay in the house of temptation. And if there is ever any danger, I will be there by your side." The youngest brother wondered how such a small child could protect him on the journey, but he remembered that he also had his parents' blessing for protection.

When he passed the house of temptation, he knew that he must not even look at it. The priest had taught him that the powers of temptation are strong and that he must use all his strength to keep from going down the path of temptation.

Moral and Religious Stories

As soon as he waded into the first river, the river of water, he started to drown in the swift, rushing current. But he remembered his parents' blessing and said, "With the blessing of my parents I will be safe. And with the protection of my master, the young child, I will not suffer harm."

As soon as he had said these words, the river of water became calm and he easily crossed it. When he climbed onto the bank he said, "When I return I shall ask my master the meaning of all this."

As he came to the second river, the river of blood, he was frightened. But as he remembered the blessing of his parents and the protection of the child, the river of blood turned into a river of water. Then he thought to himself, "When I return from this journey I must ask my master the meaning of all this."

Because of his confidence in the blessing of his parents and the protection of the child, the third river, the river of daggers, was no challenge for the youngest brother. The daggers quickly disappeared and allowed him to pass unharmed.

As he continued on his journey, he came upon an incredible sight. There before him were two large mountains crashing together. When their massive peaks and giant boulders met, the force was so violent that the whole earth shook like an earthquake.

There was only one path, and that was through the middle of the two crashing mountains. The brother closed his eyes, called upon his parents' blessing and the child's protection, and walked down the middle of the path between the two mountains. As he reached the mountains, they became still. The silence that suddenly surrounded him made him open his eyes. When he looked up he saw the two mountains, still and towering to the sky as if neither had moved since the beginning of time.

On the other side of the mountain, he came upon another wondrous sight. There before him were two open meadows with sheep in each one. In one meadow the ground was barren and dry, with no vegetation at all. In this meadow the sheep were fat, content, and healthy. In the other meadow the grass was lush and long, and the vegetation was plentiful. The sheep in this meadow, however, were skinny and ragged.

As he passed by the two meadows, he said, "What a strange journey this has been. When I return I shall ask my master the meaning of all this."

As he came to the top of the hill, he looked ahead and saw a city of light at the top of the next hill. He had never seen or imagined such a beautiful city. It truly looked like a city of gold. As he approached the city, he heard the heavenly music of angels singing. A lady came out of the middle of the light and asked if her son had sent him.

He fell to his knees and handed the letter to the lady. As soon as he had delivered the letter, he looked up, and there stood the child at the lady's side.

The child spoke to him and said, "You have done well. You have been successful in the journey, and now you shall have your reward."

The youngest brother knew that he was in the presence of a miracle, and he was thankful that the blessing of his parents had brought him this far. He then asked the child, "On my journey I have seen many wondrous things. Please explain the meaning of them to me."

The child took his hand and spoke to him. "I am *El Santo Niño*, the Holy Child. This is my mother, the Blessed Virgin. And this city is *La Gloria*, heaven itself. Your reward for completing the journey is eternal life with me here in *La Gloria*.

"The river of water is the river of baptism, through which all the faithful must pass if they are to live in eternity with me in *La Gloria*. The river of blood is the blood I shed on the cross for mankind's sins. The river of daggers is the dagger the soldier used to lance my side as I was upon the cross. The two fighting mountains are two *compadres* who do not know that my way is the way of peace. The two meadows with sheep are the lessons of the church about how the faithful are to live by my teachings. The fat sheep who live in the barren meadow are the souls of the faithful who believe the holy teachings. The skinny sheep living amid plenty are the souls of those who follow the path of the material world and forsake the teaching of the church."

The youngest brother listened to the words of *El Santo Niño*. He knew that his parents had been right. With their blessing and the teaching of the church, no harm had come to him. He asked *El Santo Niño* if his family could join him in eternal life in *La Gloria*.

The Holy Child told him that his parents, because of the holy life they had led, could join him in *La Gloria*. His two brothers, however, would suffer for all eternity because they had not believed in the words of *El Santo Niño*.

THE DEVIL'S FRIEND

Once there were three friends working in the fields. They were young and carefree and enjoyed the hot sun beating on their backs. They spent their youthful days working, laughing, and pursuing the young women of the village. Often they would compete to see who could get the most attention from the woman of their choice.

One day they were in the fields, tending to the crops, when a group of young women walked by. The boys immediately tried to get the girls' attention. They whistled and called their names and generally acted like all boys do when they are trying to get the attention of girls. However, the young women knew to pretend that they heard and noticed nothing. They had been taught by their parents to ignore such rude behavior.

One of the young men was especially attracted to the prettiest girl. She had long, black hair and coal-black eyes. He would watch her in church, and he knew that she was the one for him. When he told his friends, they laughed and laughed. They taunted him, saying, "You are much too ugly and poor for her to even look at. You will need the help of *El Diablo* to win her heart." (See fig. 16.)

The next time the young women walked by the field, the heart-struck young man called out to his intended, "Adiós, my heart! Love of my heart!"

As she walked by, ignoring him in her cool and unattainable manner, he said to himself, "She is a work of God. I would sell my soul to *El Diablo* if I could someday marry her."

The young women passed, and the sun continued on its long, hot path through the sky. When the workday was over, the friends said farewell for the day, and they all went their separate ways home.

On his way home the love-struck young man was approached by a stranger on a tall, black horse. The man looked gallant, dressed in the finest clothes. The horse had a fiery temper and reared up when the young man approached them.

The stranger looked down at the young man and said, "Good day, *Señor*. Is it true that you would sell your soul to *El Diablo* for a chance to marry the woman of your dreams?"

The young man did not know what to say. Of course he wanted to marry the woman of his dreams, but he was not really serious about selling his soul to *El Diablo*. He told the stranger, "Those were just words I said in a rash moment. My soul belongs to the Lord."

The stranger continued, "The Lord will never be able to give you the heart of the woman you desire. If you truly want her hand in marriage, I am the only way."

The young man trembled with fear. He then noticed the faint smell of sulfur. It was *El Diablo* himself! The young man had heard that *El Diablo* was in another village down the road, and he knew that *brujas* often did *El Diablo's* work on this earth, but he never imagined *El Diablo* as such a handsome man with a proud, noble horse.

El Diablo addressed the young man again, "This is your one and only chance to have the heart of the woman you desire. If you do not agree, then resign yourself to a life of longing for her from a distance. The future is written that she will marry one of your friends."

The man could not bear the thought of losing the woman he loved. He agreed to *El Diablo's* terms. He asked *El Diablo*, "When do I give you my soul, now or when I die?"

"Oh, it is not your soul I want. I usually get the souls of men like you sooner or later anyway. I have a friend who goes around collecting souls like yours for me. It is the soul of your first born that I want in return for my favors."

His first born! This was impossible. But the more the young man thought about it, the more he realized how much he wanted the love of the woman of his dreams. He told himself, "Perhaps we will not have any children at all, and I will have beaten *El Diablo* at his own game." He finally agreed to *El Diablo's* terms.

El Diablo smiled with joy at the thought of gaining another soul. He told the man, "We must write the contract right now, while the thoughts are still in your mind." He produced a contract and told the young man he must sign it in his own blood. The young man took out his knife, cut his skin, and signed the contract. The pact with *El Diablo* was complete.

The next day the men were working in the field when the young women walked by again. The young men tried to catch their attention as usual. This time the beautiful one looked at our friend in a way she never had before. She almost tripped because she was looking at the man so longingly.

"Wow, did you see that?" one of his friends exclaimed. "She almost tripped because she was looking so hard at you. I think you've won her heart, my friend. The last time we saw someone look that hard, they were married in a month." The friend continued, "All this time I was sure she was falling for me. What happened to change her so fast?"

Soon it all came true as *El Diablo* had guaranteed. The man and the woman of his dreams were married almost a month to the day after she had first returned his glance.

The years passed, and they were blessed with a child, a son. The boy grew to manhood, and his parents were proud of the man he became. But often the wife noticed her husband looking woefully at his son. She would ask, "Why do you look so sadly at our son? He is growing into a fine young man. Does he not bring you joy?"

The man would answer, "It is just a passing thought. It is nothing. Do not worry."

But the man was grief-stricken when he thought of the bargain he had made with *El Diablo* years ago. He realized that it is never possible to beat *El Diablo* at his own game. Even though he married the woman of his dreams and had a son he loved more than his own life, he realized that this son's soul was doomed. At night he prayed to the Lord, "Lord, please forgive me for my sins and send me a way to save the soul of my son."

When the child was growing up he was a quiet child, given to long periods of reflection. His parents noticed how he enjoyed reading the Bible and how he loved the ceremonies of the church. They predicted that one day he would be the priest of the family.

It was no surprise, then, when one day he announced his interest in studying for the priesthood. They gave him their blessing and turned him over to the hands of the Lord as he left for the seminary.

The day the son left for the seminary, his father fell to his knees and cried, "My prayers have been answered! My son has found a way to escape the torments of *El Diablo*. As a priest my son will have the protection of the Lord, and his soul will be safe from *El Diablo's* grasp."

Years passed and one day the son, now an ordained priest, returned home. When he walked up to his childhood home, he discovered the house abandoned and the doors blocked with steel bars. He immediately ran to the church and asked the village priest what had happened to his parents. The priest told him, "Your parents are gone, and we had to seal the house from all entry. Some time ago a man on a tall, black horse came to visit your parents. That night they disappeared, and the neighbors reported seeing the visitor ride off with them. Since that time the house has had the strong smell of sulfur. We fear your parents are in the hands of *El Diablo* himself."

The son was distraught that his parents would be in the hands of *El Diablo*. He asked if there was anyone who knew the way to the land of *El Diablo*. The village priest told him, "Deep in the woods lives a hermit. People say that he knows the path to the land of *El Diablo*. But be careful. People who have gone on your journey have never returned."

The son traveled into the woods, asking for the hermit. The people he asked always pointed even deeper into the woods. Finally the son arrived at the house of the hermit. It was deep in a dark place in the woods, and the son knew that few people ever arrived at this place in the forest.

Without any warning the hermit came out of his house. He was a small man covered in torn and dirty clothes. He approached the son and asked, "You seek to know the path to the land of *El Diablo*. Is that not true?"

The son replied, "Yes, I am on a holy journey to take back the souls of my parents from *El Diablo*. With the Lord's help I will succeed."

The hermit scoffed at what the son said. "*El Diablo* never gives up what he has taken. Even the power of the Lord is not strong enough against *El Diablo*."

"Nevertheless I must find the path to the land of *El Diablo*, old hermit. Please tell me what you know."

"Very well. But know that those who have gone down that path before have never returned." The hermit then pointed to a path leading into an even darker part of the forest. "Follow that path. Some ways down it there lives a man who is *el compadre del Diablo*, the Devil's friend. He guards the path to the land. He will show you the way."

The son thanked the hermit and gave him the Lord's blessing.

The hermit replied, "Thank you for the blessing. I am sorry it will be of no use to you when you reach the land of *El Diablo*."

The son traveled farther down the path the hermit had pointed out. Soon he arrived at another house, and a man came out. He did not look as disheveled and worn as the hermit.

The son asked the man for his help. "A hermit told me you were *El Diablo's* friend. Please show me the way to the land of *El Diablo*."

The friend of *El Diablo* looked at the son and recognized that he was a priest. He fell to his knees and said, "I have been waiting for a priest to come to me one day. My prayers have been answered. I have spent my life collecting souls for *El Diablo*. I have long wanted to confess my sins and leave the ways of *El Diablo*. Please, Father, hear my confession."

The son knelt to hear the man's confession. The friend of *El Diablo* had long lived a life of sin, collecting souls for *El Diablo*. It took the son a full month to hear the man's confession. At the end of the month, the son welcomed the man back into the ways of the Lord and asked the man to help him gain back his parents' souls from the land of *El Diablo*.

"Yes I will. I know the ways of the land of *El Diablo*, and soon we will have your parents' souls back with you."

As they approached the gates to the land of *El Diablo*, the son noticed the strong smell of sulfur. The son thought to himself, "This must be the smell the neighbors noticed the night *El Diablo* took my parents' souls." He crossed himself and said the names of Jesus, Mary, and Joseph.

The friend of *El Diablo* knocked three times on the gates. Voices from inside asked if he had souls for *El Diablo*. The friend knocked three more times, and again the voices asked if he had souls for *El Diablo*. The third time he knocked, the door opened, and he and the son walked into the land of *El Diablo*. The friend told the son to hide the cross he wore, or great harm would come to his parents. Inside the land of *El Diablo*, the son was filled with grief to see the eternal torment of the souls *El Diablo* had gathered. The more he saw, the more desperate he was to save the souls of his parents.

The son walked by *El Diablo's* helpers unnoticed because they thought he was just another soul the friend of *El Diablo* was delivering.

As they came to another part of the land of *El Diablo*, the son recognized his parents. As he saw them the friend of *El Diablo* took his hand and said, "Now it is time to free the souls of your parents. You carry your mother, and I will carry your father." Again the helpers of *El Diablo* let them pass without harm because they thought the friend was just doing *El Diablo's* work.

As they neared the gates the friend of *El Diablo* suddenly ran toward the gates, and with a great kick opened them. Both men ran out of the land of *El Diablo* carrying the bodies of the son's parents. As the helpers of *El Diablo* realized what was happening, they ran to close the gates, but it was too late.

The friend of *El Diablo* told the son, "They will not come past the gates. They are doomed to eternal torment and can never leave the land of *El Diablo*. We are safe."

The friend of *El Diablo* led the son and his parents out of the forest. As they passed the hermit's house, the son called for the hermit, to show him that with the Lord's help he had saved the souls of his parents.

The friend of *El Diablo* stopped the son, saying, "It is of no use. I saw the soul of the hermit in the land of *El Diablo* when we were inside. His soul must now suffer eternal torment because he doubted the power of the Lord. I myself will take the hermit's place as my penance for my sins. Father, you have saved my soul, and to give thanks to the Lord for sending you to me, I will forever be of aid to those who seek to free souls from the land of *El Diablo*."

The son returned to his village with his parents. He burned his childhood home because they were never able to get rid of the sulfur smell. On the morning their new home was completed, the family had a large celebration with all the people of the village. The parents gave thanks that their son, the priest, had saved their souls from eternal torment in the land of *El Diablo*. After they had spoken, the son told the story of how, with the help of the Lord, he had beaten *El Diablo* at his own game.

THE THREE BRANCHES (LAS TRES RAMAS)

Deep inside the forest on the other side of the mountain lived a hermit. The hermit had once been a man of the world, but he had left the world to live by himself in his small house in the forest, enjoying the company of nature. Living far from the troubles of the world, the hermit was happy with his life. He had chosen the life of solitude because he had dedicated himself to following the path of the Lord here on this earth. He spent his days praying, fasting, and reading the Bible. Often travelers trying to find the answers to their daily problems would seek him out, and he would always give them the same answer, "The answer to your problems is to follow the path of the Lord. There is no other way but the teachings of the Lord."

The Lord was pleased with the hermit, and every day He sent an angel to the hermit to give him food and water. The angel placed the food and water outside of the hermit's door, and when the hermit got up in the morning, he often heard the beating of the angel's wings as it flew back to heaven. In this way the hermit knew that he lived in grace in the eyes of the Lord.

One day a troop of soldiers was traveling through the forest by the hermit's house. They were transporting prisoners. The hermit could tell that these were especially bad prisoners because they were under such a heavy guard. He imagined all the terrible crimes they must have committed. As they passed his house, the hermit called out, "Their souls should be taken by the devil, for their sins have offended the Lord."

When the Lord heard what the hermit had said, the Lord was unhappy with him. He felt that the hermit had committed the sin of pride. The hermit had started to believe that he was more holy than anyone else.

The hermit had forgotten that only the Lord decides who is a sinner, for each person's sins are hidden inside the heart. The hermit was wrong to wish any person's soul to the devil. As long as there is a chance for repentance, there is a chance to be forgiven one's sins. To teach the hermit a lesson, the Lord no longer sent the angel with food and water.

The first day the angel didn't deliver the food, the hermit decided that he must have committed some small sin, so he said extra prayers that night. The second day that the angel did not deliver any food, the hermit was more worried. Once again he said extra prayers. Finally the hermit realized that the angel had stopped delivering the food, and he realized that the Lord was punishing him.

The hermit went to the priest and asked why the Lord was punishing him. The priest heard his confession and told him, "You have committed the sin of pride. You have sinned by wishing the prisoners' souls be taken by the devil."

Anguished by the thought that he had sinned, the hermit asked the priest, "I have sinned in the eyes of the Lord. What is my penance to be? Tell me, Father."

The priest gave the hermit his penance. "Take this cane. When the cane sprouts three green branches, then the Lord has forgiven you."

The hermit left the church carrying the cane the priest had given him. He traveled through the land, wandering from village to village. At each village he would ask for food and shelter. In some villages the people would take pity on his misery and would give him food and shelter. In other villages the people would chase him away. The children would throw rocks at him, and the dogs would bark after him as he left. The hermit wondered to himself, "When will my penance be over? I have traveled through the land, and still my cane shows no sign of sprouting even one branch."

One evening the hermit came to the house of a little old woman. He knocked on the door of the house, and when the little old woman answered, he said, "I am an old hermit. Would you please show me the kindness of giving me some food? I have traveled long and have not had any food for several days."

The old woman looked at the hermit, realized that he was suffering some penance, and took pity on him. She invited him into her house and fed him some warm soup. As the hermit was eating, she asked him, "Old man, why do you suffer so much? What have you done to displease the Lord so that he punishes you in this way?"

The hermit told her his story. As she listened, the old woman found the story so sad that she offered to give him shelter for the night.

"But when my three sons return home, you must hide. They have turned into very bad men, and I fear they will harm you if they see you here." She showed the hermit a place where he could hide in a barn by the house.

Later that evening the old woman's sons came back. The sons were thieves, and they brought with them the things they had stolen that day. As soon as they had returned to their house, they went to the barn to hide what they had stolen. As they were hiding their loot, they discovered the hermit.

They dragged the hermit out of the barn and argued over who was going to beat him up first. The hermit was very afraid that they would kill him. On the one hand, the hermit was glad that his life might be over because he was tired of suffering so much. But on the other hand, he did not want to die before his penance was finished because he knew that then he would never have eternal salvation.

The old woman came out of the house and stopped the thieves from beating the hermit. Her sons asked her, "Why should we do this old man any favors? He looks so miserable he deserves to die."

The old woman admonished her sons, "Leave him alone! This poor man has suffered enough. He is being punished by the Lord for the sin of pride, and he must travel as a hermit until his penance is done."

The sons took their hands off the hermit, and one of them said, "This is how the Lord punishes a man for the sins the hermit has committed. What will the Lord do to us? We are murderers and thieves!"

When the sons thought about what their punishment might be, they decided to change their ways and to follow the ways of the Lord for the rest of their lives. They thanked the hermit for coming to their house and showing them their sins while there was still time to change. The thieves asked the hermit to show them how to pray to the Lord for forgiveness. After they had prayed, they told the hermit he could stay with them until he was finished with his penance.

The next morning when they awoke, they went to find the hermit. They found him dead. He had passed away during the middle of the might. By his bed they found his cane. During the night it had sprouted three green branches. By this sign the old woman and her sons knew that the hermit had finished his penance and that his soul rested in eternal grace.

LAS TRES RAMAS
(THE THREE BRANCHES)

En la espesura del bosque, al otro lado de la montaña, vivía un ermitaño. Había sido un hombre de mundo, pero lo había dejado todo para vivir en soledad en su pequeña cabaña en el bosque, disfrutando de la compañía de la naturaleza. Así, viviendo lejos de los problemas del mundo, el ermitaño era feliz con su vida. Había escogido la soledad porque se había consagrado a seguir el camino del Señor aquí en esta tierra. Pasaba sus días rezando, ayunando y leyendo la Biblia. A menudo los viajeros lo buscaban intentando encontrar las respuestas a sus problemas cotidianos, y él siempre les daba la misma respuesta, "La solución a tus problemas es seguir el camino del Señor. No hay otra respuesta sino las enseñanzas del Señor."

El Señor estaba contento con el ermitaño, y cada día le enviaba un ángel que le traía comida y agua. El ángel dejaba el agua y la comida a la puerta de la cabaña y el ermitaño, al levantarse por las mañanas, a menudo escuchaba el roce de las alas del ángel al volar de vuelta al cielo. De este modo, el ermitaño sabía que vivía en gracia ante los ojos del Señor.

Un día una tropa de soldados, que llevaba prisioneros, atravesaba el bosque cerca de la casa del ermitaño. El ermitaño se dió cuenta de que eran prisioneros realmente malos porque iban muy fuertemente vigilados. Imaginó los terribles crímenes que debían haber cometido. Al pasar por su casa, el ermitaño dijo en voz alta, "El diablo debería llevarse sus almas porque sus pecados han ofendido al Señor."

Cuando el Señor escuchó lo que el ermitaño había dicho dejó de estar contento con él, porque había cometido pecado de soberbia. El ermitaño había empezado a creer que era más santo que nadie.

El ermitaño había olvidado que sólo el Señor decide quién es pecador, ya que los pecados de cada persona están escondidos dentro del corazón. El ermitaño estaba equivocado al desear que el diablo se llevara el alma de cualquier persona. Porque siempre que exista la posibilidad del arrepentimiento, también existe la posibilidad de que los pecados de uno sean perdonados. Para dar una lección al ermitaño, el Señor dejó de enviar al ángel con comida y agua.

Moral and Religious Stories

El primer día que el ángel no trajo la comida, el ermitaño pensó que debía haber cometido algún pecado pequeño, y aquella noche rezó algunas oraciones de más. El segundo día que el ángel no le trajo la comida, el ermitaño estuvo más preocupado. Y otra vez, rezó unas oraciones de más. Finalmente el ermitaño se dió cuenta de que el ángel definitivamente había dejado de traerle la comida y que el Señor estaba castigándole.

El ermitaño se fué al cura y le preguntó por qué le estaba castigando el Señor. El cura escuchó su confesión y le dijo, "Tú has cometido pecado de soberbia. Has pecado al desear que el diablo se llevara las almas de los prisioneros."

Angustiado por el pensamiento de que había pecado, el ermitaño dijo al cura, "He pecado ante los ojos del Señor. ¿Cuál será mi penitencia? Dígame, Padre."

El cura dió al ermitaño su penitencia. "Toma esta vara. Cuando de ella broten tres ramas verdes, entonces el Señor te habrá perdonado."

El ermitaño salió de la iglesia llevando la vara que el cura le había dado. Viajó por el país, errante, de pueblo en pueblo. En cada pueblo pedía comida y techo. En algunos pueblos la gente le tenía lástima por su desgracia y se lo daba. En otros pueblos la gente lo echaba. Los niños le tiraban piedras y los perros le ladraban al irse. El ermitaño se preguntaba, "¿Cuando se acabará mi penitencia? He viajado por todo el país, y aún la vara no muestra señales de que le vaya a brotar ni una rama."

Una tarde el ermitaño llegó a la casa de una viejecita. Llamó a la puerta, y cuando la viejecita le abrió, dijo, "Soy un viejo ermitaño. ¿Sería Ud. tan amable de darme algo de comer? He viajado mucho y no he comido nada durante varios días."

La vieja miró al ermitaño, se dió cuenta de que estaba cumpliendo alguna penitencia, y le dió lástima. Lo invitó a entrar en su casa y le dió de comer una sopa caliente. Cuando el ermitaño estaba comiendo ella le preguntó, "¿Viejo, por qué sufres tanto? ¿Qué has hecho para desagradar tanto al Señor que El te castigue de esta manera?"

El ermitaño le contó su historia. Conforme la vieja escuchaba, encontró su relato tan triste que le ofreció pasar la noche en su casa.

"Pero cuando mis tres hijos vuelvan, debes esconderte. Ya que se han convertido en hombres muy malos, y temo que te hagan daño si te ven aquí." Entonces mostró al ermitaño un lugar en el granero que había cerca de la casa donde podría esconderse.

Más tarde esa misma noche regresaron los hijos de la vieja. Los hijos eran ladrones, y traían con ellos las cosas que habían robado. Cuando estaban escondiendo su botín, descubrieron al ermitaño.

Lo arrastraron afuera del granero, y discutieron acerca de quién iba a pegarle primero. El ermitaño temió que lo iban a matar. Por una parte, estaba contento de que su vida pudiera acabarse ya que estaba muy cansado de sufrir tanto. Pero por otra parte, no quería morir antes de cumplir su penitencia porque sabía que entonces nunca alcanzaría la salvación eterna.

La vieja salió de la casa y detuvo a los ladrones antes de que golpearan al ermitaño. Sus hijos le preguntaron, "¿Por qué debemos perdonar a este viejo? Parece tan miserable, que merece morir."

La vieja regañó a sus hijos. "Dejadlo en paz. Este pobre hombre ya ha sufrido bastante. Está siendo castigado por el Señor por haber cometido pecado de soberbia, y debe viajar como ermitaño hasta que cumpla su penitencia."

Los hijos quitaron sus manos de encima del ermitaño, y uno de ellos dijo, "Así es como el Señor castiga por los pecados que el ermitaño ha cometido. ¿Qué hará con nosotros entonces? ¡Si somos asesinos y ladrones!"

Cuando los hijos pensaron cómo podría ser su castigo, decidieron cambiar y seguir el camino del Señor para el resto de sus vidas. Agradecieron al ermitaño el haber venido a su casa y mostrarles sus pecados cuando aún tenían tiempo para cambiar. Los ladrones le pidieron que les enseñara cómo rezar al Señor para ser perdonados. Después de que habían rezado, le dijeron que podía quedarse con ellos hasta que acabara su penitencia.

A la mañana siguiente cuando se despertaron, fueron a buscar al ermitaño, pero lo encontraron muerto. Había muerto en mitad de la noche. Al lado de su cama encontraron su vara. Durante la noche tres ramas verdes habían brotado de ella. Por esta señal la vieja y sus hijos supieron que el ermitaño había cumplido su penitencia y que su alma descansaba en gracia eternamente.

THE BRUJAS' DANCE

In a valley not too far from here, a young man spent his days tending to the crops on his father's farm. The family farm sat next to the mighty *Sangre de Cristo* mountains. The son was very proud of his family's farm and worked hard to insure that each year's crops provided the food they needed to eat.

The young man was very religious. He always accompanied his parents to church on Sunday and on Holy Days. He always wore the scapular he had received at his First Holy Communion. The priest had told him never to take it off because as long as he had it on, he was protected from evil by God's power.

One day the father called his son over for a man-to-man talk. He knew that his son would one day run the farm by himself and that it was time for him to start learning about the decisions that have to be made about the farm.

The father explained to the son that the work of the farm was starting to be too much for just two people. They would have to find someone to help with the work in the field, and the son would have to show that person how to do the work. The son was very proud that his father was starting to trust him with more responsibility.

Fortunately for the father and the son, a man looking for work arrived at the farm the very next day. The father and son could not believe that the man had showed up so suddenly, but they thought that he must have been sent by God.

The son and the man spent many hours working together in the fields, tending the crops. The man was a hard worker, and often the son was amazed at the good luck that had brought the man just when they needed a good worker. The son felt that the forces of heaven really do pay attention to the affairs of humans on this earth.

The son and the man soon developed a good friendship. The man obviously was a man of the world, and the son spent many hours listening to the stories of his travels. Often the son imagined what his life would be like if he traveled the world as his friend had.

One day the man told the son about a dance that was going to be held in a nearby field. He asked the son if he wanted to go. He told the son that there would be many beautiful girls there and he might be able to meet one of them.

The son had never been to a dance, and he kind of liked the idea of meeting some beautiful girls. When he told his father about the dance, his father warned him that the dance might be for older people and maybe he shouldn't go. The son convinced his father that he was going with the new worker and that everything would be all right.

On the day of the dance, the worker told the son to be ready to go as soon as darkness had fallen. He said the dance couldn't start until the sun had set. He then made a very strange request. He asked the son not to wear his scapular or to say the names of the Holy Family at the dance. The man explained that it might make the beautiful girls think the son was too religious, and they might not be interested in someone like that.

The son thought that this request was strange, but he knew the man was experienced in the ways of the world and thought perhaps he was right.

When it was dark the man came around and asked the son if he was ready to go to the dance. He also asked the son if he had removed his scapular. The son said yes, but secretly he put the scapular in his pocket, because he remembered that the priest had told him to never be without it.

They got on their horses and rode a few miles, to a field close to the mountains. When they arrived at the dance, the son saw a large fire blazing in the middle of a corn field. Around the fire were many people dancing.

The man had been right. There were many beautiful girls at the dance, but the son wondered why he didn't recognize any of the girls. He knew almost all of the families in town, and he had never seen any of these girls before. As the night continued the son danced with many of the girls, and he began to understand why men were so attracted to beautiful women.

The light of the fire suddenly grew more intense, and the flames soared up into the night sky. All of the people ran to the fire, and the son joined them, not wanting to miss anything that was happening.

As the son watched he couldn't believe what he was seeing. A large goat walking on its hind legs came out of the middle of the fire. The goat had a long, pointed tail and was followed by a huge, slithering snake. The snake's tongue flickered wildly about as it looked at the people gathered around the fire. The goat's face was fiercely lit by the fire's light. As the goat walked around the circle of people gathered by the fire, the son was astounded to see the people kiss the goat's pointed tail. Then the people kissed the snake's tongue.

The son knew that his turn would come soon, and he didn't know what to do. Suddenly he became very frightened. He had heard stories about *brujas'* dances and what happened to people who went to them. He also had heard of the balls of fire people had seen over the hills, and he knew that those balls of fire marked the places where the *brujas* held their gatherings at night. Then the son realized that the goat must be *El Diablo* himself.

Suddenly the goat was in front of the son. Everyone in the circle stopped their wild, frenzied dancing and looked at the son to see what he would do. In desperation the son reached into his pocket and took out his scapular. He held it in front of the goat's face and yelled out the names of the Holy Family, "Jesus, Mary, and Joseph!"

A crashing bolt of lightning struck the ground in front of the son. It seemed as if the whole world exploded in flames, and the son passed out from fright.

The next morning the son woke up and found himself alone in the middle of the cornfield. All the people from the night before were gone, and there was no sign that a fire had raged in the middle of the field. The son looked around for his friend and his horse, but the son was all alone.

The son walked back to his farm, still looking for his friend to ask him about everything that had happened the night before. His father told him that the man had not showed up to work that morning. When his father asked about the dance, the son said yes, there were many beautiful girls there and he had enjoyed dancing with them.

The man never returned. The son often thought about what forces had brought the man to work at his family's farm. He never told anyone about the frightening events at the *brujas'* dance. But from that day on he never took off his scapular. He had learned that, while the powers of heaven are always present in the affairs of humans on this earth, the powers of evil are also constantly active in the lives of humans.

THE GIFTS OF THE HOLY FAMILY (LOS REGALOS DE LA SAGRADA FAMILIA)

In a small house in a mountain valley there lived a poor family. The only child in the family was a little boy named Juan. The father of the family was old and sick. He had been sick for many years, and he was not able to work in the fields to grow food for his family. Every day the mother of the family had to go out into the forest to search for food.

When Juan was 12 years old, he asked his parents if he could go out into the world to discover God's plan for him. His parents hated to see their only child leave home, but they knew that the time must come for every child to go into the world. As Juan kneeled before them, they gave him their blessing and asked for God's blessing and protection for their only child.

Before Juan left his mother gave him a bag with two *tortillas* in it. The *tortillas* were his only food for his journey. She kissed him and through her tears wished him good fortune on his journey.

Juan had been gone from home for a while when he discovered that it was harder to find work than he had expected. Everywhere he went there was no work for him. He began to be discouraged and wondered if he should have stayed home with his parents.

He stopped by a river to rest and to decide what to do. As he sat there a man walked up to him. Juan had not noticed the man approaching, and he was surprised that the man appeared so suddenly. The man obviously was a weary traveler like himself, and Juan decided to be kind to the man.

Juan called to the man, "*Señor*, come over here. I have two *tortillas*, and I will share one of them with you."

The man slowly walked over to Juan and sat down by him. Juan took out one of his mother's *tortillas* and gave it to the man. He took out the other *tortilla* and ate it himself.

After they had eaten the man finally spoke to Juan. He told him, "When you cross the river you will meet two people, a man and a woman. They will have work for you."

Then the man walked away. After he had left Juan looked in his bag and saw that there were two more *tortillas* there. Juan began to wonder if his fortunes were changing. What he did not know was that the man was Jesus himself, who had come to this earth to see who among his flock had a kind and giving spirit.

Juan took his bag of *tortillas* and crossed the river. When he got to the other side, a man and a woman were waiting for him, just as the traveling man said. What Juan did not know was that this man was St. Joseph and this woman was the Blessed Virgin Mary.

The man called Juan over and asked him, "What are you looking for?"

Juan answered, "I am looking for work. I want to make money so I can take care of my parents. Also I hope to discover God's plan for me on this earth."

The man told Juan, "We have work for you if you want it. But I am only able to pay you one *centavo* a day."

Juan thought about the man's offer. He felt that if he saved his one *centavo* a day, he would soon be able to give his parents enough money to live well. Juan accepted the man's offer and went to work on his farm.

Juan worked for the man and woman for five years, but it seemed like five days to Juan. At the end of the five years, Juan went to the man and asked for his money. Juan said, "It is time for me to return to my parents. May I have the money I have earned?"

The man answered Juan, "Yes, it is time for you to go to your parents. But before you leave you must tell me one thing. What do you want the most, a bag full of money or a magic book that will give you what you want?"

Juan thought about the unexpected offer and answered, "I want the book."

The man gave Juan the book. It was a plain book, and Juan wondered if he had made the right choice. Before he left to return to his home, Juan kneeled and received the blessing of St. Joseph.

As soon as Juan had left, he decided to test the book. He asked the book for a white horse and white clothes to go with it. As soon as he had spoken, a regal white horse appeared and Juan's clothes were changed into beautiful white garments. Juan climbed on the horse and rode off to his home.

Meanwhile Juan's parents had continued their meager life on their farm. Every day they looked out of their door, hoping for Juan to return. Often the mother would ask out loud, "I wonder what life the Lord has made for our Juan?"

One day as they were looking out the door, the father saw Juan riding the regal white horse toward the house. Both parents ran out to greet their son. Both were overcome with joy to see their son again, and they fell to their knees to give thanks to the Lord for returning him safely home.

After he had been home for a while, Juan took out his book and asked it to provide a palace for his parents to live in. He also asked the book to provide his parents with everything they wanted. The book immediately provided these things for Juan and his parents.

Many years passed, and Juan and his parents lived a life full of happiness. The time came when Juan's parents were very old and had come to the end of their lives. As the time of his parents' death approached, Juan prayed for their souls to go to heaven.

Shortly after this St. Joseph came down to earth to see Juan and his parents. Juan recognized the man who had given him work and was surprised to see him at his parents' farm.

Juan approached St. Joseph and said to him, "It is good to see you again. I will always remember your kindness when I needed work and your gift of the magic book. But what brings you to my home now?"

St. Joseph came to Juan and told him, "Once you showed kindness to a man in the forest. That man was a member of my family. Because of your act of kindness, I will offer you the greatest gift possible. Your parents have lived many years. Before your parents leave this earth, I want you to tell me something. What do you want the most, more money on this earth or to go to heaven with your parents?"

Juan didn't have to think about the question at all before he answered, "It is best for me to go to heaven with my parents."

St. Joseph told Juan that he would be back for him the next day. When the next day arrived, St. Joseph came and made the palace and all the things in it disappear. He then took Juan and his parents with him to heaven.

From that time on Juan and his parents spent all eternity living in heaven with the Holy Family. Finally Juan and his parents realized God's plan for Juan. (See fig. 14.)

Moral and Religious Stories

LOS REGALOS DE LA
SAGRADA FAMILIA
(THE GIFTS OF THE HOLY FAMILY)

En una casa pequeña, en un valle en las montañas, vivía una familia pobre. El único hijo era un niño llamado Juan. El padre era viejo y estaba enfermo. Había estado enfermo durante muchos años, y no podía trabajar en los campos para alimentar a su familia. Cada día la madre tenía que ir al bosque en busca de comida.

Cuando Juan tenía doce años, preguntó a sus padres si podía irse por el mundo a descubrir los planes que Dios tenía para él. A los padres no les gustaba ver a su único hijo dejar la casa, pero sabían que llega un momento en que los hijos tienen que salir a descubrir el mundo. Juan se arrodilló delante de ellos, y ellos le dieron su bendición y pidieron a Dios que también lo bendijera y lo protegiera ya que era su único hijo.

Antes de que Juan se fuera su madre le dió una bolsa con dos tortillas. Las tortillas eran su única comida para el viaje. Lo besó y con sus lágrimas le deseó buena suerte en su viaje.

Juan había estado ausente de su casa poco tiempo cuando descubrió que era más difícil encontrar trabajo de lo que él había esperado. A todas partes que iba no había trabajo para él. Empezó a sentirse desilusionado y se preguntaba si debía haberse quedado en casa con sus padres.

Se detuvo al lado de un río para descansar y para decidir qué hacer. Mientras estaba allí un hombre se le acercó. Juan no se había fijado en él, y se sorprendió cuando apareció tan de repente. El hombre, obviamente, era un viajero cansado igual que él, y Juan decidió ser amable.

Juan lo llamó, "Señor, venga aquí. Tengo dos tortillas, y compartiré una con Ud."

El hombre anduvo lentamente hacia Juan y se sentó a su lado. Juan sacó una de las tortillas de su madre y se la dió. Entonces sacó la otra tortilla y se la comió él.

Después de que habían comido el hombre por fin habló a Juan. Le dijo, "Cuando cruces el río encontrarás a dos personas, un hombre y una mujer. Ellos tendrán trabajo para ti."

El hombre se alejó. Después de que se había ido, Juan miró en su bolsa y vió que había dos tortillas más. Empezó a preguntarse si su fortuna estaba cambiando. Lo que no sabía era que el hombre era el mismo Jesús, que había venido a la tierra para ver los que de entre su rebaño tenían un espíritu amable y generoso.

Juan cogió su bolsa de tortillas y cruzó el río. Cuando llegó al otro lado, un hombre y una mujer lo esperaban, tal como le había dicho el viajero. Lo que Juan no sabía era que este hombre era San José y la mujer era la Bendita Virgen María.

El hombre llamó a Juan y le preguntó, "¿Qué estás buscando?"

Juan le contestó, "Estoy buscando trabajo. Quiero ganar dinero para así poder cuidar de mis padres. También espero descubrir los planes que Dios tiene para mí en este mundo."

El hombre le dijo, "Tenemos trabajo para ti si lo quieres. Pero sólo te puedo pagar un centavo al día."

Juan pensó en la oferta del hombre. Creyó que si podía ahorrar su centavo diario, pronto podría dar a sus padres suficiente dinero para vivir bien. Juan aceptó la oferta y empezó a trabajar en la granja del hombre.

Juan trabajó para el hombre y la mujer durante cinco años, pero a él le parecieron como cinco días. Al final de los cinco años, Juan se fué al hombre y le pidió su dinero. Le dijo, "Es hora de que vuelva con mis padres. ¿Puede pagarme el dinero que he ganado?"

El hombre le contestó, "Sí, ya es hora de que vuelvas con tus padres. Pero antes de irte debes decirme una cosa. ¿Qué quieres más, una bolsa llena de dinero ó un libro mágico que te dará lo que le pidas?"

Juan pensó en la inesperada oferta y contestó, "Quiero el libro."

El hombre le dió el libro. Era un libro normal, y Juan se preguntó si había escogido bien. Antes de partir para volver a su casa, Juan se arrodilló y recibió la bendición de San José.

Tan pronto como Juan se había alejado, decidió probar el libro. Le pidió un caballo blanco y ropas blancas para ir vestido haciendo juego. En cuanto habló, un regio caballo blanco se le apareció, y sus ropas fueron transformadas en preciosas vestiduras blancas. Juan montó en el caballo y se fué para su casa.

Mientras tanto los padres de Juan habían continuado su vida sencilla en la granja. Cada día salían a la puerta a mirar, esperando que Juan volviera. A menudo la madre se preguntaba en voz alta, "¿Me pregunto qué vida ha dado Dios a nuestro Juan?"

Un día cuando salieron a mirar a la puerta, el padre vió a Juan montado en el caballo blanco cabalgando hacia la casa. Ambos padres salieron a recibir a su hijo. Los dos estaban emocionados por la alegría de volver a verlo, y se arrodillaron para dar gracias al Señor por habérselo devuelto sano y salvo.

Después de que había estado en casa un tiempo, Juan sacó su libro y le pidió un palacio para vivir sus padres. También le pidió que les diera todo lo que ellos querían. El libro concedió inmediatamente todas estas cosas.

Pasaron muchos años, y los tres vivieron una vida llena de felicidad. Llegó el momento en el cual los padres de Juan eran muy viejos y habían llegado al final de sus vidas. Conforme se acercaba la hora de su muerte, Juan rezaba para que sus almas fuesen al cielo.

Poco después de esto San José bajó a la tierra para ver a Juan y a sus padres. Juan reconoció en él al hombre que le había dado trabajo, y se sorprendió de verlo en la granja de sus padres.

Juan se acercó a San José y le dijo, "Me alegro de verlo otra vez. Siempre me acordaré de su bondad cuando yo necesitaba trabajo y de su regalo del libro mágico. ¿Pero qué es lo que le trae a mi casa ahora?"

San José le dijo, "Una vez fuiste generoso con un hombre en el bosque. Ese hombre era un miembro de mi familia. Por tu generosidad, te ofreceré el mayor regalo posible. Tus padres han vivido muchos años. Antes de que dejen esta tierra, quiero que me digas algo. ¿Qué es lo que más deseas, más riquezas ó irte al cielo con tus padres?"

Juan no tuvo ni que pensar en la pregunta antes de que respondiera, "Para mí lo mejor es ir al cielo con mis padres."

San José le dijo que volvería por él al día siguiente. Cuando el día siguiente llegó, San José vino e hizo desaparecer el palacio y todas las cosas que había dentro. Entonces se llevó a Juan y a sus padres con él al cielo.

Desde entonces Juan y sus padres pasan toda la eternidad viviendo en el cielo con la Sagrada Familia. Por fin, Juan y sus padres supieron los planes que Dios tenía para Juan.

EL SANTO NIÑO DE ATOCHA

In Hispanic religious imagery *El Santo Niño de Atocha,* the Holy Child of Atocha, is one of many common and popular figures. (The others are the Virgin of Guadalupe, the Holy Family, and various representations of Christ.) Christian Hispanics hold these images in great reverence. Previous generations of Hispanics commonly heard and knew the stories of the lives of the saints and the miracles of the heavenly powers. These stories deepened their belief, fortified their shared religious bond, and enhanced their understanding of their religion. The story of *El Santo Niño de Atocha* is one example of these religious stories. (See fig. 15.)

EL SANTO NIÑO DE ATOCHA

It was the time of the invasion of the Spanish peninsula by the Moors. In one town, Atocha, the Moors imprisoned all the Christian men, and no one was allowed to visit the men in prison.

The families of these men tried to bring food to their fathers and sons, but the Moors were afraid that any adults who entered the prison might help the men to escape. For this reason only children were allowed into the prison on errands of mercy. Knowing that there was little food in the prison, the families of the men prayed for the deliverance of their loved ones and for their release from suffering.

One day a child dressed as a pilgrim appeared in the town. The child went to the prison carrying a staff, a basket of food, and a gourd of water. The child gave the food and water to the prisoners and brought comfort to them. When the men had eaten and drunk their fill, the basket and the gourd were still full.

The child disappeared soon afterward, but the people of the town always prayed to *El Santo Niño de Atocha* in their time of need. To this day, *El Santo Niño de Atocha* is the patron of travelers and is known for performing miracles, rescuing people, and delivering prisoners from illness.

Los Dos Compadres Stories

THE TRUE PATH TO HAPPINESS (EL CAMINO VERDADERO A LA FELICIDAD)

Stories about two friends, *los dos compadres,* are some of the most common and popular stories in Hispanic tradition. The relationship of *compadre* is a very special friendship relationship in Hispanic culture. Technically, a *compadre* is the godparent of one's child. In everyday life, however, two fast friends are also referred to as *compadres. Los Dos Compadres* stories always contrast two opposite types of individuals. Usually one is rich and the other poor. In these stories the rich man ends up paying for his sins and evil ways, and the poor man has a reversal of fortune that allows him to change places with the rich man. At the center of a *Dos Compadres* story is a moral lesson about right and wrong.

THE TRUE PATH TO HAPPINESS
(EL CAMINO VERDADERO A LA FELICIDAD)

Once there were *dos compadres,* a religious *compadre* and a worldly *compadre.* The religious *compadre* believed that the true path to happiness on this earth was to follow the ways of the Lord. The worldly *compadre* believed that the true path to happiness on this earth was in one's own hard work. (See fig. 17.)

As usual the two *compadres* were arguing over who was right about the true path to happiness on this earth. They argued and argued until they finally agreed on one thing—there was no way they were going to solve the argument themselves because both were too stubborn. So they made a bet. They would allow the next person who walked by to be the judge of the argument. Whoever lost the argument had to spend the night in the desert tied to a cactus.

It just so happened that right at that time the devil, *El Diablo,* was standing around the corner, and he heard the argument and the bet of the two *compadres. El Diablo* often comes to earth himself to see what mischief he can cause in human affairs. And there is no greater mischief *El Diablo* can cause than to turn a religious soul away from the Lord.

El Diablo cast a spell to disguise himself as a *viejito,* a little old man. As the *viejito* came around the corner, the two *compadres* called him over and asked him to be the judge of the argument.

The religious *compadre* spoke his case. "As a man who goes to church every day, I have learned that it is better to follow the ways of the Lord to find peace and happiness on this earth."

Then it was the worldly *compadre's* turn to speak. "In my life I have had little help from some invisible spirit in the sky. I have found that my own effort and hard work have brought me the happiness I need in this life."

The *viejito* scratched his head. Then he scratched his beard. Then he scratched his nose. Finally he spoke. His voice was so faint and scratchy that the two *compadres* had to lean forward to hear what he said. "Well, I have lived a long life, and in my life I have learned a few things. One thing I have definitely learned is that it is better to follow one's own ways to find true happiness."

The worldly *compadre* let out a whoop and slapped the *viejito* so hard on the back that he almost fell over. The worldly *compadre* gave the *viejito* five pesos, thanked him, and sent him on his way.

The religious *compadre* couldn't believe that the Lord had abandoned him in his moment of need. He was certain that it was some sort of test of his faith.

"Well," gloated the worldly *compadre*, "You sure lost that one. Pick your cactus." Then he tied the religious *compadre* to a cactus and went back to the village to tell all his *compadres* about how he had bested the religious *compadre*.

As nightfall came to the desert, the religious *compadre* heard the animals of the desert coming out from the darkness. The snake. The scorpion. The spider. The coyote. He was very afraid of what he was hearing, so he somehow managed to untie himself and climb up to the top of the cactus, where no animals could get him.

In the middle of the night, he heard three voices below him talking. He looked down, and there were three devils laughing and talking about all the evil they had caused on earth that day.

The first devil told this story: "Just seven miles from here a young girl is dying. Her family doesn't know that I took the girl's soul and put it inside a snake buried seven feet under her bed. Oh, what wonderful evil I caused today!"

Then the second devil spoke up. "You call that evil. I call that nothing!" The two devils started to scuffle, but the third devil settled them down, and the second devil continued, "That is just one dying person. Seven miles in the other direction, there is a whole village dying, especially the children! No one in the village knows it, but I went up to the headwaters of the river that runs through the village, and I put a large boulder in the river and stopped the water from running into the village. They are all dying of thirst!"

Finally the third devil spoke up. He told them the simple story of how he had overheard two *compadres* arguing about whether it was better to follow the Lord's path or one's own path to find true happiness on this earth. At the mention of the Lord's name, the two other devils sat forward and listened with great attention. He told them about how he had disguised himself as a *viejito* and had caused the religious *compadre* to lose the bet and to doubt the Lord for a minute.

At this part of the story, the other devils leaped up and did a violent dance, full of yelling and shrieking. They couldn't be any happier, because nothing brings a devil more joy than news that a religious person lost faith, if only for a moment. They both agreed that the third devil had caused the best mischief on earth that day.

The third devil continued, "Right now the religious *compadre* is in this very desert, tied to a cactus. If that poor fool only knew that underneath this cactus lies a chest of Spanish gold!" And with that the three devils vanished in a fireball of smoke.

Carefully the religious *compadre* slid off the cactus branch, holding onto the limbs and lowering himself around the thorns. He sprinted to the village where the young girl was dying. He ran into the house, grabbed a shovel, and started to dig under the girl's bed. Her family thought he was crazy, but he told them he was doing the work of the Lord.

When he had dug down seven feet, a snake reared up its hissing head. The religious *compadre* took his knife and sliced off the snake's head. As soon as the head struck the floor, the spirit of the little girl returned to her body and she came back to life.

Her family was so happy that, to thank the religious *compadre*, they gave him a burro loaded with sacks of gold.

The religious *compadre* then ran to the other village. He found the headwaters of the river, and grabbing a large limb from a fallen tree, he unearthed the boulder blocking the water. As the water flowed to the village, the people ran to the river and stuck their heads in the water. They dunked their children's heads in the water, and it looked like everyone was getting baptized again.

The people of the village were so happy and thankful that they gave the religious *compadre* another burro loaded with sacks of gold.

Then the *compadre* went back to the cactus where he had been tied, and he dug up the chest of Spanish gold the devils had talked about.

As the sun rose in the village, the worldly *compadre* gathered his other *compadres* around him to finish telling them about how he had won the bet with the religious *compadre*. As they looked down the road, they saw the religious *compadre* coming down the path, leading two burros loaded with bags of gold. One of the burros even was carrying a chest of Spanish gold!

All the people of the village gathered around and asked the religious *compadre* to tell them where all the gold had come from. He just said, "It was the Lord's will that I have this gold." He then gave away all the gold to the people of the village. He gave a special amount to the church, and he kept just enough so his family would be free from worry.

All this infuriated the worldly *compadre.* He kept after the religious *compadre* to tell him the truth about how he got the gold until the religious *compadre* gave in and told him about the two villages and the chest of Spanish gold.

As nighttime fell in the village, the worldly *compadre* went out into the desert, looking for the cactus where he had tied up the religious *compadre.* He finally found one that looked right. He climbed onto it and waited for something to happen.

Pretty soon he heard three voices below him. He looked and saw three devils laughing and boasting about all the evil they had caused on earth that day. The worldly *compadre* got so excited that he began to lose his balance and started to fall out of the cactus.

When the devils heard the noise, they looked up and saw the worldly *compadre* falling out of the cactus. One of the devils was overjoyed with the discovery and said, "Well, what have we here!" All three devils grabbed the worldly *compadre,* and in a thunderbolt of lightning, all four disappeared.

To this day no one knows what happened to the worldly *compadre,* for he was never seen again in the village.

So I leave it for you to decide who won the argument between *los dos compadres:* the religious *compadre,* who said that to find true peace and happiness on this earth it is better to follow the path of the Lord, or the worldly *compadre,* who felt that the true path to happiness is through one's own work and effort.

EL CAMINO VERDADERO
A LA FELICIDAD
(THE TRUE PATH TO HAPPINESS)

Erase una vez dos compadres, un compadre religioso y un compadre mundano. El compadre religioso creía que el camino verdadero a la felicidad en esta tierra era seguir el camino del Señor. El compadre mundano creía que el camino verdadero a la felicidad en esta tierra consistía en el trabajo duro de cada uno.

Como siempre los dos compadres estaban discutiendo acerca de quién tenía razón en lo del camino verdadero a la felicidad. Discutieron y discutieron hasta que por fin estuvieron de acuerdo en una cosa, que no iban a solucionar esta discusión entre ellos porque ambos eran demasiado tercos. Así que hicieron una apuesta. Dejarían que la siguiente persona que pasara por allí decidiera la cuestión. El perdedor tendría que pasar la noche atado a un cactus en el desierto.

Justamente en ese momento el diablo estaba al otro lado de la esquina, y escuchó la discusión y la apuesta de los dos compadres. El mismo diablo a menudo viene a la tierra para ver qué maldades puede ocasionar en los asuntos humanos. Y no hay mayor maldad que el diablo pueda causar que desviar un alma piadosa del camino del Señor.

El diablo mediante un hechizo se convirtió en viejito. Cuando el viejito dobló la esquina, los dos compadres lo llamaron y le pidieron ser el juez en la discusión.

El compadre religioso explicó su postura. "Como hombre que va a la iglesia todos los días, he aprendido que es mejor seguir el camino del Señor para encontrar la paz y la felicidad en esta tierra."

Entonces le tocó hablar al compadre mundano. "En mi vida he tenido poca ayuda de los espíritus invisibles del cielo. He comprobado que mi propio esfuerzo y trabajo es lo que me ha traído la felicidad que necesito en esta vida."

El viejito se rascó la cabeza. Entonces se rascó la barba. Y entonces se rascó la nariz. Al final habló. Su voz era tan débil y áspera que los dos compadres tuvieron que inclinarse hacia adelante para escuchar lo que decía. "Bueno, he vivido una vida larga, y he aprendido algunas cosas. Una cosa que he aprendido muy claramente es que es mejor seguir el camino de uno mismo para encontrar la felicidad verdadera."

El compadre mundano soltó una carcajada y dió una palmada tan fuerte al viejito en la espalda, que éste casi se cayó. Después le dió cinco pesos y las gracias, y lo mandó por su camino.

El compadre religioso no podía creer que el Señor lo había abandonado en su momento de necesidad. Estaba seguro que esto era alguna prueba para su fé.

"Bueno," dijo el compadre mundano pavoneándose, "Has perdido la apuesta. Escoge tu cactus." Entonces ató al compadre religioso a un cactus y volvió al pueblo para contar a todos sus compadres cómo había ganado la apuesta al compadre religioso.

Conforme caía la noche, el compadre religioso escuchaba a los animales del desierto saliendo de la oscuridad. La serpiente. El escorpión. La araña. El coyote. Tenía mucho miedo de lo que estaba escuchando y, de alguna manera, consiguió soltarse y subir a lo alto del cactus para que ningún animal pudiera alcanzarlo.

En la mitad de la noche, escuchó tres voces hablando por abajo de él. Miró hacia abajo, y había tres diablos riéndose y hablando acerca de todo lo malo que habían hecho en la tierra ese día.

El primer diablo contó la siguiente historia: "A justamente siete millas de aquí una niña se está muriendo. Su familia no sabe que le quité su alma y la metí en una serpiente enterrada a siete pies por debajo de su cama. ¡Oh, qué maldad más maravillosa he hecho hoy!"

Entonces habló el segundo diablo. "Tú llamas a eso maldad. ¡Eso no es nada!" Los dos diablos empezaron a pelearse, pero el tercer diablo los tranquilizó, y el segundo diablo continuó, "Eso es solamente una persona muriéndose. ¡A siete millas en la otra dirección, hay un pueblo entero pereciendo, sobre todo los niños! Nadie en el pueblo lo sabe, pero yo subí al nacimiento del río que pasa por el pueblo, y allí puse una roca grande que impide que el agua corra y baje hasta el pueblo. ¡Están todos muriéndose de sed!"

Por fin habló el tercer diablo. Les contó la historia sencilla de cómo había oído a dos compadres discutiendo acerca de que si era mejor seguir el camino del Señor, ó el camino propio de uno mismo para encontrar la verdadera felicidad en esta tierra. Al mencionar el nombre del Señor, los otros dos diablos se inclinaron hacia adelante y escucharon con mucha atención. Les contó como él se había convertido en viejito, y había hecho que el compadre religioso perdiera la apuesta y dudara del Señor durante un minuto.

Al llegar a esta parte de la historia, los otros diablos saltaron y bailaron una danza violenta, llena de chillidos y gritos. No podían estar más contentos, porque nada produce más alegría a un diablo que la noticia de una fé perdida, aunque sólo sea por un momento. Ambos estuvieron de acuerdo en que el tercer diablo había causado ese día la mayor maldad en la tierra.

El tercer diablo continuó, "Ahora el compadre religioso está en este mismo desierto atado a un cactus. ¡Si el pobre tonto supiera que debajo de este cactus hay un cofre de oro español!" Y con eso los tres diablos desaparecieron en una bola de fuego y humo.

Con cuidado, el compadre religioso bajó del cactus, apoyándose en las ramas y evitando las espinas. Se dirigió corriendo muy de prisa al pueblo donde la niña se estaba muriendo. Entró en la casa, cogió una pala, y empezó a cavar debajo de la cama de la niña. La familia pensó que estaba loco, pero él les dijo que estaba haciendo el trabajo del Señor.

Cuando había cavado siete pies, una serpiente levantó su cabeza siseante. El compadre religioso sacó su cuchillo y se la cortó. En cuanto la cabeza tocó el suelo, el espíritu de la niña volvió a su cuerpo y la vida volvió a ella.

La familia estaba tan contenta que, en agradecimiento, dieron al compadre religioso un burro cargado de sacos de oro.

Entonces el compadre religioso se fué corriendo al otro pueblo. Encontró el nacimiento del río, y cogiendo una rama grande de un árbol caído, movió la roca que bloqueaba el paso del agua. Cuando el agua llegó al pueblo, la gente corrió hacia el río y todos metieron sus cabezas debajo de agua, las de sus hijos también, y parecía que todo el mundo se estaba bautizando de nuevo.

La gente del pueblo estaba tan contenta y agradecida que dieron al compadre religioso otro burro cargado de sacos de oro.

Entonces el compadre volvió al cactus donde había estado atado, y desenterró el cofre de oro español del que habían estado hablando los diablos.

Cuando el sol se levantó en el pueblo, el compadre mundano reunió a sus otros compadres para terminar de contarles cómo había ganado la apuesta al compadre religioso. Cuando miraron hacia el camino, vieron al compadre religioso viniendo con dos burros cargados de sacos de oro. ¡Uno de los burros incluso llevaba un cofre de oro español!

Toda la gente del pueblo se reunió y pidió al compadre religioso que contara de dónde había venido tanto oro. El sólo dijo, "Fué la voluntad de Dios que yo tenga este oro." Entonces regaló todo el oro a la gente del pueblo. Dió una buena cantidad a la iglesia, y se quedó con lo justo para que su familia estuviera libre de preocupaciones.

Todo esto puso furioso al compadre mundano, el cual insistió e insistió en que el compadre religioso le dijera la verdad de cómo había conseguido el oro, hasta que por fin éste le contó lo de los dos pueblos y el cofre de oro español.

Cuando se hizo de noche en el pueblo, el compadre mundano se fué al desierto, a buscar el cactus donde había atado al compadre religioso. Al final encontró uno que parecía el que buscaba. Trepó a lo alto y esperó a que algo ocurriera.

Pronto escuchó tres voces por abajo de él. Miró y vió a tres diablos riendo y jactándose de todo el mal que habían causado en la tierra ese día. El compadre mundano se entusiasmó tanto que empezó a perder el equilibrio y a caerse del cactus.

Cuando los diablos escucharon el ruido, miraron hacia arriba y vieron al compadre mundano cayéndose del cactus. Uno de los diablos estaba contentísimo con el descubrimiento y dijo, "Bueno, ¿qué tenemos aquí?" Los tres diablos agarraron al compadre mundano, y con un relámpago y un trueno desaparecieron los cuatro.

Hasta hoy nadie sabe qué pasó al compadre mundano, porque nunca más fué visto en el pueblo.

Así que dejo que Uds. decidan quién ganó la discusión entre los dos compadres: el compadre religioso, que dijo que para encontrar la paz y la felicidad verdadera en esta tierra es mejor seguir el camino del Señor, ó el compadre mundano, que creyó que el camino verdadero a la felicidad se encuentra en el trabajo y el esfuerzo de uno mismo.

THE COMPADRE'S SANDALS

Once there were *dos compadres,* a rich *compadre* and a poor *compadre.* The poor *compadre* was a farmer who struggled to feed his family. He was so poor he had only one skinny cow to give milk for his family. The rich *compadre* had many cows and other animals on his family farm. This rich *compadre* enjoyed aggravating his poor *compadre.* Even though they were *compadres,* he couldn't help playing a good joke on his poor friend.

One day the poor *compadre* was walking past his *compadre's* house when he saw his friend sitting on his porch reading the newspaper. Since he couldn't read, he went up to his friend and asked him, "So, what's going on in the world?"

The rich *compadre* replied, "Oh, not too much. At least not much that's worth paying attention to. Except for this story about the town where people are paying a lot of money for sandals."

The poor *compadre* asked his friend to read him the article about that town. His friend just said, "It's a town not far from here. But what difference is it to you? You don't have any sandals to sell."

The poor *compadre* walked away thinking about the town that paid such good prices for sandals. As the poor *compadre* walked away, the rich *compadre* laughed at the foolishness of his friend.

When the poor *compadre* got home, he told his wife about the town. His wife warned him not to do anything foolish, because all they had was their only cow. But late at night the poor *compadre* began to form a plan, a plan that would make him rich. Then his family could have everything they wanted, and he would no longer have to be the butt of his *compadre's* jokes.

In the morning he went out into the barn and killed his cow. He butchered the cow and made sandals out of the cow's hide. When his wife saw what he had done, she ran crying back into the house. The poor *compadre* understood her feelings, but he knew that in a few short days she would be happy beyond belief.

He gathered up his sandals and walked to the nearby town. As he walked into the town, he noticed that no one was wearing sandals. He wondered why they didn't wear the sandals they had paid so much money for. He figured it was just their way, so he started walking through the streets calling out, "Sandals for sale! Sandals for sale!" No one came up to him to buy any sandals. So he yelled out louder, "Sandals for sale! Sandals for sale!" Still no one came to buy sandals.

Finally he asked a policeman if this was the town where people paid a good price for sandals. The policeman just looked at him quizzically. He told the poor *compadre*, "Someone must be playing a joke on you. There is no such town around here. The ground is too rocky and hard to wear sandals."

The poor *compadre* knew who had played a joke on him. He gathered up his sandals and began the long, dusty walk back home. He didn't know what he was going to tell his wife. Not only had she been right, but now their only cow was slaughtered and all he had to show for it was a bunch of sandals.

As he walked home he became more and more depressed. Perhaps it was God's will that he stay poor all his life. He just wished his family didn't have to suffer because of his bad luck.

He stopped by a river to drink some water and rest. It was very hot out in the sun. He spotted a nearby cave, and he went into it to rest in the shade. As he walked into the cave, he noticed a great labyrinth of tunnels going deeper into the cave. He was curious about the tunnels and began to explore them. The tunnels went every which way. Many times the poor *compadre* thought he was lost. But eventually he found his way, and soon he began to know his way around the cave.

To his surprise he came to several large rooms. He investigated the largest room and found it filled with leather bags. As he opened one of the bags, he saw it was filled with gold coins.

Quickly he looked around. He didn't see anyone or any sign of the bags' owners. The bags seemed to have been abandoned for a very long time. As he ran his fingers through the gold coins, he thought to himself, "Perhaps my luck is changing!" He thanked the Lord for his good luck, gathered up several of the bags, and ran out of the cave as fast as he could.

When he got home he told his wife all about the sandals and the joke the rich *compadre* had played on him. He didn't tell his wife about the gold coins right at first. Then, just as his wife began crying again about the dead cow, he whipped out one of the bags of gold coins.

His wife was astounded to see so much money. When the poor *compadre* told her how he had found the coins, she fell to her knees and thanked God for their good luck.

Soon it became apparent to the rich *compadre* that his friend had come into some money. Since the rich *compadre* was a very greedy and jealous man, he kept questioning his friend about his sudden change of fortune. Finally the poor *compadre* could stand it no longer, and he told his friend about the cave he had found. He thought that his friend had so much money that he would never go looking for the cave and its bags of gold coins.

But he really didn't know his friend that well. For soon afterward his friend set off to look for the cave. The rich *compadre* soon found the cave and began searching through the dark and labyrinthine tunnels. The rich *compadre* was lucky and quickly found the room with the bags of gold. When he saw all those bags of gold coins, he could not control his happiness, and he shouted out with joy.

Now, it just so happened that some thieves who lived in the caves heard the rich *compadre's* shouts and knew that they had caught the man who had carried off some of their loot. They ran to the cave room and saw the rich *compadre* running his hands through the gold. The thieves captured the rich *compadre* and accused him of stealing their bags of gold coins. The rich *compadre* tried to explain that he was not their man, but the thieves thought he was lying and decided to punish him for stealing their gold coins.

For a few days no one missed the rich *compadre*. Often he traveled and no one knew where he had gone. But after a few weeks, everyone knew that the rich *compadre* was not on a trip but was missing.

When his friend did not return home, the poor *compadre* guessed what had happened. He was sorry that his friend's greed had cost him his life, so he went to the church and gave some money to the priest in honor of his lost friend. The poor *compadre* and his family lived a life of happiness from that time on.

THE GREEDY COMPADRE

Once there were *dos compadres,* a greedy *compadre* and a poor *compadre.*

The winter had been especially long and hard for the poor *compadre.* He and his wife had suffered without much food for many cold nights. He was a hard worker, but no matter how hard he worked, he never seemed to have enough money. Finally the poor *compadre* decided to go ask his neighbor, the greedy *compadre,* to loan him some money so he could buy some food. The poor *compadre* was sure that he would be able to pay the greedy *compadre* back when the spring crops came in.

Swallowing his pride the poor *compadre* went to his neighbor's house and asked him for a small loan to buy food. The greedy neighbor just laughed and said, "If you worked harder, you wouldn't be so poor. Just look at me. I have all I want because I have always worked hard. No, I won't give you any money."

The poor *compadre* went home and told his wife what had happened. Both he and his wife felt humiliated. They knew that they were hard workers and were just down on their luck. Most of all they felt that the greedy *compadre* needed to be taught a lesson. They thought and thought all night until they came up with a plan that they thought would work.

The next day the poor *compadre* went out into the field and trapped two rabbits. He hid one of the rabbits in the shed in back of his house. He kept the other rabbit in the house until the greedy *compadre* walked by.

Soon the greedy *compadre* did walk by. As he passed by the front of the poor *compadre's* house, he saw the poor *compadre* brushing a rabbit. He asked his friend, "Why are you doing such a careful job of brushing that rabbit?"

The poor *compadre* answered, "This is no regular rabbit. This is a special rabbit I have trained to follow orders and run errands for its master."

The greedy *compadre* did not believe his friend's story. But he was curious enough to ask for a demonstration. He said, "If this rabbit can do what you say, then prove it."

The poor *compadre* replied, "I will prove it. Is there anything you need delivered? If there is, then give it to me. If the rabbit does not deliver it, then I will give you all my belongings and my farm."

The greedy *compadre* had always wanted his neighbor's farm. He knew that this would be a very easy way to get it. So he agreed. He brought over a package of jewels that he had planned to take to a store in town the next day. He gave the jewels to the poor *compadre* and watched as the poor *compadre* strapped the jewels onto the rabbit's back.

The poor *compadre* then commanded the rabbit, "Take this package to town. When you have done this, come back with a note from the store to prove you have delivered the jewels." When he let go of the rabbit, it raced off through a field toward town.

The *compadres* waited several hours for the rabbit to return. While they were waiting the poor *compadre's* wife went out into the road and released the second rabbit that had been hidden in the shed. She tied a note onto the rabbit's back to fool the greedy *compadre* into thinking this second rabbit was the first rabbit that had run off with the jewels on its back.

The greedy *compadre* was astounded when he saw the rabbit running up the road with a note attached to its back. The poor *compadre* caught the rabbit and gave the note to the greedy *compadre*. The note said, "I have received the package."

The greedy *compadre* decided that he had to own the rabbit. He pleaded and pleaded with the poor *compadre* to sell. The poor *compadre* refused to sell the rabbit, but the greedy *compadre* persisted. Finally the poor *compadre* agreed to sell the rabbit for a goodly sum of money. The greedy *compadre* wanted the rabbit so much that he agreed to the sum of money. He gave the money to the poor *compadre*, and as he walked away with the rabbit under his arm, the poor *compadre* and his wife danced for joy because their plan had worked so easily.

As he was walking home, the greedy *compadre* met the owner of the store where he had sent the jewels. He ran up to the store owner and exclaimed, "Wasn't it amazing! Imagine this rabbit delivering the jewels to you. And now I own the rabbit, and people are going to pay me a lot of money just to see it."

The store owner asked the greedy *compadre*, "What are you talking about? No rabbit delivered anything to me. Don't you know that it is impossible for a rabbit to do such a thing?"

The greedy *compadre* began to suspect that he had been fooled. He immediately ran back to the poor *compadre's* house. When the poor *compadre* saw his neighbor running up the road, he and his wife made a quick second plan.

The greedy *compadre* didn't even knock at the poor *compadre's* door. As he burst right into the front room of the house, he was shocked by what he saw. In the middle of the room on the floor was the poor *compadre's* wife. She appeared to be quite dead.

The greedy *compadre* asked, "What happened? Is she dead?"

The poor compadre replied, "Yes, she is dead. She had a sudden heart attack a few minutes ago. It was terrible to watch, but I am not worried. The *curandera* gave me a magic flower that can bring the dead back to life."

He then took out a yellow flower and held it to his wife's nose. As he waved the flower under her nose, she began to stir. The more he waved the flower, the more she moved on the floor. Finally she raised up, and with a shaking in her legs, walked around the room.

The greedy *compadre* knew that he had witnessed a miracle. He also knew that he had to have that flower. He thought to himself, "Once people know what this flower can do, they will pay a lot of money, even give me everything they have, for just one whiff of this flower." He pleaded with his neighbor to sell him the flower.

The poor *compadre* refused to sell him the flower. He told the greedy *compadre*, "The *curandera* warned me to take care of the flower. Its powers are very strong, too strong for most men to handle."

But again the greedy *compadre* would not give up until he got what he wanted. Finally the poor *compadre* relented and sold the flower to the greedy *compadre*.

When the greedy *compadre* got home he felt he had to test the flower. He killed his wife, and as she lay dead on the floor, he waved the flower under her nose.

Nothing happened. He waved the flower under his wife's nose again. Nothing happened. He ground up the flower and blew it into his wife's nose. Still nothing happened.

The greedy *compadre* knew that he had been tricked a second time by his neighbor. He stormed over to his neighbor's house to get his money back.

The poor *compadre* and his wife never imagined that the greedy *compadre* would kill his wife to test the flower, and they were surprised when he came back so soon.

The greedy *compadre* grabbed the poor *compadre* and threw him into a sack. He dragged him out of the house, yelling, "You have tricked me out of my money for the last time. Now you are going to drown in the river!"

He pulled the sack with the poor *compadre* in it over to his ranch. He told one of his workers to put the sack on a horse while he went and saddled his own horse.

While he was gone the poor *compadre* called out for the worker to let him out of the sack. He told the worker, "Help me. I am being carried off against my will to marry the rich sister of your ranch owner. I am a married man, and I don't want to marry his rich sister. Please change places with me."

Now, the ranch worker was a very poor worker himself and had always wished his luck would change. He knew that this might be his only chance to change his fortune. He quickly untied the bag and released the poor *compadre*. Then he climbed into the bag and let the poor *compadre* tie it back up.

The greedy *compadre* returned and rode off with the sack toward the river. When he got to the river, he tossed the bag in and left it to sink to the bottom. Fortunately for the ranch worker, the poor *compadre* had deliberately tied the sack loosely, and the worker was able to escape and swim to the banks of the river. Happy to be alive he ran off and never returned to his job at the ranch.

Meanwhile the poor *compadre* returned to his home. On the way he found the package of jewels that had fallen off the first rabbit as it ran through the fields. The poor *compadre* picked up the package of jewels and took it home to show to his wife.

The next day the greedy *compadre* was walking by the poor *compadre's* house and was surprised to see the poor *compadre* on the front porch, inspecting a pile of jewels. The greedy *compadre* walked up to his neighbor and said, "I thought you had drowned. How come you are alive, and where did you find my jewels?"

The poor *compadre* looked up and answered his *compadre,* "You didn't throw me into a very deep part of the river. When I didn't drown the river people, who live at the bottom of the river, rescued me. They have immense collections of jewels, and they told me they had found these on my rabbit. They let me take all the jewels I wanted because they have so many."

The greedy *compadre* knew that there was still a chance for him to come out ahead of his neighbor. He asked the poor *compadre* to throw him into the river so that he could be rescued by the river people.

The poor *compadre* refused to have any part of the greedy *compadre's* plan. Instead he just kept sorting the jewels. But the greedy *compadre* made such a pest of himself that finally the poor *compadre* took the greedy *compadre* to a spot on the river and threw him in. Unfortunately the greedy *compadre* couldn't swim, and he drowned right away.

Because he was the greedy *compadre's* neighbor and because the greedy *compadre* had no living relatives, the poor *compadre* was given possession of all the property and riches of the greedy *compadre.* To this day the poor *compadre* and his wife live a comfortable and happy life, and they share their wealth with any relative, friend, or needy person who asks for help.

Chistes

ONE FOR YOU, ONE FOR ME (UNA PARA TI, UNA PARA MÍ)

Once two thieves stole some money from a village, and as they escaped they looked for a place where they could divide their fortune. They ran past the cemetery and decided that it was the perfect place. One told the other, "No one will ever look for us here!"

In their hurry they dropped two bags of money outside the cemetery. "Wait, we dropped two of the bags," one thief said.

"We'll get them later, when it's dark. Hurry up!" the other replied.

Later a man was walking by the cemetery, and he heard the two thieves dividing the money. "One for you, one for me. One for you, one for me."

The man thought, "It must be the devil and the Lord dividing up the souls! I must run and tell my *compadre.*"

He ran to his friend's house and told him what he had heard. They decided to sneak over later that night, in the dark so nobody could see them.

When they were outside the cemetery wall, they heard the voices from within. "One for you, one for me. One for you, one for me."

The man who had first heard the voices told his friend, "See, I told you. It is the devil and the Lord dividing up the souls."

Just then one of the thieves said, "Let's go get those two outside the cemetery wall."

The two *compadres* took off running. One yelled back to the other, "Run faster! You don't know if you're in the Lord's lot or the devil's!"

UNA PARA TI, UNA PARA MÍ
(ONE FOR YOU, ONE FOR ME)

Sucedió que una vez dos ladrones robaron un dinero de algún pueblo, y en su huída buscaron un lugar donde poder dividir el botín. Pasaron corriendo al lado del cementerio y decidieron que era el lugar perfecto. Uno dijo al otro, "¡Nadie nos buscará aquí jamás!"

En su prisa se les cayeron dos bolsas de dinero afuera del cementerio. "Espera, se nos han caído dos bolsas," dijo un ladrón.

"Las cogeremos más tarde, cuando esté oscuro. ¡Date prisa!" contestó el otro.

Más tarde un hombre pasó por el cementerio, y escuchó a los dos ladrones repartiéndose el dinero. "Una para ti, una para mí. Una para ti, una para mí."

El hombre pensó, "¡Deben ser el diablo y el Señor repartiéndose las almas! Debo correr a decírselo a mi compadre."

Y se fué corriendo a la casa de su amigo a contarle lo que había oído. Los compadres decidieron ir al cementerio más tarde aquella noche, cuando nadie los pudiera ver en la oscuridad.

Cuando llegaron al muro del cementerio, escucharon las voces desde dentro. "Una para ti, una para mí. Una para ti, una para mí."

El compadre que había escuchado las voces primero dijo al otro compadre, "Ves, te lo dije. Son el diablo y el Señor repartiéndose las almas."

Justo en ese momento uno de los ladrones dijo, "Ahora vamos a por esas dos que están afuera del cementerio."

Los dos compadres salieron corriendo. Uno gritó al otro, "¡Corre más de prisa! ¡Que no sabemos cuál de los dos está en el lote del Señor ó en el del diablo!"

YOU FIRST!

Once in a village nearby there lived a little old couple. They had lived long and full lives, and their children were long since raised and gone. For the past several years, they had nothing but each other and the ailments of old age.

After one especially long and painful day, the husband told his wife, "I am so tired of living. How I wish for my youth and my health back."

His wife answered, "What you say is so true. Those were such wonderful days. But you know as well as I do that those days will never return. All we have to look forward to are more long days and more great pains."

"That is so true. How I wish the Lord would take mercy on me and take me to my eternal reward. I would gladly go first."

"No, husband, I wish the Lord would take me first!"

Just then a friend of the devil came by. He overheard their conversation and decided to play a trick on the couple. He went up to the house and knocked on one of the outside walls.

The husband called out, 'Who is knocking on my house?"

Disguising his voice the friend of the devil said, "I am an angel of the Lord. I have been sent to take you to your final reward. Who will go first?"

The husband looked at his wife and said, "You can go first."

DON CACAHUATE, MR. PEANUT

Don Cacahuate, Mr. Peanut, is a comic character who usually appears in short stories that make fun of his ways. Sometimes he is by himself, sometimes with his wife. She usually plays the straight character to his buffoon.

One spring day Don Cacahuate was riding in the pasture, checking on any cows that might have run off in last night's storm. As he passed over a stream, the horse suddenly bolted and threw Don Cacahuate. Picking himself up from the ground, Don Cacahuate dusted himself off and said to the horse, "Thank you, horse. That is where I wanted to get off."

One day Don Cacahuate and his wife were going on a trip to visit relatives. Don Cacahuate bragged to his wife, "I have some free tickets to use at the train station."

When they got to the train station, Don Cacahuate started walking down the tracks.

His wife ran to catch up with him and asked, "We're walking? I thought you said you had free tickets!"

He looked at her and said, "Oh, I forgot to tell you. It's only free if we walk."

Later in the day they decided that if they were ever going to get to their relatives' house, they would have to hop on a train as it rushed past. As the train passed by, Don Cacahuate's wife easily hopped on board. Right behind her Don Cacahuate missed his grip. He was dragged, dangling, until he managed to get on the train.

His wife asked him, "What were you doing back there?"

Don Cacahuate answered, "Oh nothing. I was just keeping the train from falling over while you got settled."

Don Cacahuate was in jail. He asked his wife, "Please bring me some coffee."
Since Don Cacahuate had been in jail he had not been working, and there was no money in the house to buy any coffee. So his wife asked him, "And what am I supposed to get the coffee with?"
He answered, "With milk. You know I don't like it any other way."

One afternoon Don Cacahuate's wife was hungry. She asked Don Cacahuate, "Is there anything in the house to eat? I'm hungry."
Don Cacahuate answered, "There's *tortillas*. Have a *tortilla*."
She answered back, "I don't want a *tortilla* by itself."
He told her, "Well, then, have two!"

IS HE LOST?

Once there was a man who lived a very wild life. He was always gambling and spending his time down at the *cantina*. Ever since he was a little boy, he had always had a wild streak to him. He was always getting into trouble with the law, and usually if something had been done that was wrong, he was somehow involved. People just got used to blaming him, even for things he didn't do.

He never married but enjoyed the company of women just like him. He had never been to church in his life. His family was always trying to get him to change his ways and go to church. He resisted their pleas for years, until the family finally gave up trying.

As the man got older, he started to slow down. He spent fewer and fewer nights at the *cantina*. He even talked about starting to go to church. His family was overjoyed. Their prayers had been answered.

One Sunday the man announced that he would like to go to church. The family members told him that because of the life he had led, he would have to speak to the priest and maybe go to confession before he went to church. They warned the priest that he was coming to confession.

The priest was very happy to see the man finally coming to church. He felt that if this man could be saved, then anyone could be saved. When the man entered the church, the priest welcomed him. He told the man that they would begin with the teachings of the church.

The priest decided that since the man had never been to church, he should begin with some very easy questions to see how much the man knew. He asked the man, "Where is God?"

The man answered in a hurt voice, "I don't know. Is he lost? I always get blamed for everything!"

LIKE FATHER, LIKE SON
(DE TAL PALO, TAL ASTILLA)

Once there was a family that consisted of the father, the mother, the grandpa, and the little child. The grandpa had lived with his son, the father of the family, for many years. His wife, the grandma of the family, had died during an especially hard winter long ago. When his wife died, the grandpa was thankful that he had a son with whom he could live. As the years passed and he grew older, he especially enjoyed the company of his grandson.

During the years when he was younger, the grandpa was able to help with the chores of running the farm. During these years he was active in the life of the family, and he felt he had a place in his son's home.

With the passing of the years, however, he grew ill and was not able to help with the work of the farm. Gradually he was able to do less and less. The wife started to complain that the grandpa was nothing but work and maybe they should think about getting him to live someplace else.

The son did not want to send his father away, but then he thought, "Maybe my wife is right. He is not much use any more, and he might be happier somewhere else." He called his young son over and said, "Go get a blanket and put it in the barn for your grandpa. He is old and useless, so he is moving to the barn."

The young son got the blanket and then got a pair of scissors and started to cut the blanket in two.

The father asked the boy, "What are you doing? That is a perfectly good blanket."

The boy answered his father, "I am cutting the blanket in two pieces so when you get old like grandpa, I will have a blanket to give you when you move into the barn."

From that day on the grandpa continued to live in the house with the family.

DE TAL PALO, TAL ASTILLA (LIKE FATHER, LIKE SON)

Erase una vez una familia que consistía en el padre, la madre, un abuelo, y un hijito pequeño. El abuelo había vivido con su hijo, el padre de la familia, durante muchos años. Su esposa, la abuela de la familia, había muerto durante un invierno muy frío y duro hacía mucho tiempo. Cuando su esposa murió, el abuelo estaba agradecido de tener un hijo con quien vivir. Conforme pasaban los años y envejecía, disfrutaba grandemente de la compañía de su nieto.

En los años cuando era más joven, el abuelo podía ayudar en las tareas de la granja. Durante estos años se mantuvo activo en la vida de la familia, y creía que tenía un lugar en la casa de su hijo.

Sin embargo, con el paso de los años se fué enfermado y no podía ayudar con el trabajo de la granja. Poco a poco fué haciendo menos y menos. La esposa empezó a quejarse de que el abuelo sólo daba trabajo, y quizás debían pensar en que se fuera a otro sitio a vivir.

El hijo no quiso enviar a su padre a ningún sitio, pero después pensó, "Quizás mi esposa tenga razón. El ya no es de mucha ayuda, y a lo mejor sería más feliz en otra parte." Llamó a su hijito y le dijo, "Ve a coger una manta y ponla en el granero para tu abuelo. Porque como es viejo y no ayuda en nada, allí es donde va a vivir."

El hijito cogió la manta y entonces con unas tijeras empezó a cortarla en dos piezas.

El padre preguntó al hijo, "¿Qué estás haciendo? ¡Esa manta está perfectamente bien!"

El hijo contestó a su padre, "Estoy cortándola en dos porque así cuando tú seas viejo como el abuelo, yo tendré una manta para darte cuando te mudes al granero."

Desde ese día en adelante, el abuelo continuó viviendo en la casa con la familia.

THE THREE SIMPLETONS (LOS TRES SIMPLONES)

Once there were three simpletons who decided to go to the city. They all wanted to learn how to speak Spanish, and they figured the easiest way to learn would be to listen to the people of the city speak Spanish. So they listened to the people in the city speaking, and pretty soon each simpleton knew how to say one phrase in Spanish. They were so proud that they couldn't wait to tell the others what they had learned.

The first one had learned to say *nosotros*, or we.

The second had learned to say *porque quisimos*, or because we wanted.

The third had learned to say *muy justo es*, or it is very just.

It just so happened that while they were in town a man was killed. The police searched the town for the killer. They found the three simpletons and brought them before the judge for questioning.

The judge asked the first one, "Who killed the man?"

The first simpleton thought about the question and then answered with the only Spanish he knew, "*Nosotros.*"

Then judge asked the second simpleton, "Why did you kill the man?"

The second simpleton also answered with the only Spanish he knew, "*Porque quisimos.*"

The judge looked at the three simpletons and said, "Then we will have to put all of you in jail and hang you."

The third simpleton proudly answered in his new Spanish, "*Muy justo es.*"

LOS TRES SIMPLONES
(THE THREE SIMPLETONS)

Erase una vez tres simplones que decidieron ir a la ciudad. Querían aprender a hablar español, y pensaron que lo más fácil sería escuchar cómo hablaba la gente de la ciudad. Así que escucharon a la gente hablar, y pronto cada uno supo decir una frase en español. Estaban tan orgullosos que no podían esperar para contar a los demás lo que habían aprendido.

El primero había aprendido a decir, "nosotros."

El segundo había aprendido a decir, "porque quisimos."

El tercero había aprendido a decir, "muy justo es."

Sucedió que mientras estaban en la ciudad un hombre fué asesinado. Cuando la policía buscaba al asesino, encontró a los tres simplones que fueron llevados a presencia del juez para ser interrogados.

El juez preguntó al primero, "¿Quién mató al hombre?"

El primer simplón pensó en la pregunta y contestó con lo único que sabía en español, "Nosotros."

Entonces el juez preguntó al segundo simplón, "¿Por qué mataron a ese hombre?"

El segundo simplón también contestó con lo único que sabía en español, "Porque quisimos."

El juez miró a los tres simplones y dijo, "Entonces tendremos que meterlos a los tres en la cárcel y ahorcarlos."

El tercer simplón contestó orgullosamente en su nuevo español, "Muy justo es."

THE THREE SIMPLETONS, EVEN DUMBER!

In another part of the country, the three simpletons were walking in the forest. They were hungry. They tried to catch some wild rabbits to eat, but every time they tried to creep up on a rabbit, they made so much noise that they scared the rabbit away before they could even get close.

Finally they decided to give up trying to catch rabbits and to eat whatever they could find. They came upon some bushes full of ripe berries. They all sat down and began to pick the berries off the bushes. They ate and ate and ate until their mouths were stained with the red juice of the berries.

As they were eating some robbers came over the hill. They saw the three simpletons and ran toward them. As soon as the simpletons saw the robbers, they ran for their lives and hid.

But the robbers were too fast, and they caught one of the simpletons. They robbed him and beat him up. After they had tied up the simpleton, they noticed he was bleeding and that his blood was very red. One of the robbers commented, "Look how red this blood is. I wonder how come his blood is so red."

The second simpleton was hiding behind a big rock nearby. When he heard the robber's question, he yelled out, "His blood must be so red because of all the berries he was eating."

Of course the robbers easily found the second simpleton. They robbed him, beat him, and tied him up. One of the robbers said to the others, "What a foolish man! If he had kept quiet, we never would have found him."

When the third simpleton, who was hiding behind some trees nearby, heard what the robber said, he called out, "That's why I am staying so quiet!"

THE THREE DREAMERS

During an especially long summer, a poor shepherd earned extra money by taking men from the city on hunting and camping trips. On one trip he took two men out in the wilderness to camp.

The shepherd brought along several of his sheep for food. The men would help slaughter the sheep, and then they would cook the meat over the open fire and eat it.

After one meal the men were full and decided not to eat the sheep's head. They thought it would be best to bury the sheep's head for the night and eat it the next day.

One of the men came up with an interesting plan. He told the other man, "Here is my plan. In the morning we will tell each other the dreams we dream tonight. Whoever has the best dream will be the winner and will get to eat the sheep's head. What do you say?" The other man agreed to the plan, and they both went to sleep.

During the night the shepherd woke up, saw that the two men were sleeping, and dug up the sheep's head and ate it.

The next morning the two men told each other their dreams. One began by saying, "Last night I had the most glorious dream. I dreamed that I was being carried up to heaven by a host of heavenly angels to spend all eternity in heaven by the side of God himself."

The second man said, "That's the same dream I had!"

They decided the dreams were equal and went to dig up the sheep's head. When they discovered that someone had already dug it up, they turned to the shepherd and demanded an explanation.

The shepherd grinned and said, "Last night I dreamed that I saw both of you being carried up to heaven by a host of heavenly angels, and I thought you would never be coming back, so I got up and ate the sheep's head!"

THE SHEPHERD AND THE SKUNK

Once a shepherd came into town to buy some supplies. As he walked through the town, everyone he met cleared a path for him. Some people even crossed the street when they got close to him. Most gave him a funny look as he walked by.

Now, he knew that all shepherds have their own smell and that their sheep can find them by that smell. But he was sure that only sheep could smell that smell.

The shepherd had been out in the fields tending to his sheep for many weeks, but he did not think that he was that dirty. Why, every so often he even went to the river and washed his face! In fact he had done just that before coming to town. He could think of no good reason why the people of the town were treating him so.

As he walked down the road to the general store, he saw a large crowd gathered in a field. People were yelling, and there was a large commotion. The shepherd worked his way to the front of the crowd to see what was going on.

A skunk was trapped inside a shed. All the men were arguing over who was the bravest and who could stay in the shed with the skunk for the longest time. Two men were leading the arguments, a doctor and a lawyer.

The doctor said loud enough for all to hear, "I am the most educated and bravest man in the town. To prove it I will go inside that shed and stay until the skunk leaves first."

The lawyer countered, "I am the most educated and bravest man in the town, and I will prove it by going into that shed and not coming out until tomorrow."

The argument between the two men was not going anywhere when the shepherd spoke up. He said, "Why don't each of you go in the shed and see who wins?"

Neither the doctor nor lawyer liked the idea of a shepherd telling them what to do, but everyone was standing around watching who would go in first. So the doctor went in first. He was in only a few minutes when he came running out, yelling and holding his nose. The lawyer laughed out loud and made a disparaging remark about the doctor's courage. With great nonchalance he went into the shed. He had been in the shed slightly longer than the doctor when he came running out, crying and holding his nose.

Both the doctor and lawyer had been humiliated. Turning their anger on the shepherd, they said, "If you are so brave, why don't you go in the shed?"

The shepherd looked around and didn't know what to do. He had just come into town to get some supplies. But with a shrug and without a word, he went into the shed.

Minutes passed and people began to wonder if the shepherd was O.K. Suddenly the door to the shed flew open. Out ran the skunk, holding his nose and running as fast as a skunk can run.

The shepherd came out of the shed and shrugged his shoulders again. He went on into town to buy his supplies. He still noticed, however, that people cleared a path for him as he walked around the store. To this day he doesn't know why.

Photographs

Fig. 1. Quetzalcoatl—*Codex Borbonicus* (The Five Suns). © Fondo de Cultura Económica, S.A. De C.V.

Fig. 2. Tezcatlipoca— *Codex Borgia* (The Five Suns). © Fondo de Cultura Económica, S.A. De C.V.

Fig. 3. Huitzilopochtli—*Codex Borbonicus* (The Five Suns). © Fondo de Cultura Económica, S.A. De C.V.

Fig. 4. Mictlantecuhtli—*Codex Borbonicus* (The Five Suns). © Fondo de Cultura Económica, S.A. De C.V.

Fig. 5. Quetzalcoatl and Mictlantecuhtli—Stevon Lucero (The Five Suns).

Fig. 6. Moon with Rabbit—*Codex Borgia* (The Five Suns). © Fondo de Cultura Económica, S.A. De C.V.

Fig. 7. The Four Suns—Aztec Calendar (The Five Suns).
© Fondo de Cultura Económica, S.A. De C.V.

Fig. 8. La Llorona—Arlette Lucero.

Fig. 9. La Llorona—
Stevon Lucero.

Fig. 10. Our Lady of
Guadalupe—Denver Art
Museum. Courtesy of The
Denver Art Museum.

Fig. 11. Our Lady of Guadalupe—Carlota Espinoza.

Fig. 12. Doña Sebastiana—Denver Art Museum. Courtesy of The Denver Art Museum.

Fig. 13. Doña Sebastiana—Meggan De Anza Rodriguez.

Fig. 14. The Holy Family—
Carlos Santistevan.

Fig. 15. El Santo Niño
de Atocha—Carlota
Espinoza.

EL DIABLITO

Fig. 16. El Diablito—Mexican *loteria* game (The Devil's Friend).

Fig. 17. Dos Compadres—Tony Ortega.

Fig. 18. Coyote—Carlos Martinez.

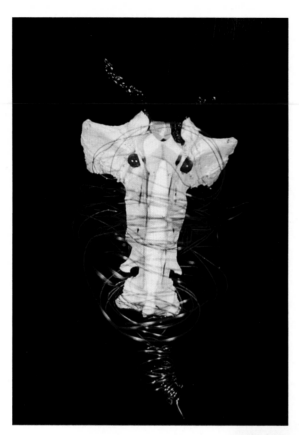

Fig. 19. The Dust Devil—
Al Cardanas.

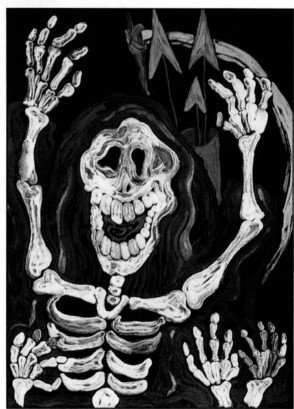

Fig. 20. La Calavera—
Meggan De Anza Rodriguez.

Fig. 21. The Corn Woman—Daniel Luna (*Cuento* of the Corn).

Fig. 22. La Coqueta—Tony Ortega (La Coqueta de Piedras Negras
Y El Barrilero).

Fig. 23. El Apache—Carlota Espinoza
(La Coqueta de Piedras Negras Y El Barrilero).

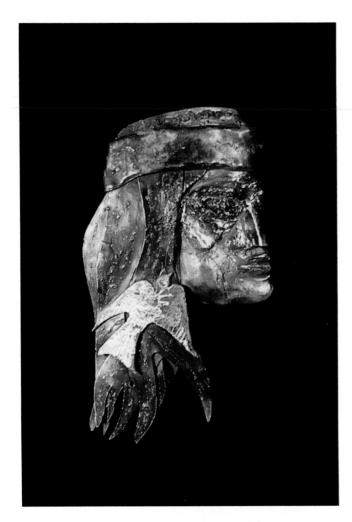

Fig. 24. El Apache—Al Cardanas (La Coqueta de Piedras Negras Y El Barrilero).

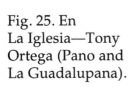

Fig. 25. En La Iglesia—Tony Ortega (Pano and La Guadalupana).

Tales of Transformation, Magic, and Wisdom

THE THREE PIECES OF GOOD ADVICE (LOS TRES BUENOS CONSEJOS)

This common story, sometimes called "The Three Councils," is a very well documented *cuento*. The story exists in many versions, which differ in the reason why the traveler leaves home, the nature of the advice he receives, who is the man he finds embracing his wife, and even the number of pieces of advice he gets. Sometimes he receives two pieces of advice, sometimes three. In *Folktales of Mexico,* Américo Paredes presents a version in which the traveler receives five pieces of advice. The version told here is the most common in the Southwest.

THE THREE PIECES OF GOOD ADVICE
(LOS TRES BUENOS CONSEJOS)

Once there were three men, poor farmers, who lived in a barren part of the valley. They struggled and struggled to make the dry earth give forth enough food to feed their families. Eventually they decided to leave home to see if they could find work elsewhere. They knew that if they were able to find work, they could send money home to their families. Even though it broke their hearts to have to leave their families, they felt it was for the best.

Soon after they had begun their journey, they came upon an old man walking along the road. The old man had three bags of money. The poor farmers were very excited to see them. They asked the old man, "Where did you get those bags of money? We are looking for work to make some money, and if there is some job paying with bags of money, we want to know about it!"

In a creaky but wise voice, the old man replied, "Oh, I didn't get this money from some job. I got it by following good advice. In fact, I have a proposition for you. I will give each of you a bag of money or I will give you three pieces of good advice."

Two of the farmers laughed at the old man. "Money or advice. What type of foolish choice is that, old man? You've been out in the hot sun too long." These two men took a bag of money and congratulated each other on their good luck.

But the third man had been raised to respect his elders, and he had a feeling that the old man knew some important wisdom that might be helpful as he was looking for a way to make money. He knew that one bag of money would not go very far and that one day it would run out.

When he told the old man that he would take the advice, his two friends laughed even harder. "Now you are as *loco* as this old man. Will advice feed your children?" they scoffed.

But the third man did what he felt was the best. The old man leaned forward and secretly told him this advice:

1. Keep to the main road, the well-traveled road. Do not go down strange roads, for they lead to danger.

2. Mind your own business. Keep quiet and only watch the affairs of others.

3. Think before you act. Don't do things without first looking carefully.

The third farmer had hoped that he would get better advice than that, but he thanked the old man anyway. The travelers continued on their way. The two farmers who had chosen the bags of money could not stop laughing about how foolish the third farmer had been. Then they came to a fork in the road and had an argument about which way to turn.

The first two farmers thought the shortcut would be the better path. "If we take the long road, it will be dark before we get to the village."

The third farmer remembered the first bit of advice the old man had given him. "Well, I think it would be safer to take the long road. It is more traveled."

The other two farmers again laughed at him. "What do you know? You know so little, you turn your nose up at money in favor of a few words from an old man at the side of the road. We're going down the short path, and we'll arrive at the village with time to eat and rest before you even get over the mountain." And with that they said good-bye and started down the short path.

It just so happened that a gang of thieves had been hiding in the forest close to the short path that day, robbing any person who came down the path. The thieves attacked the farmers, stole their money, and left them tied up at the side of the road.

Much later, when the third farmer arrived in the village, he was surprised that his two friends were not there. He immediately sensed that he had been right in following the old man's advice to keep to the main road.

In the village he asked if there was any work, and the owner of the inn said that he needed a man to help in the kitchen.

Once he began working in the kitchen, the third farmer noticed that the owner's wife was terribly thin. He also noticed that the owner didn't let his wife eat anything but *tortillas*. The farmer was very curious about all this, but he remembered the second bit of advice the old man had given him, so he decided to mind his own business. The job at the inn was a good one, and it allowed him to send money home to his family. He still wondered what was wrong with the owner's wife, but he minded his own business and kept quiet.

After he had worked at the inn for several years, the owner of the inn called him over for a talk. "I am a rich man, and I am tired of working. I am going to give you this inn and half of my money."

The poor farmer was speechless. He stammered, "But why me?"

The owner answered him, "Because you have minded your own business. I know you have always been curious about my wife and why she is so thin and eats only *tortillas*. But you never asked and only did your work. Years ago I made up my mind to give my money and my business to the man who was able to mind his own business. You are that man."

The farmer was overcome with joy. Now he knew that he was right to follow the advice of the old man, for now he could have his family come to live with him, and he could take care of them the way he had always wanted to.

He rushed back to his farm to tell his family the good news. As he came up to his house, he saw a man, a priest, embracing his wife. He was angered that his wife would be unfaithful to him and that a priest would behave in such a way. He took out his gun, and then he remembered the third bit of advice the old man had given: Think before you act. He put his gun away and went into his house. Then he recognized that the man was his son, who had grown up and become a priest while he was away.

His family rejoiced at his return and at his story of good fortune. The farmer was now a rich man, and he and his family lived happily ever after.

LOS TRES BUENOS CONSEJOS
(THE THREE PIECES OF GOOD ADVICE)

Erase una vez tres pobres granjeros que vivían en una parte estéril del valle. Luchaban y luchaban para hacer que la tierra seca diera suficiente comida para alimentar a sus familias. Por último decidieron dejar sus hogares para ver si podían encontrar trabajo en alguna parte. Sabían que si encontraban trabajo, podrían mandar dinero a sus familias. Aunque les dolía en el alma dejar sus hogares, pensaron que era lo mejor.

Poco después de comenzar su viaje, encontraron a un viejo andando por el camino. El viejo tenía tres bolsas con dinero. Los pobres granjeros se pusieron muy contentos al verlas. Preguntaron al viejo, "¿dónde ha conseguido esas bolsas? ¡Estamos buscando trabajo para ganar dinero, y si hay algún trabajo en el que paguen con bolsas de dinero, queremos saberlo!"

Con voz ronca pero sabia, el viejo contestó, "Oh, Yo no gané este dinero en un trabajo. Lo gané siguiendo un buen consejo. De hecho, tengo una proposición para Uds. Le daré a cada uno una bolsa de dinero ó les daré tres buenos consejos."

Dos de los granjeros se rieron del viejo. "Dinero ó consejo. ¿Qué tipo de opción tonta es esta, viejo? Ud. ha estado demasiado tiempo al sol ligero." Estos dos hombres cogieron una bolsa de dinero cada uno y se congratularon por su buena suerte.

Pero el tercer hombre había sido criado en el respeto a los mayores, y presintió que aquél viejo poseía cierta sabiduría que podría serle útil mientras buscaba la manera de ganar dinero. Sabía que una bolsa de dinero no duraría mucho tiempo y que algún día se acabaría.

Cuando dijo al viejo que él escogería los consejos, sus dos amigos se rieron aún más fuerte. "Ahora tú estás tan loco como este viejo. ¿Dará el consejo de comer a tus hijos?"

Pero el tercer hombre hizo lo que le parecía mejor. El viejo se inclinó hacia él y secretamente le dió estos tres consejos;

"Quédate en el camino principal, el camino más frecuentado. No vayas por caminos extraños, porque conducen al peligro.

Preocúpate de tus propios asuntos. Manténte callado y sólo observa los asuntos de los demás.

Tales of Transformation, Magic, and Wisdom

Piensa antes de actuar. No hagas nada sin mirar cuidadosamente primero."

El tercer granjero había esperado recibir mejores consejos que estos, pero dió las gracias al viejo de todos modos. Los viajeros continuaron su camino. Los dos granjeros que habían escogido las bolsas de dinero no podían dejar de reírse de lo tonto que había sido el tercer granjero. Entonces llegaron a un cruce en el camino y tuvieron una discusión acerca de la dirección que iban a tomar.

Los primeros dos granjeros pensaron que sería mejor seguir por el atajo. "Si tomamos el camino largo, se hará de noche antes de que lleguemos al pueblo."

El tercer granjero recordó el primer consejo que el viejo le había dado. "Pues, yo creo que sería más seguro seguir por el camino largo. Es el camino más frecuentado."

Los otros dos granjeros se rieron de él otra vez. "¿Qué sabes tú? Sabes tan poco que rechazas dinero por unas pocas palabras de un viejo que encuentras por el camino. Nosotros vamos a seguir por el atajo, y llegaremos al pueblo con tiempo para comer y descansar antes de que tú hayas cruzado la montaña." Y con esto le dijeron adiós y siguieron por el atajo.

Y casualmente sucedió que ese día había una banda de ladrones escondida en el bosque cercano al atajo, robando a todo el que por allí pasaba.

Los ladrones atacaron a los granjeros, les robaron su dinero, y los dejaron atados a un lado del camino.

Más tarde, cuando el tercer granjero llegó al pueblo se sorprendió de que sus dos amigos no estuvieran allí. Inmediatamente supo que había hecho lo correcto al seguir el consejo del viejo de tomar el camino principal.

En el pueblo preguntó si había algún trabajo, y el dueño de la posada le dijo que él necesitaba un hombre para ayudar en la cocina.

Una vez que había empezado a trabajar, el tercer granjero notó que la esposa del dueño estaba terriblemente delgada. También notó que el dueño no permitía a su esposa comer nada excepto tortillas. El granjero sintió mucha curiosidad sobre todo esto, pero recordó el segundo consejo que el viejo le había dado, y decidió preocuparse de sus propios asuntos. El trabajo en la posada era bueno, y le permitió enviar algún dinero a su familia. Aunque seguía preguntándose qué pasaba a la mujer del dueño, sin embargo se dedicó únicamente a sus propios asuntos y se mantuvo callado.

Después de que había trabajado en la posada algunos años, el dueño lo llamó para hablar. "Soy un hombre rico, y estoy cansado de trabajar. Te voy a dar esta posada y la mitad de mi dinero."

El pobre granjero se quedó sin habla. Y tartamudeó, "¿pero por qué a mí?"

El dueño le contestó, "Porque te has preocupado de tus propios asuntos. Sé que siempre has sentido curiosidad por mi esposa y por qué está tan delgada y come sólo tortillas. Pero nunca preguntaste y sólo cumpliste con tu trabajo. Hace varios años hice la determinación de dar mi dinero y mi negocio al hombre que fuera capaz de preocuparse de sus propios asuntos y no meterse en los de los demás. Tú eres ese hombre."

El granjero estaba emocionado por la alegría. Entonces supo que fué correcto seguir el consejo del viejo, porque ahora podría traer a su familia a vivir con él, y cuidarla como él siempre había querido.

Volvió corriendo a su granja a contar a su familia la buena nueva. Cuando se aproximaba a la casa, vió a un hombre, un cura, abrazando a su esposa. Le enojó mucho que su mujer le fuese infiel y que un cura se comportase de aquella manera. Sacó su pistola, y entonces recordó el tercer consejo que el viejo le había dado: "Piensa antes de actuar." Así que guardó la pistola y entró en la casa. Entonces se dió cuenta de que el hombre era su hijo, que se había hecho mayor y se había convertido en cura en su ausencia.

Su familia se alegró de su regreso y de su buena fortuna. El granjero era ahora un hombre rico, y él y su familia vivieron felices para siempre.

THE BOY WHO KILLED THE GIANT (EL MUCHACHO QUE MATÓ AL GIGANTE)

Many years ago in a distant land, there lived a boy who thought he was old enough to leave home and seek his fortune in the world. He gathered up his belongings and went to his parents to ask for their blessing on his journey.

"Mama, papa," he kindly asked, "May I have your blessing to go into the world to seek my fortune?"

"Oh, no, *jito.* You are much too young to leave home. Go outside and play with your toys," they replied.

A full year passed, and the little boy really felt he was old enough to leave home. He approached his parents and again asked for their blessing. "Mama, papa," he pleaded, "Please let me leave home."

But again they answered, "Oh no, you are much too young to leave home. Go outside and play in the yard. Maybe later, when you grow up."

Another year passed, and the boy was finally turning into a young man. This time even his parents knew that it was time for him to leave home to seek his fortune in the world. When the boy asked for their blessing, they gladly gave it to him.

"You have our blessing. Remember that if you are ever in trouble, call on the blessing we give you today and you will be safe. And if you do find your fortune, come back and tell us about your great adventures."

As the boy packed his belongings, he was especially careful to tie his magic pouch to his belt. He had had his magic pouch since childhood, and whenever he found something with special magic, he always put it in his pouch for safekeeping.

He had been gone from his home for a few hours when he came over a ridge and saw the most incredible fight between four animals. In a field below him a lion, an eagle, a bear, and a dog were fighting over the body of a dead animal they had found. The animals were arguing over who deserved to eat the animal.

The lion growled, "I am the king of the beasts. I deserve to eat this animal."

The bear bellowed, "No, I am the strongest of all the animals. The animal is mine!"

The eagle screamed, "I am the fiercest hunter of the skies. I saw the animal first, so it should be mine."

The dog howled, "Because of my great speed I was the first one to get to the animal. I was already eating it when all of you showed up. The animal is mine!"

The little boy knew that this fighting was wrong. It would only lead to more bloodshed and maybe even the death of one of the animals. So he stepped into the middle of the animals and stopped the fight.

"Wait! Stop!" he yelled at the animals, trying to get them to stop fighting long enough to listen to him. "This is no way to solve a fight. In my world, the world of people, we use cooperation to solve fights. Just listen to my plan, and all of you will end up happy instead of angry."

The animals could not believe what was happening. They had never seen a foolish person foolish enough to walk into the middle of a pack of fighting animals. They were so surprised that they were unable to move.

"Listen," continued the boy, "this is what you should do. Divide the animal into four pieces, and then you will each get a share of the meat."

The animals had never heard of such an idea. Imagine wild animals dividing food instead of fighting for it! But the little boy seemed to have a powerful force behind him, so they did what he said. When they had finished eating the animal, they all marveled at what a good idea the little boy had given them. They decided that since the boy had been so brave and wise, they would each give him a reward.

The lion was the first. "Here is a strand of golden hair from my mane. If you ever need my help, cry out, 'A Dios y León,' to God and the Lion, and I will come and help you."

Then the bear pulled off one of his huge, powerful claws. "If you ever need my help, just call out, 'A Dios y Oso,' to God and the Bear, and I will come and help you."

Tales of Transformation, Magic, and Wisdom

The eagle looked at the boy with his fierce eyes and said, "Here is the most precious object I can give you." Giving the boy one of his golden feathers, the eagle told the boy, "If you ever need my help, just hold this feather tightly and call out, 'A Dios y Águila,' to God and the Eagle, and I will be at your side."

Finally, the dog pulled a hair from his tail and gave it to the boy. "If you ever need my help, just call out, 'A Dios y Perro,' to God and the Dog, and I will be there to help you."

The boy could not believe his good luck. He had been out in the world seeking his fortune for only a few hours and already he had four magic treasures. He carefully put the treasures in his magic pouch, and bidding the animals farewell, he continued on his journey.

He went a little farther when he came upon the castle of the King. He had never been away from his home, and he was very surprised that the King's castle was so close to his home. As he walked up to the front gate of the castle, he came upon a *viejita*, a little old woman, wrapped in a black shawl, crying.

"Excuse me, but why are you crying?" he asked the little old woman.

"Haven't you heard? The giant has stolen the princess. The king has sent all of his bravest and strongest soldiers to save the princess, but the giant has killed them all. Now we know that we will never see her again. That is why all the people of the castle spend all their days crying."

Excitedly the boy told her, "I am in the world seeking my fortune, and I just received four magic treasures from the animals. I know I can save the princess."

"Oh, little boy," the woman interrupted, "The giant has already killed all the King's soldiers. Go and play with your magic treasures. You are too young and too small to be of any help. Go play with your toys."

The little boy didn't like that the old woman seemed to be making fun of him. Later that night he was trying to fall asleep underneath a tree in the field outside the castle when he heard the saddest song. Far off in the distance, he could see the giant's castle on top of a scary mountain. The singing was the voice of the princess, carried by the wind all the way to the little boy's ears. The song was so sad that the little boy knew he just had to do something, no matter what the old woman had said.

He reached into his pouch and pulled out the eagle feather. "*A Dios y Águila,*" he cried out. Immediately the eagle flew by and swooped him off the ground. The eagle knew just what the little boy wanted. He flew the little boy to the giant's castle, right into the room where the princess was being held prisoner in a golden cage.

The princess was shocked to see the little boy. In a very frightened voice, she told the boy, "Run away! If the giant sees you, he will kill you! And by the way, how did you get here?"

As the boy began to tell her about the eagle and the magic feather, he heard the heavy footsteps of the giant. Boom! The door slammed open. The little boy quickly hid behind one of the heavy curtains in the room.

"Who has been here?" yelled the giant.

"No one," said the princess in a shaking little voice.

"Good!" said the giant. "Because if someone was here I would have to kill him!"

The giant left the room, slamming the door so hard the whole castle rattled.

The boy came out from behind the curtain. "Boy, he sure is mean. I've never seen a giant before. Wow, and is he smelly!"

"But how can you help me?" asked the princess.

"Don't worry. I have magic treasures. But first we must find out where the giant keeps his powers. Trick him into telling you where he keeps his powers. Then I will be able to destroy them."

"Oh, you will never kill the giant. I have seen how powerful he is. You will . . . Oh, here he comes again! Run and hide, quickly, before he gets you!"

Boom! The door slammed open again.

"Who were you talking to?" shouted the giant.

The princess tried to answer calmly, but her voice cracked with fear. "No one, giant. Really, no one. I was just talking to myself. It gets so lonely up here." Trying not to look at the ugly face of the giant, the princess continued to be brave. "Giant, you are the strongest giant in the whole world. Where do you get such great powers? Surely one day someone will find where you keep your powers."

Now, the giant really was powerful and fearsome. He really was ugly and smelly. But most of all he was dumb. When he heard that someone might find his powers he went into a rage.

Tales of Transformation, Magic, and Wisdom

"No one will ever find my powers! I have already killed all the King's men, and there is no one left who could find them. And do you know why? In a lake far away from here, too far for any person to get to, there is a beast. And that beast is a giant, terrible beast. And if someone could kill that beast, which they can't, the beast has seven hides; and if someone could cut through those hides, which they can't, inside the beast is a rabbit; and if someone could catch that rabbit, which they can't, inside that rabbit is a pigeon; and if someone could catch that pigeon, which they can't, inside that pigeon is an egg; and if someone could get that egg, which they can't, inside that egg is where I keep my powers. And that is why no one will ever get my powers!"

As he finished he laughed with a cruel and evil look in his eye. Coming closer to the princess, he warned her, "So don't even begin to think you will ever leave this room, because you won't!" Then he stomped out of the room, laughing so hard the rafters in the castle started to shake.

The boy came out from behind the curtain. He had heard every word the giant had said. He told the princess, "You were really brave. I was scared to death he would find out about your trick. Wish me luck!"

And then he once again took out the eagle feather and held it tight to his chest. "*A Dios y Águila*," he called. Immediately the eagle was at his side, and they were flying off to the giant's hidden lake.

When they got to the lake, they saw why the giant was so sure that no one would ever get to the beast in the lake. The lake was in the middle of a volcano, and the lake was on fire. The eagle carefully put the boy down by the lake. As the boy approached, the ground started to tremble as if an earthquake was coming. Suddenly the beast rose out of the middle of the lake. The beast was huge and fierce.

As the beast rushed to kill the boy, the boy took the lion hair from his pouch. "*A Dios y León!*" he called out in his most desperate voice.

From nowhere the lion appeared and began to fight the beast. The lion used all of his strength, digging his claws into the beast, but the beast was too strong. Seeing that the lion needed help, the boy took out the bear claw and called, "*A Dios y Oso!*"

Now the beast was big and strong, but so was the bear. The beast was fierce, but so was the bear. And the beast was savage, but so was the bear. And the bear had the help of the lion, while the beast was all alone. After a ferocious battle the lion and the bear finally killed the beast. As the beast fell to the ground, the whole earth became still. The fires on the lake went out, and the lake became as smooth as a mirror.

The boy took out his knife and began to cut through the layers of hide on the beast. One, two, three, four, five, six, seven!

When he had cut through the last layer, a rabbit popped out and began to run away as fast as the wind. The boy tried to chase the rabbit, but the rabbit was too fast. Then the boy remembered the gift the dog had given him. He took out the dog hair and cried, *"A Dios y Perro!"* Just as he had promised, the dog was right there at the boy's side. The dog easily caught the rabbit, and the moment the dog grasped the rabbit in his teeth, a pigeon flew out of the rabbit's mouth.

Now this was the easiest part of all. The eagle swooped down and caught that pigeon right in the sky. An egg came out of the pigeon and started to fall to the ground. As the egg fell the boy ran to it and caught it just in time.

When the boy returned to the princess, he showed her the egg. With great excitement in his voice, he told her, "Inside this egg are the powers of the giant."

Boom! The door slammed open, and there stood the giant. "Give me that egg!"

The boy was terrified. He backed up against the wall.

"Give me that egg!" the giant thundered again.

As the giant reached down to grab the egg, the boy, in a sudden and desperate move, hurled the egg against the giant's forehead. The instant the egg hit the giant's head, it burst into a thousand parts and the room was filled with thunder and lightning. When all the smoke had cleared, the giant was dead on the ground.

A short while later the *viejita*, little old lady, was walking in the King's castle, and as she looked up she saw something she couldn't believe. She saw an eagle flying into the King's castle, carrying the princess on its back. With the princess was that little boy with the magic treasures.

When the King saw that the princess was home safe, he called for a celebration of all the people in the castle. At the celebration he gave the little boy half of his kingdom.

Later the little boy returned home to his parents. As he came up to his childhood home, his parents ran out and hugged and kissed him. They were so happy he had returned to them.

The boy told his parents all about the adventures he had had since he left home. He told them about the four fighting animals. He told them about the four magic treasures. He told them about the King's castle. But most of all he told them about the giant, the beast, and the princess.

His parents were amazed by the story of his adventures. After they had heard the stories, they told the boy, "We are so glad you came home safe after your great adventures. And if you ever want to go into the world to seek your fortune again, go ahead!"

EL MUCHACHO QUE MATÓ AL GIGANTE (THE BOY WHO KILLED THE GIANT)

Hace muchos años, en un país lejano, vivía un niño que creía que era suficientemente mayor para dejar su casa e ir a buscar fortuna por el mundo. Recogió sus cosas y se dirigió a sus padres para pedir su bendición para el viaje.

"Mamá, papá, ¿Puedo tener vuestra bendición para ir por el mundo en busca de fortuna?" preguntó amablemente.

"Oh, no, jito. Eres demasiado joven para irte de casa. Sal afuera y juega con tus juguetes," le contestaron.

Pasó un año entero, y el niño creyó que ya era suficientemente mayor para dejar su casa. Se dirigió a sus padres y pidió su bendición de nuevo. "Mamá, papá," les rogó, "Por favor, dejad que me vaya de casa."

Pero otra vez le contestaron, "Oh no, aún eres demasiado joven para irte de casa. Sal afuera y juega en el jardín. Quizás más adelante cuando hayas crecido."

Otro año pasó, y el niño por fin se estaba convirtiendo en un muchacho. Esta vez incluso sus padres sabían que ya era hora de que se fuera de la casa en busca de fortuna por el mundo. Cuando el muchacho les pidió su bendición, se la dieron felizmente.

"Ahora tienes nuestra bendición. Y si alguna vez tienes problemas, recuerda la bendición que te damos hoy y estarás a salvo. Y si tienes suerte y haces fortuna, vuelve y cuéntanos acerca de tus grandes aventuras."

Mientras el muchacho empaquetaba sus cosas, tuvo especial cuidado en atar su bolsita mágica a su cinturón. La había tenido desde su niñez, y desde entonces cuando encontraba algo con una magia especial, siempre lo guardaba en la bolsita.

Había estado ausente de la casa sólo unas pocas horas cuando llegó a la cima de una montaña y vió la pelea más increíble que imaginarse pueda entre cuatro animales. Abajo en un campo, un león, un águila, un oso, y un perro estaban peleándose por un animal muerto que habían encontrado. Los animales estaban discutiendo acerca de quién de ellos merecía comérselo.

El león gruñó, "Yo soy el rey de los animales. Merezco comerme a este animal."

El oso rugió, "No, yo soy el más fuerte de todos los animales. ¡Este animal es mío!"

El águila gritó, "Yo soy el cazador más fiero de los cielos. Ví al animal primero, por eso debe ser mío."

El perro aulló, "Por mi gran velocidad fuí el primero en llegar al animal. Ya me lo estaba comiendo cuando todos Uds. aparecieron. ¡El animal es mío!"

El muchacho sabía que tanto pelear era malo. Sólo llevaría a más derramamiento de sangre, y quizás incluso a la muerte de alguno de los animales. Así que se puso en medio de ellos y detuvo la pelea.

"¡Esperen! ¡Deténganse!" gritó a los animales, intentando hacer que dejaran la pelea el tiempo suficiente para escucharle. "Así no se resuelve una pelea. En mi mundo, el mundo de las personas, usamos la cooperación para resolver las disputas. Escuchen mi plan, y todos terminarán contentos en vez de enfadados."

Los animales no podían creer lo que estaba ocurriendo. Nunca habían visto a una persona tonta, tan tonta como para ponerse en medio de unos animales peleándose. Estaban tan sorprendidos que no eran capaces de moverse.

"Escuchen," continuó el muchacho, "esto es lo que deben hacer. Dividan al animal en cuatro partes, y cada uno tendrá su porción de carne."

Los animales nunca habían oído de tal idea. ¡Imaginar que animales salvajes se repartan la comida en vez de pelearse por ella! Pero el muchacho parecía tener una fuerza poderosa con él, así que hicieron lo que dijo. Cuando habían terminado de comerse el animal, se maravillaron de la buena idea que el muchacho les había dado. Decidieron que como el muchacho había sido tan valiente y sabio, cada uno de ellos le daría una recompensa.

El león fué el primero. "Toma un pelo dorado de mi melena. Si alguna vez necesitas mi ayuda, grita, 'A Dios y León,' y yo vendré a ayudarte."

El oso sacó una de sus enormes y poderosas garras. "Si alguna vez necesitas mi ayuda, grita, 'A Dios y Oso,' y yo vendré en tu ayuda."

El águila miró al muchacho con sus fieros ojos y dijo, "Toma lo más precioso que te puedo dar." Y dándole una de sus plumas doradas, le dijo, "Si alguna vez necesitas mi ayuda, coge esta pluma fuertemente y grita, 'A Dios y Aguila', y yo estaré a tu lado."

Finalmente, el perro sacó un pelo de su rabo y se lo dió al muchacho. "Si alguna vez necesitas mi ayuda, grita, 'A Dios y Perro', y yo estaré allí para ayudarte."

El muchacho no podía creer en su buena suerte. Sólo había estado por el mundo en busca de fortuna unas pocas horas y ya tenía cuatro tesoros mágicos. Con mucho cuidado puso los tesoros en su bolsita mágica y, diciendo adiós a los animales, continuó su viaje.

Fué un poco más lejos y se encontró con el castillo del rey. Nunca había estado fuera de su casa, y se sorprendió al saber que el castillo del rey estaba tan cerca. Cuando se acercaba a la entrada principal del castillo se encontró con una viejita, la cual iba vestida con un mantón negro y estaba llorando.

"Perdóne, pero, ¿por qué está llorando?" preguntó a la viejita.

"¿No has oído? El gigante ha raptado a la princesa. El rey envió a sus soldados más valientes y fuertes para salvarla, pero el gigante los ha matado a todos. Ahora sabemos que nunca más la volveremos a ver. Por eso, es por lo que todo el mundo en el castillo pasa sus días llorando."

Con entusiasmo el muchacho le dijo, "Estoy en el mundo buscando fortuna, y acabo de recibir cuatro tesoros mágicos de los animales. Sé que puedo salvar a la princesa."

"Oh, muchacho," le interrumpió la viejita, "El gigante ya ha matado a todos los soldados del rey. Vete a jugar con tus tesoros mágicos. Eres demasiado joven y demasiado pequeño para poder ayudar. Vete a jugar con tus juguetes."

Al muchacho no le gustó que la viejita pareció reírse de él. Más tarde esa noche cuando intentaba quedarse dormido bajo un árbol, en un campo a las afueras del castillo, escuchó la canción más triste que nunca había escuchado. Muy lejos, en la distancia, podía ver el castillo del gigante en lo alto de una montaña siniestra. El canto era la voz de la princesa, llevada por el viento hasta los oídos del muchacho. La canción era tan triste que el muchacho supo que tenía que hacer algo, sin importarle nada lo que había dicho la viejita.

Metió la mano en su bolsita y sacó la pluma del águila. "A Dios y Aguila," gritó. Inmediatamente el águila llegó volando y lo levantó del suelo. El águila sabía exactamente lo que quería el muchacho. Lo llevó al castillo del gigante, justamente a la habitación donde éste tenía a la princesa prisionera en una jaula de oro.

La princesa estaba asombrada de ver al muchacho. Con voz asustada, le dijo, "¡Vete corriendo! ¡Si el gigante te ve, te matará! Y, a propósito, ¿cómo has llegado hasta aquí?"

En cuanto el muchacho empezó a contarle acerca del águila y la pluma mágica, escuchó los pesados pasos del gigante. ¡Puum! La puerta se abrió de golpe. Rápidamente el muchacho se escondió detrás de una de las grandes cortinas que había en la habitación.

"¿Quién ha estado aquí?" gritó el gigante.

"Nadie," dijo la princesa con voz temblorosa.

"¡Bueno!" dijo el gigante. "¡Porque si hubiera alguien aquí yo tendría que matarlo!"

El gigante salió de la habitación, dando un portazo tan fuerte que sacudió todo el castillo.

El muchacho salió de detrás de la cortina. "Pues sí que es malo en verdad. Nunca antes había visto a un gigante. ¡Y también huele mal!"

"Pero, ¿cómo puedes ayudarme?" preguntó la princesa.

"No te preocupes. Tengo tesoros mágicos. Pero primero, debemos averiguar donde guarda el gigante sus poderes. Engáñale de algún modo para que te cuente dónde guarda sus poderes. Entonces podré destruirlos."

"Oh, nunca matarás al gigante. He visto lo poderoso que es...Oh, ¡Aquí viene otra vez! ¡Corre y escóndete, rápido, antes de que te coja!"

¡Puum! La puerta se abrió de golpe otra vez.

"¿Con quién estabas hablando?" gritó el gigante.

La princesa intentó contestarle con calma, pero su voz temblaba de miedo. "Con nadie, gigante. Con nadie, de verdad. Sólo estaba hablando conmigo misma. Aquí arriba estoy tan sola." Intentando no mirarlo a su cara fea, la princesa continuó siendo valiente. "Gigante, tú eres el gigante más fuerte del mundo entero. ¿Dónde consigues poderes tan grandes? Seguramente algún día alguien averiguará dónde guardas tus poderes."

El gigante era realmente poderoso y terrible. Era realmente feo y maloliente. Pero, sobre todo, era tonto. Cuando escuchó que alguien podría encontrar sus poderes montó en cólera.

"¡Nadie encontrará jamás mis poderes! Ya he matado a todos los hombres del rey, y no queda nadie que pueda encontrarlos. ¿Y sabes por qué? Porque en un lago, muy lejos de aquí, demasiado lejos para que llegue ninguna persona, hay una bestia. Y esa bestia es una bestia terrible y gigantesca. Y si alguien pudiera matar a esa bestia, lo cual no se puede, la bestia tiene siete pieles; y si alguien pudiera cortar esas pieles, lo cual no se puede, dentro de la bestia hay un conejo; y si alguien pudiera atrapar a ese conejo, lo cual no se puede, dentro del conejo hay una paloma; y si alguien pudiera atrapar a esa paloma, lo cual no se puede, dentro de esa paloma hay un huevo; y si alguien pudiera coger ese huevo, lo cual no se puede, dentro de ese huevo es donde guardo mis poderes. ¡Y por eso es por lo que nadie jamás los encontrará!"

Y cuando terminó se rió y su mirada era cruel y malvada. Acercándose a la princesa, le advirtió, "Así que ni siquiera pienses que vas a salir nunca de esta habitación, ¡Porque no lo harás!" Entonces se fué dando pisotones, riéndose tan fuerte que las vigas del castillo comenzaron a temblar.

El muchacho salió de detrás de la cortina. Había oído cada palabra que el gigante había dicho. Y dijo a la princesa, "Fuiste realmente valiente. Yo tenía mucho miedo de que el gigante descubriera tu engaño. ¡Deséame suerte!"

Y otra vez sacó la pluma del águila y la apretó contra su pecho. "A Dios y Aguila," gritó. Inmediatamente el águila apareció a su lado, y se fueron los dos volando al lago oculto del gigante.

Cuando llegaron al lago, vieron por qué el gigante estaba tan seguro de que nadie nunca llegaría hasta la bestia. El lago estaba en medio de un volcán, y se encontraba en llamas. Con cuidado el águila dejó al muchacho en el suelo al lado del lago. Conforme el muchacho se acercaba, la tierra empezó a temblar como si hubiera un terremoto. De repente la bestia salió del centro del lago. Era enorme y feroz.

Cuando la bestia se precipitó sobre el muchacho para matarlo, éste sacó el pelo del león de su bolsita. "¡A Dios y León!" gritó con voz muy desesperada.

De la nada apareció el león y empezó a combatir con la bestia. El león utilizó toda su fuerza, clavando sus uñas en la bestia, pero ésta era demasiado fuerte. Viendo que el león necesitaba ayuda, el muchacho sacó la garra del oso y gritó, "¡A Dios y Oso!"

La bestia era grande y fuerte, pero también lo era el oso. La bestia era feroz, pero también lo era el oso. Y la bestia era salvaje, pero también lo era el oso. Y el oso tenía la ayuda del león, mientras que la bestia estaba sola. Después de una batalla tremenda el león y el oso al final mataron a la bestia. Cuando la bestia cayó al suelo, toda la tierra quedó inmóvil. Los fuegos en el lago se extinguieron, y el agua se puso tan lisa como un espejo.

El muchacho sacó su cuchillo y empezó a cortar las siete capas de piel. Una, dos, tres, cuatro, cinco, seis, ¡siete!

Cuando había cortado la última capa, un conejo saltó afuera y empezó a correr tan rápido como el viento. El muchacho intentó perseguirlo, pero el conejo era demasiado rápido. Entonces el muchacho recordó el regalo que el perro le había dado. Sacó el pelo del perro y gritó, "¡A Dios y Perro!" Tal como había prometido, el perro apareció allí mismo al lado del muchacho. El perro atrapó al conejo fácilmente, y en el momento en que lo tuvo entre los dientes, una paloma salió volando de la boca del conejo.

Ahora venía lo más fácil de todo. El águila se lanzó en picado y atrapó a la paloma en vuelo. De la paloma salió un huevo que empezó a caer al suelo. Conforme caía el huevo, el muchacho corrió y lo cogió justo a tiempo.

Cuando el muchacho regresó junto a la princesa, le enseñó el huevo. Con gran emoción en la voz, le dijo, "Dentro de este huevo están los poderes del gigante."

¡Puum! La puerta se abrió de golpe, y allí estaba el gigante. "¡Dame ese huevo!"

El muchacho estaba aterrorizado. Se echó para atrás contra la pared.

"¡Dame ese huevo!" tronó el gigante otra vez.

Cuando el gigante alargó la mano para coger el huevo, el muchacho, en un movimiento repentino y desesperado, lo lanzó contra la frente del gigante. En el instante en que el huevo dió en la cabeza del gigante, explotó en mil pedazos y la habitación se llenó con truenos y relámpagos. Cuando todo el humo se había disipado, el gigante yacía muerto en el suelo.

Un poco más tarde, la viejita iba andando por el castillo del rey, y al mirar para arriba vió algo que no podía creer. Vió un águila volando hacia el castillo con la princesa en su lomo. Con la princesa venía el muchacho de los tesoros mágicos.

Cuando el rey vió que la princesa estaba de regreso sana y salva, invitó a todos los habitantes del castillo a una fiesta para celebrarlo. En la fiesta el rey dió al muchacho la mitad de su reino.

Más tarde el muchacho regresó a la casa de sus padres. Cuando llegó a la casa donde transcurrió su niñez, sus padres salieron corriendo para recibirle, y lo abrazaron y lo besaron. Estaban muy contentos de la vuelta de su hijo.

El muchacho contó a sus padres acerca de las aventuras que había tenido desde que se fué de casa. Les contó acerca de los cuatro animales que encontró peleándose. Les contó acerca de los cuatro tesoros mágicos. Les contó acerca del castillo del rey. Pero de lo que más les contó fué acerca del gigante, la bestia, y la princesa.

Sus padres estaban asombrados por el relato de sus aventuras. Después de que habían escuchado todas las historias, le dijeron, "Estamos muy contentos de que hayas regresado a casa sano y salvo después de tus grandes aventuras. Y si alguna vez quieres irte por el mundo en busca de fortuna otra vez, ¡Adelante!"

DON JACINTO

Don Jacinto was the richest man in all the land. He always wore the finest custom-made clothes. His stable of horses was the largest in the land. Whenever his horses were racing, people came just to watch such fine animals. When he walked through the plaza on his Sunday stroll, the people of the city would come up to pay their respects to Don Jacinto. Don Jacinto especially liked children. When the children came up to him, he would always slip coins into their little hands. People knew he was at least a millionaire, but no one really knew how much money he had.

Don Jacinto also liked to gamble. There was not a bet he would turn down. The higher the stakes the better. In fact, most of Don Jacinto's money had come from gambling. Only the most foolhardy would enter into a bet with Don Jacinto. Many a man had lost his fortune to some foolish wager with Don Jacinto. Don Jacinto liked to brag that there was not a man alive he couldn't beat in a bet.

One night a man came into the *cantina* where Don Jacinto was gambling. This stranger challenged Don Jacinto to a card game, winner take all. This was the type of game Don Jacinto liked the most. He figured he could easily beat the man, and then he would be all the richer.

Soon after they began playing, Don Jacinto realized that this would be the most difficult card game he had ever played. The stranger had a hard look to his face, and when Don Jacinto shook the man's hand, a cold shiver went down his spine.

From the very first hand, the stranger seemed to have luck as good as Don Jacinto's. Whenever the stranger needed a particular card, it turned up in his hand. People throughout the city whispered that at last Don Jacinto had met his match.

The card game was very close as hands went back and forth between Don Jacinto and the stranger. Finally, at the end of a month of playing, the stranger had won everything. In one month Don Jacinto had gone from being the richest man in the land to being a beggar on the streets. For a year Don Jacinto wandered through the streets, looking for something to eat. He was so hungry that, almost crying, he said, "I'd sell my soul to the devil for four coins to buy something to eat."

As he turned the corner, there stood the man who had beat him at cards just one short year ago. Now Don Jacinto knew who his worthy opponent had been. It was *El Diablo* himself.

El Diablo offered to take Don Jacinto up on his offer. In his smooth and enticing voice, he said, "I will gladly give you four coins for food in exchange for your soul."

Don Jacinto hesitated, then he said, "I didn't really mean it and besides, my soul is worth more than four coins."

"But these are not just any coins. You should know my powers by now. These coins will never go away. As soon as you spend one, another takes its place in your pocket."

Now these were the type of coins Don Jacinto needed. With these coins he didn't need his soul. Don Jacinto told *El Diablo*, "I agree. Give me the coins."

The coins changed hands, and *El Diablo* told Don Jacinto about the last part of the agreement. "You will have 30 more years. At the end of that 30 years, go to the City of Shells and Marble Trees. That is my city, and I will be waiting for you there."

With his four coins Don Jacinto returned to his former wealth and gambling ways. During the 30 years he gave little thought to his agreement with *El Diablo*. He just enjoyed the life that an endless supply of money made possible. At the end of the 30 years, the coins suddenly vanished, and Don Jacinto knew it was time for him to keep his part of the bargain.

On the way to the City of Shells and Marble Trees, Don Jacinto crossed paths with an ant who was starving. Don Jacinto remembered that long year when he was starving, and he felt sorry for the ant. Reaching down he gave the ant the bread he was carrying for the journey to the City of Shells and Marble Trees.

When the ant had eaten the bread, he told Don Jacinto, "You have shown me great kindness. If ever you are in trouble, call on me and I will come and help you." Don Jacinto knew that he would need help with *El Diablo*, but he didn't know how a little ant could ever help him.

As he approached the outside walls of the City of Shells and Marble Trees, Don Jacinto found an eagle who was caught in a trap. Don Jacinto felt like he, too, was caught in a trap with *El Diablo*. His heart was touched by the plight of the poor bird, and he freed it. As it soared away it told Don Jacinto, "Thank you for your great kindness. If you ever find yourself in trouble, call on me and I will come and help

Tales of Transformation, Magic, and Wisdom

you." Don Jacinto thought that the only way the eagle could help him was to teach him to fly so he could escape from the devil's plan for him.

Once he was inside the walls of the city, Don Jacinto passed a fountain that had lost its water. Inside the dry fountain was a fish that was dying in the hot sun for lack of water. Don Jacinto knew that soon he too would be in a very hot place, dying of thirst. Once more he felt sadness for a suffering animal. He scooped up the fish and placed it in another fountain that was full of water.

The fish slowly came back to life, and when it had regained all of its strength, it told Don Jacinto, "Thank you for your kind act. If you are ever in trouble, call on me and I will come and help you."

Finally Don Jacinto was inside the city, and just as he had promised 30 years ago, *El Diablo* was waiting for him. Now that his moment of death was at hand, Don Jacinto began to lament that he had wasted his life on money and gambling. He remembered the little animals he had helped and wished he had dedicated his life to helping those in need.

He asked *El Diablo*, "Is there any way for me to get out of my agreement with you? Any way at all?"

Now, it just so happened that *El Diablo* always enjoyed a good bet—even a last-minute bet. So he made this proposition to Don Jacinto: "I will give you three more nights. If I can't guess where you slept on each of those nights, then you shall have your soul back. But if I do guess where you slept, then your soul and the souls of your family are mine for all eternity."

Don Jacinto did not like the idea of betting on the souls of his family, but he knew that this was his only and last chance. Besides, he thought, there had to be someplace he could hide from the devil for one night.

Don Jacinto remembered the eagle that he had helped. He called for the eagle, and the eagle flew down from the sky.

"Eagle, please help me. Take me somewhere tonight where no one will know where I am."

The eagle put Don Jacinto on his back and flew high into the night sky. The eagle flew higher and higher, until he had flown behind the moon itself. The eagle and Don Jacinto spent the night hidden behind the bright, full moon.

The next day Don Jacinto went to meet the devil. *El Diablo* greeted Don Jacinto with a cheery smile and asked, "How goes it, *amigo?*"

Don Jacinto responded carefully, "It goes fine, *amigo.*"

Then *El Diablo* called out, "City of Shells and Marble Trees, moon, sun, stars, birds of the air, where did Don Jacinto spend the night last night?"

The eagle flew to *El Diablo* and said, "Behind the moon."

Don Jacinto knew that *El Diablo* had power over the eagle, and he forgave the eagle for revealing his secret.

On the second night Don Jacinto called for the fish. He explained to the fish that he needed to spend the night in a place where no one could find him. The fish opened up her mouth and let Don Jacinto spend the night inside her.

On the second day Don Jacinto went to find *El Diablo,* but *El Diablo* always seemed to find him first. Again *El Diablo* greeted Don Jacinto with a cheery smile and asked, "How goes it, *amigo?*"

Don Jacinto responded carefully, "It goes fine, *amigo.*"

Then *El Diablo* called out, "City of Shells and Marble Trees, moon, sun, stars, fish of the sea, where did Don Jacinto spend the night last night?"

The fish swam to *El Diablo* and said, "Inside of me."

Don Jacinto knew that *El Diablo* had power over the fish, and he forgave the fish for revealing his secret.

El Diablo laughed at Don Jacinto and said, "How goes it, *amigo?* You are losing your soul and the souls of your family. You have one night left."

Don Jacinto did not know if he could trust the ant, but he had no one else to turn to. He called out for the ant, and when it arrived he asked the ant to help him. He asked the ant if he was in the devil's power.

The ant reassured him, "I am from another part of this country. If you remember, you met me first, at the beginning of your journey, far away from here. Come with me now. I know a perfect place for you to hide. *El Diablo* will never think of looking for you where I will hide you tonight." Following a long, winding path, the ant took Don Jacinto down into the cellar of a large house.

When Don Jacinto's eyes had adjusted to the darkness, he saw a figure chained to a post. It was a woman. She cried out to Don Jacinto, "Please save me! *El Diablo* keeps me chained up to this post and tries to make me break my holy vows to the Blessed Virgin. Please help me!"

Then Don Jacinto knew where the ant had taken him—to the devil's own house! *El Diablo* would never imagine that Don Jacinto would hide in his own house. What a great plan the ant had.

Don Jacinto heard *El Diablo* coming down the steps to the cellar, and he hid under a sheepskin in the corner. Peeking out from under the sheepskin, he saw *El Diablo* try to get the woman to break her vows to the Blessed Virgin, but he was unsuccessful. Don Jacinto knew that the woman must be a holy woman because only a woman with the Lord inside her could resist the devil's threats and temptations. Finally *El Diablo* gave up and left.

Don Jacinto told the woman, "Holy woman, if I am able to save my own soul, I will return and free you also."

The next morning *El Diablo* was waiting for Don Jacinto as usual. "How goes it, *amigo?*"

Don Jacinto answered, "It goes fine, *amigo.*"

El Diablo then called out, "City of Shells and Marble Trees, moon, sun, stars, birds of the air, fish of the sea, where did Don Jacinto spend the night last night?"

There came no answer from anywhere. Looking around worriedly *El Diablo* called out again, "City of Shells and Marble Trees, moon, sun, stars, birds of the air, fish of the sea, where did Don Jacinto spend the night last night?"

Again no answer. The ant had told the truth. He was from another place, and the devil had no power over him.

El Diablo threw a fit that made the sky shake with thunder and flash with lightning. He knew that he had lost the bet with Don Jacinto. He challenged Don Jacinto to one more bet, but Don Jacinto told him, "I have escaped with my soul and the souls of my family. I will bet no more."

El Diablo threw one last fit and stormed away, swearing to never again give someone a second chance.

Don Jacinto hurried down the path that led to the devil's house. Taking the short cut the ant had shown him, he got there before *El*

Diablo. He rushed into the cellar and freed the imprisoned woman. Thanking Don Jacinto for his great kindness, she said, "Surely you are a man of the Lord. Only such a man could beat the devil at his own game."

Don Jacinto tried to make his story sound as good as possible for the woman. "Yes, I have befriended children and small animals in my life, and I am dedicating the rest of my life to doing good deeds."

Running as fast as they could, they escaped from the City of Shells and Marble Trees. They returned to their homes, where they lived the rest of their lives with their souls free.

THE MAGIC VIOLIN

One day a little shepherd boy was in the field, tending to his sheep. He enjoyed being out in the field with the sheep because the world was always so peaceful there. The animals got along, and on some days the smell of the flowers made the little boy think he was in heaven itself. When the evening sunset came, with its beautiful painted sky, he knew that the Lord was in heaven, looking after his own flock on earth.

The little boy was an orphan child. His parents had been killed right after he was born, and he had been taken in by the wealthiest man in the valley. The man owned the largest ranch around; he was well known in the valley for his land and the size of his herds.

The man had taken in the little boy as an act of charity. At the time he had said, "I can always use another shepherd, as long as he doesn't eat too much." The man had always thought this was the funniest joke, but as the little boy grew older, he hated hearing it because it reminded him that he was an orphan child.

The little boy would go out with the sheep and would not come back to the ranch for days on end. He felt much better being with the sheep, where he didn't have to listen to his master make jokes about him. The little boy told himself that one day he would be able to go out on his own and stop living with his master. He knew that this would be the happiest day of his life.

One day while he was out with the sheep, he heard singing coming from the top of the hill. He had never heard such beautiful singing, and he was surprised that anyone would be as far out in the field as he was. He had chosen that spot to feed the sheep because it was so far away from everything.

He climbed to the top of the hill, and there was a woman dressed in a shimmering white gown. Around her head was a circle of light, and she seemed to be floating off the ground.

The little boy asked the lady, "Who are you? And why are you here, so far from everything?"

The lady answered in a voice that seemed to be as light as the air, "I am the Blessed Virgin Mary, the mother of Jesus Christ. I have been watching over you since your parents died. Your parents are in heaven now, and they asked me to watch over you. I know how lonely you have been, and I have come to give you a present to entertain you during your long times alone."

She gave him a violin. It was a small violin, just his size, made of light brown wood. The little boy told the Virgin, "But I don't how to play the violin."

The Virgin comforted him with her words. "You will learn how. Besides, this is not an ordinary violin. It is a special violin. Whenever you play it, everyone will dance. They will keep dancing until you stop playing. Enjoy your gift and know that I am watching after you."

The little boy started to say something to the Virgin, but she just disappeared while he stood there watching her. He could not believe that he had been so lucky. This violin would be his special friend, and he would play it to make the sheep happy.

During his long days and nights with the sheep, he played the violin, and a peacefulness came over the land whenever he played.

When he finally returned to the ranch, he found all of his things packed up and thrown outside the bunkhouse. He asked who had done this, and the ranch boss told him, "The master said you are getting too old and eating too much. He's fired you, and you are to go on your own way."

The little boy didn't care that he had been fired. He was old enough to go out on his own, and anyway, this was the day he had been waiting for. He went to the master and asked for the wages that the master owed him.

The master told him, "Wages! I don't owe you anything. I took you in when you were an orphan baby, and all these years I have fed you and given you a place to sleep."

The boy protested, "But you promised me my wages when I started taking care of the sheep. You owe me my wages!"

The master cuffed the boy on the head and said, "Get out before I call the sheriff and tell him you've been stealing."

The boy knew that it was wrong for the master to refuse to pay him, but he was so frightened he ran away as fast as he could. He took his belongings and his little violin and left the ranch forever.

He went into town and asked if there was any work. The owner of an inn said that he needed a boy to wash dishes and he could have the job if he wanted it. The boy was really happy that he had found a job so easily, and then he remembered that the Virgin was watching over him. He went to church every day to thank the Virgin and to pray for the souls of his parents.

One evening the master came to the inn to eat. As usual he brought a lot of friends with him, and they had a large dinner party. The master did not know that the boy was working in the back of the kitchen of the inn.

During a break from his work, the boy took out his violin and played a soft and gentle song. The people in the inn heard the tune and were so moved by its beauty that they began to dance. The dancing wound around the tables, and everyone began to sing along with the song, until the inn became very noisy with the sound of singing and dancing.

The boy heard all the noise, and when he peeked out the door of the kitchen, he saw his old master leading the dancing with his group of friends. The boy found this so funny that he began to play faster and faster. The master and his friends soon got tired of dancing and tried to stop, but they couldn't. The sound of the violin kept making them dance, and they couldn't stop, no matter how hard they tried.

The boy came out of the kitchen with his violin and told his master, "I will stop playing when you pay me the wages you owe me."

The master was about to collapse from exhaustion, and he was willing to promise anything to get the music to stop. He told the boy, "Yes, I will pay you. Just stop playing the music." The boy believed the master and stopped playing the violin. All the people collapsed right where they were dancing, and the owner of the inn rushed over to ask if everyone was okay.

The master pushed himself up and bellowed, "I am not okay! That boy tried to kill me. Call the sheriff and have him arrested."

The master was so powerful that the owner of the inn immediately did what the master ordered. The sheriff came, arrested the boy, and took him to jail. He warned the boy not to try to escape and told him his trial would be in the morning.

The next morning the judge opened the trial of the boy. The master had come to give testimony that the boy had tried to kill him. When everyone heard the master's testimony, they knew that the boy must be convicted. The judge ended the trial early and sentenced the boy to prison and a life of hard labor. The little boy wondered if the Virgin was still watching over him, but he kept his faith and knew that in the end things would turn out for the best.

He asked the judge for one last request. "Before I am sent to jail, could I have my little violin to play just one more time?" The judge knew that the boy had been convicted only because of the power of the master, and he felt sorry for the boy, so he said yes.

The master tried to jump up and tell the judge not to say yes, but it was too late. The little boy had started playing.

Soon everyone in the courtroom was dancing. The more the boy played, the more they danced. Everyone was begging the boy to stop.

The boy shouted, "I'll stop playing as soon as the master tells the truth!"

By this time the master really was afraid he might die if the music didn't stop. He finally told everybody, "Yes, I promised him his wages and then I didn't pay him, but now I'll pay him double if he'll stop playing that horrible violin!"

The little boy stopped playing the violin. All the people in the court fell in their places, trying to catch their breath. Some even said, "I really liked that music. It just went on too long."

The master tried to escape out the door, but the sheriff stopped him. The judge had heard the master's confession and was going to hold him to his word. Before he left the courtroom, the master paid the boy double his wages.

The boy took his belongings and his little violin and went out into the world to seek his fortune, knowing that the Virgin was watching over him.

JUJUYANA, THE DEVIL'S DAUGHTER

For years Juan had asked his parents if he could leave home to seek his fortune in the world. Finally, with great sadness in their hearts, his parents gave him their blessing. As he traveled through the land, he heard many stories about young men like himself who were looking for work. Often these men would disappear, never to be heard from again. These stories did not bother Juan because he had received his parents' blessing when he left home. And besides, he had always been lucky. As he listened to these stories, he knew that it was just a matter of time before he would be lucky enough to find work.

After one especially hot day of traveling, Juan found a mountain stream and sat down beside it to rest. He cupped his hands and drank its fresh water. From his pack he took some food that a kind old lady had given him at his last stop, and he began to eat.

As he sat beside the stream, listening to the gentle sound it made as it flowed over rocks, he was suddenly very homesick. Perhaps it had been a mistake to leave home. After all, his cousin had ended up staying on his father's farm and was now starting his own family.

As he was deciding whether or not to return home, he heard a sound among the trees. The sound of breaking twigs alerted him to an approaching stranger.

Out of the woods came another traveler. This traveler was not a young man like Juan. He looked more like an old hermit who had spent many nights sleeping on the ground under the trees. His hair was long and uncut, and his beard was gray and tangled. Indeed, Juan thought he might be a forest *duende*.

Juan had heard legends of the *duendes*. They were little people who lived in the forest and played tricks on travelers. As the man came closer, Juan kept a close eye on his belongings.

"Good day, *Señor*," Juan said to the man.

The man did not answer Juan. He just sat down next to him and began to eat Juan's food. Now, Juan had learned that it was kind to share one's food with the needy, but he was really worried that the man might eat all of his food and that it would be days before he could get any again. He would have to eat the berries off of trees like a wild animal.

Suddenly the man stopped eating and looked at Juan. His eyes were green and twinkled with a mischievous sparkle. Juan looked into the eyes and thought, "Now I know this is a *duende*. So far so good, though. All he has done is eat some food. Perhaps he will leave and not do anything more."

The man gestured for Juan to come closer. Juan inched a little closer, but not much. The man leaned over and began to speak to him, "So you are looking for work. Well, you are lost in the forest. No work around here. Except down that path." He gestured to a path that Juan had not noticed before. The path was barely noticeable, but it definitely led away from the river.

The man continued, "But I wouldn't go down that path. It is called The Place of Smoke from which No One Returns. No, I wouldn't go down that path."

Then the little man got up and walked down the path himself.

Juan knew that this was some trick a *duende* was playing on him. His grandma had told him about the tricks these little people played on travelers, but he had not believed her. Now Juan had to decide whether or not to go down the path.

He thought out loud, "What if it really is The Place of Smoke from Which No One Returns? I have heard stories of travelers getting lost and never being heard from again. But I'm not lost. I know the next village is just over the hill. No harm could come from exploring the path a little way. I can always run back at the first sign of danger." Finally Juan's youthful curiosity got the best of him, and he gathered his belongings and headed down the path the little man had pointed out.

As soon as he had traveled down the path a little way, he smelled smoke. The smoke had the slight smell of sulfur, but he was not alarmed, so he continued down the path. Soon he came to a clearing and saw a house in the middle of a meadow. As he approached the house a young woman came out. She ran to Juan and began to warn him of great danger.

"How did you find this place? You must leave right away. My father is gone, but he will return soon. He leaves to do his work in the world, but he will return unexpectedly. If he finds you here, he will kill you. You must leave right away!"

Juan looked at the woman and saw her great beauty. He could not believe that he had found her so deep in the forest. It was almost as if a spell had been cast on him. Juan felt that his journey had suddenly turned into one of the fairy tales his grandmother used to tell him when he was a child. Or perhaps this was still part of the trick by the *duende*.

Juan knew that the woman was telling the truth, but he couldn't make himself leave. He asked the woman, "Who are you, and who is your father, such a mean man that he will kill a stranger who has done him no harm?"

"I am Jujuyana, and my father is . . ."

Just then the smell of sulfur became very strong, and Juan noticed that there was smoke everywhere. Juan tried to catch Jujuyana's hand, but he lost her in the smoke. As soon as the smoke cleared, Juan saw a large man standing next to Jujuyana.

The man asked Juan, "Why are you here? Didn't my daughter tell you to leave?"

Juan was immediately afraid of the man. He looked like he could do something terrible in an instant. Juan was afraid that the man would harm Jujuyana. Gathering up his courage Juan told the man, "Yes, she did. But I am in the world seeking my fortune, and I am looking for work. Is there any work for me to do here?"

The man roared with laughter. "Seeking your fortune! They always say that, don't they, Jujuyana? Well, I will give you the same chance I have given the others. For three days I will give you a job. If you have completed the job in three days, you may leave. If not, then I will have to kill you. What do you say, fortune seeker?"

Juan knew that he was trapped. But most of all he felt sorry for Jujuyana, for she was trapped, too. He wondered what had happened to the others who had come here before him, but he didn't want to think about that too much. He remembered his parents' blessing and his good luck, and he knew he had no other choice. He told the man, "I will do the work you ask."

Again the man roared with cruel laughter. "Here is your first job. See that lake over there?" He pointed to a huge lake in another part of

the valley. "Take this thimble and use it to carry all the water in the lake to that open field over there." Now he pointed to another field with a large hole dug in it. "Finish this job before I return or I will have to kill you." And with that he whirled around and disappeared.

Jujuyana came over to Juan and grabbed him. "I told you to run. Now you will die because of the impossible job my father has given you."

Juan tried to tell her that he could do the job. "I know the job seems impossible, but while God is in His heaven, there is a way. My question to you is, why you have never left this place? And why do you still live with your father, who is such a cruel man?"

"Often I have tried to leave, but my father is a powerful man. He has always stopped me, and that is why I am still here."

Juan told her, "I will do this job. And when I am done I will help you escape from here."

Juan took the thimble the father had given him and started to carry the water from the lake. He worked as hard as he could, but soon he began to realize that the job really was an impossible one, and he knew he was doomed. He sat down under a tree and began to cry because his luck had abandoned him and because his parents' blessing offered no protection in this evil place.

Jujuyana had watched Juan's valiant effort to move the water. As she watched him crying, her heart was touched, and she decided to use her own powers to help Juan. She knew that it was dangerous to cross her father, but she felt that the time had come for the end of her own torment.

As Juan cried Jujuyana took out her brush and began to brush his hair. She cradled Juan in her arm, and her soothing comfort soon put him to sleep.

When Juan awoke he frantically grabbed the thimble and ran to continue his job. When he reached the lake he stood at its banks in amazement. All the water was gone. He looked over to the other part of the field, and there stood a lake where before was the huge hole. Juan looked for Jujuyana, but as soon as he turned, there stood her father.

The man looked at the new lake and said, "This must be the work of Jujuyana, or else you have more power than I do. Tomorrow your next job will not be so easy. See that barren ground over on the side of the mountain? You are to clear that ground, plant seeds, grow wheat, harvest it, grind the wheat, and have bread for me to eat before I return. You still have your life now, but I will kill you if there is not bread when I return."

As Juan listened to the man, his despair grew deeper. He knew it was an impossible job, but he also knew he had no choice.

The next morning Juan ran to the field and tried to move the rocks, but they were impossible to move because of their great size. Once again Juan knew that his efforts were useless. He went over to the new lake and fell down by it to rest. As he lay in the grass by the lake, Jujuyana came to him and once more began to brush his hair. Soon Juan was asleep.

As before, when he awoke Juan dashed to the field to make one last attempt to do his assigned work. When he got there he stopped in amazement. The field was clear of rocks, and the land had been planted and harvested. As he turned around there stood Jujuyana. She gave him a loaf of bread and told him to give it to her father.

When her father looked at the loaf of bread, he said, "This is the work of Jujuyana. This will not happen again. Your third job will not be so easy!" Then he stormed off into the house.

Jujuyana raced to Juan and said, "He has gone into the house for the night. Believe me, the third job will be impossible to do. It will be too difficult even for my powers. We must run from here if there is to be any chance of escaping his anger. He will kill you because I have helped you."

Jujuyana hurried to her room and grabbed a bag she had in the corner. Before she left the house, she went to the fireplace and spit three times into it. Then she ran from the house.

When Jujuyana's father heard the noise of her leaving, he called out, "Jujuyana, are you there?"

The spit she had left in the fireplace answered, "Yes, I am here."

Later the father called out again, "Jujuyana, are you there?"

For a second time the spit she had left in the fireplace answered, "Yes, I am here."

Still later in the night the father called out, "Jujuyana, are you there?"

By this time the fire had evaporated Jujuyana's spit, and there was no answer. The father knew that Jujuyana was gone and that she had run away with Juan. He jumped on his horse and galloped up the path to catch them before they escaped from his land.

Because of Jujuyana's trick, she and Juan had a head start on the path that led away from the valley and her father's house.

The Traditional *Cuentos*

Jujuyana looked behind them and saw that her father was getting closer. She reached into her bag, took her brush, and threw it behind her. The brush turned into a church by the side of the road. She cast a spell on Juan and turned him into a little old bell ringer. She turned herself into a statue inside the church.

When her father rode up, he asked the bell ringer standing outside the church, "Bell ringer, have you seen a young man and woman run past here?"

The bell ringer looked up and said, "No. I have seen no one as you describe. But please come into the church. Mass is about to begin."

The father rode up to the church, but as he neared it, his horse reared up and would go no closer. The man rode the horse past a window and looked inside. All he saw was a statue of a saint in the center of the room. The face of the saint looked familiar, but he was in such a hurry to catch up with Juan and Jujuyana that he did not stop to look closer. He kicked his horse, and they bolted down the road.

Juan and Jujuyana continued down another path in their effort to escape from the land of her father. Jujuyana was so afraid, she couldn't breathe. With desperate gasps she begged Juan, "Hurry, or we'll never escape!"

Jujuyana looked behind her again and saw that her father, still wondering about the church, had come back to the path they were on. As her father got closer to them, she threw her comb into the road. Immediately the comb turned into a field of corn. This time she turned Juan into a scarecrow in the middle of the field. She turned herself into a stalk of corn beside him.

When her father passed by the field of corn, he stopped and gazed at the scarecrow. It seemed strange to him that a stalk of corn should grow so close to the scarecrow, but once again he had just lost sight of Juan and Jujuyana, and he was impatient to catch them. He kicked his horse and thundered down the road.

Jujuyana told Juan, "We are almost free. Only a little farther."

But she spoke too soon. Her father had gotten suspicious about the field of corn and returned to it. When he saw Juan and Jujuyana, he raced to catch them.

Jujuyana saw that her father was almost upon them. She reached into her bag and took out a mirror, the final object in the bag. She threw the mirror into the middle of the road. Instantly the mirror became a

Tales of Transformation, Magic, and Wisdom

large lake, its waters so still and smooth that they reflected the sky and clouds.

When her father got to the lake, all he saw was two ducks, a male and a female, swimming peacefully in the middle of the lake. Suddenly the ducks lifted off the lake and flew away. As they flew the father knew they were Juan and Jujuyana and they were beyond his grasp. As they disappeared he shouted one last curse. "You may have escaped, Jujuyana, but you will never have his love! I place a curse on both of you. The first person to embrace him will cause him to forget you forever!"

Jujuyana heard the curse and vowed never to allow Juan to be embraced. When she told Juan about the curse, he agreed to be eternally careful, for had fallen in love with Jujuyana.

Still shaking from their desperate escape, Juan told Jujuyana that they could return to his parents' farm. They would be safe there, and he wanted her to meet his family.

As they got closer to his childhood home, Juan told Jujuyana to wait outside the house. He wanted to go in first to tell his family that he had returned from his travels and that he had brought back a young woman with him.

As Juan entered his house, his family was so excited and filled with joy to see him that they all came rushing over to hug him. Juan tried to stop them, but it was too late. His mother embraced him, and at that moment he lost all memory of Jujuyana.

Jujuyana waited outside the house until she realized what had happened. She went closer to the house and saw Juan inside, talking and laughing with his family. Her heart was broken because her father's evil curse had been fulfilled. She traveled to a nearby village and lived there in hopes that one day the curse could be broken.

As time passed Juan decided to stay at his parents' farm. Nearby was a neighbor who had a daughter who was having misfortune with her husbands. Each time she married a man, he immediately died. Everyone in the valley talked about how the woman must have a curse on her. Of course the curse was worse for the husbands.

Juan met the woman and found her to be a wonderfully kind person. It was clearly not her fault that her husbands had died. Over time Juan fell in love with her, and they agreed to be married. Juan's family was not at all for the wedding because of the rumors of the curse. But Juan felt that the curse was just gossip and wanted to go ahead with the wedding.

Meanwhile Jujuyana had been watching Juan, and she knew that the rumors of the curse were true. When the woman was a little girl, her family had angered a *bruja*. The *bruja* put a curse on the little baby girl so that whenever she married, her husband would die even before their wedding night. Jujuyana knew that, even if she could never have Juan's love, he must not marry this woman.

On the day of the wedding, Jujuyana went to the church and asked if she could give a gift to Juan and his soon-to-be bride. The families had seen Jujuyana in the village and knew her to be a good person. They agreed to let Jujuyana in to give a gift to Juan and his bride.

From those times when Jujuyana had brushed Juan's hair, she had kept a lock of it. She took one strand of his hair and made it into a dove. She then took a strand of her own hair and made it into another dove. She put these two doves into a cage and took them as a present to Juan and his bride.

When she gave them the present, the doves began to sing. The doves sang about a girl named Jujuyana and her escape from a faraway land. As Juan listened to the birds' song, he slowly regained his memory of Jujuyana. When he turned around to see who had given him the birds, he recognized his lost love. The curse was broken.

Juan told his family about Jujuyana and their close escape from her father. Juan's family found the amazing story hard to believe. Jujuyana then confessed to using her magic powers with the doves to awaken Juan's love for her. Finally, as an act of kindness for the cursed woman, Jujuyana used her power to break the curse. In time the woman fell in love with another man and married happily.

After her years of longing and loneliness, Jujuyana was able to have the happiness she had wished for. She and Juan were married, and as all good *cuentos* end, they lived happily ever after.

THE MOST INTERESTING GIFT
OF ALL

The three Ornales brothers were in love with the same woman. She lived in the city and they lived on a farm. Even though they lived in different worlds, each of the three Ornales brothers thought that he had a chance to win the love of the woman they called *La Coqueta*. The youngest brother had given her the name because she was such a flirt whenever she was around them, and the other two brothers picked up on it and started using it themselves.

One day the three brothers decided that it was time to declare their intentions to *La Coqueta*. They dressed up in their finest clothes and started off to town. The oldest brother told the others, "Today you learn why women prefer the older, more mature, man. I do not hold it against you that you love the same woman as me, but after she has chosen, you must give up your feelings for her because she will be mine."

The middle brother couldn't help but laugh out loud. "Oh brother," he said, "I give you my respect as my older brother, but I do not see *La Coqueta* saying yes to you. She is kind to you out of respect for your age, but I have seen her looking at me whenever she has the chance. Brother, I am afraid you are going to make a fool out of yourself today. But I agree with you on one thing. After today you must give up your feelings for her if we are to remain brothers."

The youngest brother had heard too much. "You two sound like a couple of *viejitos* who don't know that their time for young women is over. *La Coqueta* is young and fun-loving. Even if she doesn't choose me, she would never choose someone as old as either of you. You both are wise from experience, but that is not what *La Coqueta* wants in her husband. Her uncle or father, yes. But not her husband. You will see. I am the only one with a real chance at *La Coqueta*."

They all had a good laugh at what the others had said because they were close brothers and good friends, but each of them in his heart hoped that he was the one for *La Coqueta*.

When they arrived at the house of *La Coqueta*, they first talked to her father. They paid him their respects and asked for his permission to ask his daughter for her hand in marriage. Her father did not know quite what to make of the situation. He had never heard of three brothers asking for the hand of a woman before. But he knew the Ornales family, and he knew that the brothers were men of honor. He also knew the size of their farm, and he knew that his daughter would be well cared for. He gave them his permission, but he warned them, "My daughter is a very headstrong woman. I give you my permission to ask, but she might say no all three of you!"

The brothers thanked the father, and each prepared his speech. *La Coqueta* had requested to meet with each of them alone so that she could get the true measure of the man without him being in competition with the others.

First to go in was the oldest brother. He cleared his throat and began, "Good afternoon *La*, oops, I mean, *Señorita*. I have come to ask for your hand in marriage. Please know that I love you, and all that I have, which is considerable, being the oldest son of my family, will be yours. I know that I am older than my brothers, but I am finished with my wild days, and I will make you a good and trustworthy husband."

When the older brother was finished, he came out of the room and had to sit down, his heart was beating so fast. He couldn't even look at his brothers for fear that they would see how nervous he was.

Then it was the second brother's turn. He walked carefully into the room and began to talk to *La Coqueta*. "Good afternoon, *La* . . . I mean, *Señorita*. I have come to ask for your hand in marriage. What I have to offer you is all my love and the promise that I will honor and take care of you for all of my life. If you choose me as your husband, you will make me the happiest man in the world. Know that I will always make sure that your family is cared for and that as long as I am alive, they will be welcome at my house."

When the second brother was finished, he had to go outside to get some fresh air. He had been so hot that he thought he was going to faint while he was talking to *La Coqueta*.

Finally it was the youngest brother's turn. As he walked into the room, he stopped short because *La Coqueta* looked so beautiful to him. After he had gathered his thoughts, he began, "Good afternoon *La* . . . I mean, *Señorita*. Thank you for giving me the honor of asking for your hand in marriage. I know that as the youngest brother I do not have as much to offer you as my brothers. But know that I am a hard worker and that someday I will have as much as my brothers have and that you will never want for anything. Since I am the youngest, we will have our full lives together. We will be able to enjoy our youth and grow into old age together. I have never been with any woman, and if you accept my offer of marriage, I will never be with any woman but you."

When the third brother had finished, he went outside to join his brothers while they waited for *La Coqueta*'s decision. Each was still nervous, but they all got a good laugh out of each of them almost calling her *La Coqueta*.

Sooner than they expected, *La Coqueta* came out and gave them her decision. She told them, "I am very honored and flattered that three such fine men would want my hand in marriage. To tell the truth, it is too hard for me to make up my mind. I need a little more time to think about it. Meanwhile I give you a challenge to help me decide. Come back in a week, and whoever brings me the most interesting gift will greatly help his case with me."

La Coqueta's father just looked at the three brothers and shrugged his shoulders as if to say, "I told you so."

The three brothers immediately set out to find the most interesting gift in the world. The oldest brother had once traveled with a circus, and he knew a magician who had the most wonderful things: balls that could multiply, scarves that could disappear, rings that would link together and come apart in unseen ways. Once the magician had even cut a woman in half. Surely he would have something for the oldest brother.

When the oldest brother finally found the circus, he said to the magician, "Good friend. You know that I have done many favors for you. Now it is time for me to ask one of you. I am in love with a woman and have asked for her hand in marriage. To win her hand I need the most interesting gift in the world."

The magician got a glimmer in his eye and rubbed his hands together with glee. "I have just the thing!" he told the oldest brother.

"I have never used it in the act because I didn't want anyone to know I had it. Once on a journey in another part of the world, I met a dying magician, and he gave me this gift with the promise that I would use it well. I can't think of a better use for it than to help my old friend win the heart of his loved one."

He took the oldest brother out behind the circus camp and uncovered an old, broken-down carriage. Excitedly he told him, "I know it doesn't look like much, but that's the secret of it! It can fly and take you anywhere in the world you want to go! But don't let anyone see you use it, or they'll know your secret."

The oldest brother thanked his friend and set off for home, pulling the carriage.

Meanwhile the second brother had gone into the forest to visit a *bruja.* Usually he would never go to see a *bruja* by himself, but he was desperate. As he came up to her house, he made a lot of noise so she would come out and talk to him. When she heard the noise she yelled out, "Come in."

"Oh no," thought the middle brother, "that is just what I didn't want her to say."

As he carefully walked into the *bruja's* house, he made the sign of the cross. Once inside it took a few minutes for his eyes to adjust to the darkness. As he looked around he was surprised by what he saw. The house looked completely normal. He had imagined all sorts of terrible things, like dead animals and weeds, hanging from the walls. But there was nothing there, just a few pictures like those in his own house.

Then he had a terrible thought. What if she isn't a *bruja?* What if the rumors are nothing but rumors? Oh no! I am doomed. I will never have the hand of *La Coqueta* in marriage now.

The old woman asked the middle brother, "What is it that you want from a little old woman in the forest? There is not much I can give you. As you see, I have very little."

The middle brother began to talk to the woman, hoping for once that she was a real *bruja.* "*Señora,* I have asked a woman for her hand in marriage. She has challenged me to find the most interesting gift in the world before she accepts my offer. Is there any way you can help me? There is nothing I can give you in return, but I promise that one day I will pay you back."

The little old woman sat up, then got out of her chair. In a crackling voice she replied, "Perhaps I can help you. I do have a few special things. And don't worry about paying me back. In cases like this one I usually get what I want sooner or later."

She went into her bedroom and came back out with something wrapped in a piece of black velvet. When she unwrapped it there was a mirror.

The hopes of the second brother immediately sunk. A mirror, he thought to himself. It isn't even a gold mirror.

"No, it isn't even a gold mirror, my young man."

The middle brother was startled by what she had said. He thought, "Maybe there's hope yet."

"Young man, there is always hope. This is a very special mirror. Whenever you look into it, you will see whatever you want to see. Take care of it. If you drop it, the person you are looking at will die." ·

The middle brother thanked the little old lady, and for once in his life, he was happy that she was a *bruja*.

The youngest brother had gone to see the *curandera*. He had seen the *curandera* bring people back from the death bed, and he knew that she had very special healing herbs and plants.

He explained to her, "*Curandera*, I have asked a beautiful young woman for her hand in marriage. Would you please help me win her hand? I need to find the most interesting gift in the world."

The *curandera* said, "You have come to the right place. I have just the thing to turn a young woman's fancy in your favor."

She reached under a cabinet and pulled out a bottle filled with bright red leaves. She held them up to the light and told the youngest brother, "Just one of these leaves ground up will bring the dead back to life. Take them, but use them carefully. Once people think you have the power of the *curandero*, they will never leave you alone. Remember, you do not have the power. I am just giving you a few leaves."

The youngest brother thanked the *curandera* and went back to the city.

It just so happened that each of the three brothers took the same road back to the city. They met up with each other and shared the stories of how they had gotten their gifts. Each one was sure that his gift would be the most interesting gift.

They all decided to look in the magic mirror to see their beloved, soon-to-be wife. As the image formed in the mirror, they saw a lot of people gathered around *La Coqueta*. It looked as if she were dead because everyone was dressed in black.

The brothers panicked. They all jumped in the magic carriage and told it to take them to the home of *La Coqueta*. Immediately they were there. When they walked into *La Coqueta's* room, her father stopped them. He said that she had suddenly fallen very ill and they had already called for the priest.

The youngest brother took out one of the red leaves the *curandera* had given him. He ground it up in his hand and blew the powder on *La Coqueta*. She sat right up in bed like nothing had ever been wrong, and when she saw the three brothers, she asked what they had brought for her.

Each told her of the wonderful gift he had brought. When *La Coqueta* heard about the gifts, she said, "This has only made it harder to choose. Now we must do something else to help me make up my mind. Go out in the field and each of you shoot an arrow into the sky. Whoever shoots the arrow the farthest will help his cause in asking for my hand in marriage."

The brothers groaned, and *La Coqueta*'s father just shrugged his shoulders.

The three brothers went out into the field with their strongest bows and their lightest arrows. With all their might they drew back the bowstrings and sent three arrows flying as far as they could.

And now this story comes to an end. To this day the arrows have not come down, and the three brothers and *La Coqueta* are still waiting to see who won the hand of *La Coqueta*.

Pablo lost his parents when he was born and was raised by his grandparents. His grandparents were good people and they loved him, but they were too old to give him the discipline he really needed. Pablo grew up doing whatever he wanted to do. He would come and go whenever he wanted. He would stay up as late as he wanted. He would go to school whenever he wanted.

When Pablo was a young child, his grandparents tried to make sure that he was raised the right way. They took him to church on Sunday and taught him the importance of respecting his elders. But as Pablo got older his grandparents began to worry that he was out of their control. They were afraid that pretty soon he would fall in with the wrong crowd and end up at the boy's reformatory outside of town.

Every Saturday they would see the reformatory boys being marched down the middle of the street, dressed in their gray reformatory uniforms, and they would say to Pablo, "See, if you don't straighten up you'll end up like them."

Pablo wasn't scared, though. He knew he'd never end up in the reformatory. "Besides," he said to himself, "I'm not afraid of anything." Deep in his heart he was a good boy. He was just growing up wild.

Finally his grandparents decided that they needed help raising Pablo. They talked to the priest, and the priest agreed to let Pablo live with him. The grandparents were very happy that Pablo was going to live with the priest, who was a stern man and might be just what Pablo needed. They even imagined that Pablo might fall under the teachings of the church and one day become a priest. The family still needed a priest in it.

When Pablo first went to live with the priest, things went very smoothly. Pablo helped clean the church, and soon the priest was teaching Pablo how to be an altar boy. When his grandparents went to Mass and saw Pablo helping the priest, they were very happy and knew they had made the right decision.

Even though it appeared that things were working out for Pablo, there still was one problem. Occasionally Pablo still did crazy things. One day he climbed to the top of the bell tower just to see what the bell looked like. When the priest scolded Pablo for that dangerous stunt, Pablo replied, "I wasn't scared."

One night Pablo sneaked out of the church and spent the night in the cemetery without telling anyone. The priest had thought Pablo had run away and looked for Pablo all night. When he found Pablo sleeping in the cemetery, he scolded him again and told him how dangerous it was to spend the night in the cemetery. Again Pablo replied, "I wasn't scared."

One Saturday afternoon the priest found Pablo sitting with the reformatory boys at the movies. The priest reprimanded Pablo and warned him that the reformatory boys were criminals. Once more Pablo replied, "I wasn't scared."

Even though the priest knew Pablo was a good boy in all other respects, and had even come to enjoy Pablo's company, he felt it was time to teach Pablo a lesson. If he didn't stop taking such foolhardy risks, one day he might really get hurt.

The priest talked to some people in the town, and they helped him with his plan. They were going to scare Pablo so much that he would think twice about doing anything dangerous again.

In the town was an old, abandoned house. The people of the town said that the house was haunted by a ghost. A few brave men who had gone into the house had come running out and told people that they heard a voice calling them.

The priest made up some excuse for Pablo to have to go to the house. He told Pablo, "Go over to the haunted house and knock on the door. People are saying a hermit traveler has moved into the house, and I want to know if that is true." He didn't want Pablo to get hurt, so he made sure to tell him, "But whatever you do, don't go in the house."

Meanwhile the people of the town had put bones and scary masks on the front porch to frighten Pablo.

When Pablo went to the house, he was curious about what a hermit traveler looked like. As he went onto the porch of the haunted house, he looked through a crack in the boarded-up windows, but he couldn't see anything. As he knocked on the porch door, he saw the bones and masks the townspeople had put there, and he laughed. "I'm not scared. I saw those masks last Halloween."

He knocked on the door, and it swung open. It creaked as if it hadn't been opened in years. Even though the priest had told him not to go into the house, Pablo's curiosity was too much for him. Pablo carefully stepped into the house.

Every room was filled with dust and cobwebs. Because all the windows were boarded up, there was very little light. Every now and then a shaft of light came through a hole in the boarded-up windows, and Pablo could see little particles of dirt doing their dance in the air.

When Pablo got into the living room, he pulled off the sheet covering the sofa. Dust flew everywhere but soon settled down, and things were ghostly quiet again. Pablo sat down on the sofa and looked around the room.

Suddenly he heard a voice crying out, "I'm falling. I'm falling."

Pablo answered, "Go ahead. I'm not afraid." He figured it was just a trick to scare him.

Without any more warning, a bone of a skeleton fell down from the ceiling. The voice said again, "I'm falling. I'm falling."

Now Pablo was really curious. He got up from the sofa and looked at the ceiling, but he saw nothing up there except some old, dusty cobwebs. So he yelled out, "Go ahead. I'm not afraid."

Another bone fell from the ceiling. This continued until there was a pile of bones lying on the floor in front of the sofa. Pablo could not believe that the townspeople would go to this much trouble to scare him. As he went to pick up the bones, they began to rattle and move. First one bone and then another. Pablo figured that a mouse was scurrying underneath them.

But soon the bones began to rise up into the air and knock into each other. Pablo could do nothing but stand and watch with his mouth wide open. Finally all of the bones reassembled themselves into a human skeleton. Pablo looked at the skeleton and said, "This isn't a trick of the townspeople!" (See fig. 20.)

The skeleton moved its mouth and began to talk to Pablo. "Thank you for being so brave. You saved my life."

Pablo answered, "Saved your life? You're already dead. You're a skeleton!"

The skeleton laughed and said, "I know that. I didn't mean my life. I meant my soul. I am the owner of this house, and when I died years ago and went to heaven, St. Peter told me I had to return to earth to do penance for my sins before I could get into heaven. I've had to stay in the house as a broken skeleton until some brave person

144

helped me find my shape again. I have tried to get others before you to help me when they came into the house, but they always got scared when I called to them. Pretty soon no one ever came again."

Pablo knew that nobody would believe his story about the skeleton, but he didn't care because it was the best adventure he'd ever had.

The skeleton continued, "Now my soul can rest in peace. As a reward I will tell you where there is a treasure chest filled with gold coins hidden in the walls of the house."

The skeleton showed Pablo where the treasure was hidden and thanked Pablo again for helping him free his soul. Then the skeleton disappeared right in front of Pablo's eyes.

Meanwhile the priest had been expecting Pablo to run in, scared to death, and promise that he would never do anything frightening again. Was he surprised when Pablo walked in carrying a chest filled with gold coins! He asked, "Where did you get this treasure? Did you steal it?"

Pablo assured the priest that he did not steal the money. When he told the priest about the skeleton, the priest just laughed and said, "What an active imagination the boy has!" But he did believe Pablo when he said that he found the money hidden in the walls of the haunted house, because the townspeople said that long ago thieves had hidden their stolen loot there. Everyone had been too afraid to go into the house to look for it. Now the money belonged to Pablo.

Pablo let the priest think what he might, but he knew the true story. The next Sunday at church he said a small prayer, asking that the soul of the skeleton find eternal rest in heaven.

Pablo gave most of the gold to the church and to his grandparents. He let the priest keep some of it for his own use. The rest he asked the priest to keep for him until he finished growing up. From that day forward the townspeople called Pablo, The Boy Without Fear.

PEDRO DE ORDIMALAS

Trickster tales appear in every culture's stories. The exploits of the trickster give people imaginary license to overcome obstacles, confound and puncture authority, and give new shape to everyday events. Through its active, creative, and often playful manipulation of people and events, the trickster can reorder peoples' lives. The legendary antics can even give hope to a people struggling with difficult circumstances.

Often the trickster reinterprets knowledge for humans struggling to understand the events of life. Like the fools in Shakespeare's plays, the trickster is often the only one who speaks truthfully and sees the truth behind people's actions.

In some cultures the trickster is a gifted shaman. In the western United States, the trickster is Coyote. The Raven is the trickster of the Pacific Northwest. Germany has its Till Eulenspiegel.

The Hispanic trickster is Pedro de Ordimalas. Pedro is a rogue whose anecdotal stories can contain both serious and comic descriptions of his deeds. His most popular story concludes with Pedro tricking heaven and hell to gain a place in heaven.

PEDRO DE ORDIMALAS

Once Pedro de Ordimalas was taking care of a farmer's pigs. As he was taking care of them, he came up with a plan to get the farmer's pigs for himself.

First he cut off their tails and buried them in the mud. He then ran to the farmer and told him that his pigs had sunk in the mud.

The farmer ran to the pigpen and saw the pigs' tails sticking out of the mud. Desperately he tried to save his pigs by pulling them out of the mud by their tails. With each mighty tug, all he pulled up was a tail. He finally gave up his pigs for good and thanked Pedro for at least warning him about what had happened.

Pedro took the farmer's pigs out of hiding and took them home for himself.

One day Pedro's mother died. Pedro tied his mother on a horse and led the horse to the church. As he approached the church, the priest's dogs came running out and spooked the horse, causing Pedro's mother to fall off the horse. When the priest came running out, Pedro told the priest that the dogs had startled the horse, causing his mother to fall and be killed. The priest felt responsible and paid for the funeral of Pedro's mother.

Pedro met a man who had heard of the tricks of Pedro de Ordimalas. He asked Pedro to show him some of his famous tricks. Pedro told the man that he had his tricks at home, but if the man loaned Pedro his horse, Pedro would go home and bring back some tricks. The man gave Pedro his horse. As Pedro rode off with no intention of returning, he called back to the man, "This is one of my tricks!"

Once Pedro was down to his last 10 *centavos*. He had no work and didn't know how he would get any more money. So he went into the forest and stuck the coins to the branches of a tree with tar. Soon some travelers came by and were amazed to see the coins on the tree branches. Pedro convinced the travelers that the money had grown on the tree and that he was the owner of the tree. By the end of the conversation, Pedro had sold the tree to the travelers for 500 *pesos*. He even talked the travelers into leaving him the *centavos* as seeds for a new tree!

Once Pedro had a magic drum that would not let the person who was beating it stop until Pedro released the person from the powers of the drum. It just so happened that death herself came for Pedro one night. She told Pedro that it was time for his long trip into eternity.

Pedro asked permission to say good-bye to all his *compadres*. To speed things up, he asked death to beat the drum to call his friends together while he got his belongings ready. Because Pedro had been a good sinner, death agreed to help him. She started beating the drum. When she tried to stop, she found that she couldn't. The more she tried to stop, the louder her drumming became. Finally she begged Pedro to help her. She would give Pedro anything for his help. Of course Pedro asked for 10 more years of life on earth. In this way Pedro tricked death out of 10 years.

Once, when Pedro was walking through the forest, he heard the footsteps of a giant approaching. Not wishing to be killed by the giant, he did some quick thinking. He tore his clothes and took off his shoes. As the giant got closer, Pedro threw his shoes high in the air.

When the giant saw Pedro, he asked him why his clothes were so torn. Pedro told the giant that he had been in a fight with a man and had thrown the man high in the air to kill him.

Just then Pedro's shoes came falling to the ground. Pedro told the giant that they were the man's shoes, falling back to earth, and the man's body would follow later.

When no body came falling down, the giant believed that Pedro must be a ferocious fighter to be able to throw a man so high, and he decided to leave Pedro alone.

When Pedro died he arrived at the gates of heaven and asked to be admitted to eternal glory with the Lord. When St. Peter looked in the good book, he saw that Pedro was a sinner not worthy to enter the gates of heaven. For Pedro to do some final penance for his sins, St. Peter sent Pedro to purgatory.

While he was in purgatory, Pedro decided to help the sinners who were doing penance there pay for their sins and get into heaven faster. He took out his whip and began whipping the sinners. The screams of the whipped sinners caused such a commotion in heaven that St. Peter decided that Pedro could not stay in purgatory any longer, so he sent him to limbo.

While he was in limbo, Pedro began to feel sorry for all the babies there who would never get to heaven because they had died without being baptized. So he began to dunk the babies in the river. The babies screamed and cried so loud as Pedro almost drowned them, that St. Peter had to come down to limbo to see what was the matter. When he saw that Pedro was behind the commotion, he said to Pedro that there was only one place left, hell.

When Pedro arrived at hell, the devils laid out the red carpet. They were very excited to have such a renowned sinner as Pedro join them.

The first day Pedro was in hell, *El Diablo* himself heard a tremendous commotion coming from the devils' lunchroom. He ran out and saw Pedro saying his prayers over his food. Pedro told *El Diablo* that he had been raised a good Catholic and that he always said his prayers before eating. Each time Pedro said the names of the Holy Family, "Jesus, Mary, and Joseph," the devils yelled out in agony.

El Diablo decided that Pedro could not stay in hell. He kicked him out and told him to go any place else but stay out of hell.

Because he was dead Pedro could not return to earth. With no place to go, he went back to heaven and once more asked St. Peter to be let in. By now St. Peter knew that Pedro had no place to go but had to be somewhere. So St. Peter went into heaven to talk the problem over with the Lord.

Finally St. Peter came out and told Pedro that he could stay outside the gates of heaven with St. Peter, but he would be turned into a rock.

Pedro agreed and asked St. Peter if he could be a rock with eyes. St. Peter was frustrated that Pedro had yet another request so he asked him, "Why with eyes?"

Pedro answered, "Because of the life I've led I know all the sins people can commit. With eyes I will be able to look into the souls of people who come before you and tell you if they are worthy to enter *La Gloria*.

St. Peter thought about it and finally agreed the idea was a good one.

So when our time comes to go see St. Peter, we will approach the gates of heaven, and we will see Pedro as a rock with eyes, looking deep into our souls to see if we are worthy to enter *La Gloria*.

Animal Stories

THE LITTLEST ANT

According to the classification categories of folktales, this story is what is known as a cumulative tale. At the end of the tale, all the repeated phrases of the story are strung together to form one long conclusion. In different versions of the story, the components of the cumulative ending vary, and in some versions the ant does not get any help and learns his lesson in another way.

One version of this story was told to me by New Mexico National Heritage Storyteller Cleofes Vigil. In addition to his especially animated telling of the story, *Señor* Vigil ended the story in a most inventive way. When he got to the last part of the tale, he broke out into song and finished with a wonderful rhyming, rhythmic singing of the cumulative ending. He had told the story up to this point in English, but the song was in Spanish. When I asked him the origin of the song, he answered with a shrug, "I learned it somewhere."

THE LITTLEST ANT

Once there was a little baby ant. This little ant loved to play outside and hardly ever came into the anthill when his parents called him. He liked nothing better than to stay outside and play in the dirt. His parents were always telling him that it was time for him to grow up and help with the work of the ant colony, but the little ant didn't pay any attention and just kept playing.

Winter was coming, and all the ants were busy collecting food to store in the anthill. The little ant's parents were busy with the work of collecting food. They told the little ant not to wander away from the anthill because winter was coming and he would be caught in a snowstorm.

As usual the little ant did not pay any attention to his parents. He just kept playing and playing. Before long he had wandered far away from the anthill. He looked around and did not recognize where he was. As he looked up at the sky, he noticed that it was getting darker and darker. Soon snow began falling.

The ant hurried to get back home, but he had lost his way. He sat down to try to figure out what to do when a large snowflake fell on him. The snowflake was very heavy, and it trapped the little ant. No matter how hard he tried, he could not budge it. Soon he tired of the struggle and just lay there, trapped under the snowflake.

Soon the little ant grew very thirsty. Since it was too cold for the snow to melt into water, the little ant called out, hoping someone would hear him, "¡Agua! ¡Agua! Water! Water!" But he was very far out in the forest, and there was nobody around to hear him. He called out even louder, "¡Agua! ¡Agua!"

Finally he gave up and tried to think of a way to get free. As he looked around he saw that there was almost no way he could get loose. He begged and begged the snowflake to get off of his leg.

"Snowflake, get off my leg so I can go home."

But the snowflake didn't move. Then the little ant saw the sun up in the sky.

"Sun, melt the snowflake until it gets off my leg so I can go home."

But the sun just looked down from the sky and did nothing. Then the little ant saw a cloud in the sky.

"Cloud in the sky, cover the sun until the sun melts the snowflake, until the snowflake gets off my leg so I can go home."

But the cloud did nothing. Then the little ant called out to the wind.

"Wind, blow around the cloud in the sky until the cloud covers the sun, until the sun melts the snowflake, until the snowflake gets off my leg so I can go home."

But the wind did nothing. Then the little ant called out to the wall of an abandoned house he saw nearby.

"Wall, block the wind until the wind blows around the cloud in the sky, until the cloud covers the sun, until the sun melts the snowflake, until the snowflake gets off my leg so I can go home."

But the wall did nothing. Then the little ant saw a mouse scurrying by.

"Mouse, gnaw at the wall until the wall blocks the wind, until the wind blows around the cloud in the sky, until the cloud covers the sun, until the sun melts the snowflake, until the snowflake gets off my leg so I can go home."

But the mouse did nothing. Then the little ant saw an owl.

"Owl, chase the mouse until the mouse gnaws at the wall, until the wall blocks the wind, until the wind blows around the cloud in the sky, until the cloud covers the sun, until the sun melts the snowflake, until the snowflake gets off my leg so I can go home."

But the owl did nothing. Becoming desperate, the little ant called out to a cat hiding under the bushes.

"Cat, scratch the owl's eyes until the owl chases the mouse, until the mouse gnaws at the wall, until the wall blocks the wind, until the wind blows around the cloud in the sky, until the cloud covers the sun, until the sun melts the snowflake, until the snowflake gets off my leg so I can go home."

But the cat did nothing. Then the little ant saw a dog walking along the path.

"Dog, chase the cat until the cat scratches the owl's eyes, until the owl chases the mouse, until the mouse gnaws at the wall, until the wall blocks the wind, until the wind blows around the cloud in the sky, until the cloud covers the sun, until the sun melts the snowflake, until the snowflake gets off my leg so I can go home."

But the dog did nothing. The ant looked around and saw a stick nearby.

"Stick, beat the dog until the dog chases the cat, until the cat scratches the owl's eyes, until the owl chases the mouse, until the mouse gnaws at the wall, until the wall blocks the wind, until the wind blows around the cloud in the sky, until the cloud covers the sun, until the sun melts the snowflake, until the snowflake gets off my leg so I can go home."

But the stick did nothing. Getting more and more desperate, the littlest ant saw a fire blazing on a nearby hill.

"Fire, burn the stick until the stick beats the dog, until the dog chases the cat, until the cat scratches the owl's eyes, until the owl chases the mouse, until the mouse gnaws at the wall, until the wall blocks the wind, until the wind blows around the cloud in the sky, until the cloud covers the sun, until the sun melts the snowflake, until the snowflake gets off my leg so I can go home."

But the fire did nothing. By now the littlest ant was about to give up hope. He was so thirsty that he began to call for water again, "¡Agua! ¡Agua! Water! Water!"

To his great surprise a little stream of water flowed right by him. His prayer had been answered.

He called out to the water, "Water, go and put out the fire until the fire burns the stick, until the stick beats the dog, until the dog chases the cat, until the cat scratches the owl's eyes, until the owl chases the mouse, until the mouse gnaws at the wall, until the wall blocks the wind, until the wind blows around the cloud in the sky, until the cloud covers the sun, until the sun melts the snowflake, until the snowflake gets off my leg so I can go home."

And the water did just what the littlest ant asked it to do.

The water put out the fire, and the fire burned the stick, and the stick beat the dog, and the dog chased the cat, and the cat scratched the owl's eyes, and the owl chased the mouse, and the mouse gnawed at the wall, and the wall blocked the wind, and the wind blew around the cloud in the sky, and the cloud covered the sun, and the sun melted the snowflake.

The littlest ant thanked the water for its help and finally managed to find his way back home. His parents asked him if he had learned his lesson, and he said that he had. From that day on the little ant was one of the hardest workers in the ant colony.

Once, in a part of the forest far away from here, a lion and a bear got married. All of the animals of the forest came to the wedding. They came out of respect for the lion, who was the king of the beasts. After the wedding each animal came up to the happy couple and wished them good fortune in their marriage. Secretly the animals wondered how long it would be before the bear and the lion had an argument, because both were known for their stubborn ways.

Now to us it seems that this type of marriage is not possible, but I must tell you that it did happen and that they were very happy together.

We all know that the lion is the king of the beasts. Every morning he arises and wakes all the animals with his powerful roar. The bear was very proud to be married to the king of the beasts.

One day the lion took a long walk through the forest. When he returned home he was hot and tired. He lay down in the shade and stretched his feet out in the cool grass.

When the bear returned home she immediately noticed a strong smell. She sniffed around, coming closer and closer to the lion. Finally she was right by the lion's side, and she recognized the smell.

"Lion!" she exclaimed. "Your feet really smell. Go down to the river and wash them off!"

The lion was very offended. As king of the beasts, he was not accustomed to being spoken to in this manner. He told the bear firmly, "My feet do not smell. You must be smelling something else."

"Your feet do smell."

"My feet do not smell!"

Finally the bear said, "You are the king of the beasts. Call all of the animals together and we will have them tell us if your feet smell or not."

When all of the animals had been gathered together, they were excited because this was the argument they had been expecting. But they did not expect they would have to be part of the argument!

The lion made all of the poor animals come up and smell his feet. Whenever one of the animals would say the lion's feet *did* smell, the lion would give that animal a tremendous slap on the head with his mighty paw and say, "They do not smell!"

Whenever one of the animals would say that the lion's feet *did not* smell, the bear would give that animal a savage blow to the head with her mighty paw and say, "They do smell!"

Finally it was the fox's turn to smell the lion's feet. All of the animals, suffering from the blows they had received from the lion and the bear, were very curious about what the fox would say, for the fox had a reputation for being clever.

The fox came close to the lion's feet and sniffed and sniffed. Then she sniffed and sniffed some more. Then she sniffed even some more. But all this time she didn't say a word.

Finally the lion roared in exasperation, "How come you aren't saying anything?"

The fox replied, "I'm sorry, O Mighty King of the Beasts. I have a cold, and my nose is all stuffed up, and I can't smell a thing. I really can't say if they smell or not."

All of the other animals howled with laughter at the cleverness of the fox. And in this way the fox escaped without being cuffed by either the lion or the bear.

THE LANGUAGE OF THE ANIMALS

In a valley not too far from here, a shepherd was out in the fields tending to his sheep. As the day wore on, he became sleepy and lay down underneath a tree to rest in the shade. He looked around for any coyotes who might try to steal his sheep, but he saw none.

Soon he was awakened by the screams of something trapped and crying for help. He ran through the field, following the screams for help. At the far end of the field, he saw a tree that had been hit by lightning. The tree was on fire. Trapped under a fallen burning limb was a snake. The shepherd took off his shirt and beat out the fire on the fallen limb. Then he used another fallen limb to raise the heavy branch and free the snake.

When the snake was free, he began to thank the man for rescuing him. The man was astonished to hear the snake talk. He had never even imagined that snakes could talk.

The snake was so thankful to the man for saving his life that he said, "You must come with me to see the mother of all snakes. She is very powerful, and she will give you a handsome reward."

The man followed the snake to a dark part of the forest. They came to a cave, and the snake went in. The man heard the hissing of a thousand snakes in the cave and was afraid to enter. The snake came back out and told him, "You will be safe. I have told the mother of all snakes about your good deed, and she wishes to reward you. But you must come into the cave."

The man did not know whether to trust the snake, but he felt that the snake was speaking the truth, so he carefully stepped inside the cave. Inside the cave the man's eyes adjusted to the darkness, and soon he found himself standing before an enormous, glistening snake. The man started to shake, he was so scared.

The snake spoke to him. "You have saved my child, and because you are brave enough to stand before me now, I will give you a special reward. I give you the power to understand the language of the animals."

The mother of all snakes brought her head close to the man's face. She hissed, "Stick out your tongue." The man did as she asked. She touched his tongue with her forked tongue. As her tongue touched his, he felt a sharp, burning sensation flash through his mouth. His mouth felt paralyzed.

The mother of all snakes spoke to him. "Now you have the power to understand the language of the animals. But there is a price for this power. You are never to tell another person about this power—or you will die. Now go."

The man stumbled out of the cave, fell to the ground, and passed out. When he came to, he looked around for the snake. He saw nothing, and he thought that he had just had the most amazing dream.

As he walked back to his flock of sheep, he heard two large sheep saying, "Here comes our master. Where has he been all this time? We could have been eaten by a coyote and all he is doing is sleeping under a tree. We'd be better off taking care of ourselves."

It had not been a dream! It was true. He *could* understand the language of the animals. He rushed over to the corral. As he arrived all out of breath, he heard one horse say to another, "Here comes that crazy shepherd. Why do you think he is running over here so fast?"

Then he heard two black crows as they flew overhead. One said, "Look at that poor shepherd. If only he knew that under that fallen piñon tree lies buried treasure."

Buried treasure! The shepherd danced with joy over his new power.

The next day the shepherd took a shovel, went out to the fallen piñon tree, and began digging. As he was digging under the tree, he hit something that felt very solid. Digging some more he unearthed a large chest. Upon opening it he found it filled with gold and jewels. It must have been buried years earlier by thieves.

He took the gold and jewels to his family and showed them all he had found. They could not believe his good fortune. They asked him how he had found the treasure chest. He was just about to tell them when he remembered what the mother of all snakes had said: "You are never to tell another person about this power—or you will die." He caught himself just in time. He told his family that he had just gotten lucky while he was clearing the land around some fallen trees.

One day the man and his wife were out riding on their horses. One of the horses said to the other, "What a hot day this is. I can't wait to dump this heavy load back at the farm."

The man thought this was very funny and began to laugh. His wife asked with annoyance, "What is so funny? More and more often you laugh to yourself with no explanation. I am beginning to feel that you are laughing at me."

"Oh no, dear wife. I am not laughing at you." The man had to think quickly because he knew he could never tell his wife about his special ability. "I was just remembering something funny, but I can't tell you."

His wife was very hurt and confused by her husband's behavior. Trying to hold back tears, she told him, "If you wish to lead a life of secrets, then we do not have the marriage I thought we had. Since you want to have such a secret world, perhaps it is best if we live apart."

The man did not know what to do. He loved his wife more than anything in the world. He even thought that maybe he should tell his wife about his secret power. He would die if he did, but at least his wife would know he still loved her.

One day while the man was feeding the chickens, he overheard a dog talking to a rooster who was crowing. The dog said to the rooster, "Why do you keep singing so much? Here comes our master. Don't you realize that he may die soon? He has such sadness nowadays. He does not know what to tell his wife, and his life is so confused."

The rooster replied, "What is he confused about? Why, look at me. I have to be in charge of 15 hens. And do you know how I do it? I let them know there is only one rooster in the house!"

When the man heard the rooster, he immediately went into his house to talk to his wife. As he walked into the kitchen, he took hold of his wife and told her, "There is only one rooster in the house." His wife looked at him as if he'd gone crazy. He continued, "As the only rooster in the house I should be allowed to have a few thoughts to myself."

His wife, laughing to herself as she listened to him, thought about what he had said for a moment and answered her husband, "Yes, it is true, you are the only rooster in the house. From now on, if you wish to have some thoughts to yourself, then I will understand."

From that day on there was love and peace in the household. The man kept the secret of his power to himself, but he still enjoyed many moments of laughter when he overheard the animals talking. But he was always careful to control himself in front of his wife.

THE RABBIT AND THE COYOTE
(EL CONEJO Y EL COYOTE)

One day Coyote was out looking for food when he came upon Rabbit hiding in the tall grasses of the open meadow. Coyote had not eaten for several days, and he knew that it might be several more days before he came upon a rabbit again. Slowly he crept up on Rabbit because he didn't want to give Rabbit a chance to escape.

Rabbit was busy eating the long grass when he heard rustling behind him. He stopped eating. His little eyes looked all around, and his little nose tested the air. Sensing that all was safe, he went back to eating.

Meanwhile Coyote had come to a frozen standstill, making sure that he was upwind from Rabbit. He knew that catching a rabbit was a game of wits. He often lost, but this time he was so hungry that he was being very careful with his every move.

Without warning Coyote jumped high in the air and came down right on Rabbit. He had caught him!

Rabbit tried to squirm out of the terrible clutches of Coyote, but Coyote was holding on too tightly. Rabbit could feel the power in Coyote's paws, and he knew there was no hope in struggle.

Coyote looked at Rabbit and taunted poor Rabbit. "Well, Rabbit," he said, "Looks like I'm going to have Rabbit for supper tonight. I hope you're nice and tender."

Rabbit remained as cool and collected as he possibly could under the circumstances. "Good day, Mr. Coyote. I can see that you are very hungry, so I must tell you about a great procession that will be passing by here in just a few moments. Some of the people in the procession will be carrying a large feast. There will be plates of meat piled so high that it takes three people just to carry one of them. I'm sure that a great Coyote like yourself will find it easy to scare the people and to steal three or four plates of meat. I am afraid that if you waste any more time here with me, you might miss the procession."

Coyote felt that this was some trick on Rabbit's part, but the thought of those plates of meat was too much for him. "Where is this procession? I don't hear anything at all. And I don't see a single person."

"Oh Coyote, the procession is just around the hill. Can't you hear it? See, there it is right over there."

Coyote looked as hard as he could, but he still couldn't see anything. "The grass is too tall to see anything," he complained.

Rabbit quickly replied, "Then you must do what I do when I want to see things better. This is a secret of the rabbits, because we are always so low to the ground we need extra help to see if any of our enemies are creeping up on us."

Coyote laughed, "Your secret didn't do you much good this time!"

"That is because I was foolish and didn't use it. But there is still time for you to use it and get the plates of meat."

Every time he heard about the plates, Coyote could almost taste the meat in his mouth. "What secret? I never heard of any rabbit secret."

Rabbit chuckled to himself and told Coyote, "That's because it's a secret! Let go of me and I'll show you where we keep the secret."

Coyote loosened his grip on Rabbit just enough for Rabbit to lead him across the field. "Don't try to run off, or I'll eat you right on the spot," Coyote warned Rabbit.

They arrived at a stream that ran through the tall grasses. By the banks of the stream was a tar pit. Rabbit led Coyote to the tar pit and told him, "Here is the secret. We rub some of this magic pitch on our eyes, and we can see for miles around. Just put some on your eyes, and you'll see right where that procession is. Can't you smell the plates of meat already?"

Coyote put his nose high in the air and imagined that he did smell the plates of meat. He quickly rubbed the pitch on his eyes and raised his head to look for the procession.

Rabbit immediately wrestled himself out of Coyote's paws and ran out of his reach.

Coyote spun around and found that the pitch had sealed his eyes shut! He couldn't see a thing. He howled at Rabbit for tricking him, and he vowed that he would never let Rabbit trick him again.

But Rabbit just laughed because he knew that he would never be so careless as to let Coyote catch him again. Rabbit bounded off, and Coyote spent the rest of the day trying to get the pitch out of his sealed-shut eyes.

EL CONEJO Y EL COYOTE
(THE RABBIT AND THE COYOTE)

Cierto día Coyote andaba por ahí buscando comida cuando, sorprendió a Conejo escondido entre las hierbas altas del prado. Coyote no había comido en varios días, y sabía que podrían pasar aún varios días más antes de encontrarse con Conejo otra vez. Lentamente se deslizó hacia Conejo porque no quería darle la posibilidad de escapar.

Conejo estaba ocupado comiendo hierba cuando escuchó algo de moverse detrás de él. Dejó de comer. Sus ojitos miraron alrededor, y su naricita comprobó los olores en el aire. Pensando que se encontraba a salvo, continuó comiendo.

Mientras tanto, Coyote se había quedado muy quieto, asegurándose que el viento estuviera a su favor y no llevara su olor a Conejo. Sabía que atrapar a un conejo era un juego de ingenio que él a menudo perdía, pero esta vez estaba tan hambriento que estaba siendo muy cuidadoso con cada uno de sus movimientos.

Sin previo aviso Coyote dió un gran salto en el aire y cayó justamente encima de Conejo. ¡Lo había atrapado!

Conejo intentó escapar de las terribles garras de Coyote, pero éste lo apretaba demasiado fuerte. Conejo podía sentir la fuerza de las patas de Coyote, y sabía que no había esperanza en la lucha.

Coyote miró al pobre Conejo y se burló de él. "Bueno, Conejo," dijo, "Parece que voy a cenar conejo esta noche. Espero que estés sabroso y tierno."

Conejo permaneció tan tranquilo como le fué posible dadas las circunstancias. "Buenos días, Señor Coyote. Veo que tiene mucha hambre, así que debo decirle que un gran desfile va a pasar por aquí en tan sólo unos momentos. Alguna gente del desfile traerán mucha comida. Habrá platos con carne apilada tan alta que harán falta tres personas sólo para llevar uno de ellos. Estoy seguro que para un gran coyote como Ud. será fácil asustar a la gente y robar tres ó cuatro platos de carne. Me temo que si malgasta más tiempo aquí conmigo, podría perderse el desfile."

Coyote pensó que esto era algún truco de Conejo, pero el pensamiento de aquellos platos de carne era demasiado para él. "¿Dónde está ese desfile? No escucho nada en absoluto. Y no veo a nadie."

"Oh, Coyote, el desfile está al otro lado de la colina ahora mismo. ¿No lo escucha? Ve, está allí mismo."

Coyote miró lo mejor que pudo, pero no vió nada. "La hierba está demasiada alta y no veo nada," se quejó.

Conejo rápidamente le contestó, "Entonces debe hacer lo que yo hago cuando quiero ver mejor. Esto es un secreto de los conejos, ya que, como siempre estamos pegados a la tierra, necesitamos un poco de ayuda para ver si alguno de nuestros enemigos intenta sorprendernos."

Coyote se rió, "¡Tu secreto no te sirvió de mucho esta vez!"

"Porque fuí tonto y no lo usé. Pero Ud. aún tiene tiempo para usarlo y conseguir los platos de carne."

Cada vez que escuchaba lo de los platos, Coyote casi podía saborear la carne en su boca. "¿Qué secreto? Nunca he oído de ningún secreto de conejos."

Conejo se rió entre dientes y dijo a Coyote, "¡Eso es porque es un secreto! Suélteme y le enseñaré dónde guardamos el secreto."

Coyote dejó de apretar a Conejo lo suficiente para que éste lo guiara a través del campo. "No intentes salir corriendo, o te comeré aquí mismo," le advirtió Coyote.

Llegaron a un riachuelo que corría entre hierbas altas. En las orillas había un pozo de alquitrán. Conejo llevó a Coyote al pozo y le dijo, "Este es el secreto. Nos frotamos con un poco de este alquitrán mágico en los ojos, y podemos ver desde muy lejos. Ponga un poco en sus ojos, y verá exactamente dónde está el desfile. ¿No huele ya esos platos de carne?"

Coyote levantó su hocico al aire e imaginó que olía los platos de carne. Rápidamente se frotó los ojos con el alquitrán y alzó la cabeza para buscar el desfile.

Conejo inmediatamente se liberó de las garras de Coyote y corrió lejos de su alcance.

¡Coyote se dió la vuelta y se encontró con que el alquitrán había tapado sus ojos! No podía ver nada. Aulló a Conejo por haberle engañado, y juró que nunca volvería a dejarse engañar por él.

Pero Conejo se rió porque sabía que nunca más sería tan descuidado como para permitir que Coyote lo atrapara otra vez. Conejo se alejó brincando, y Coyote pasó el resto del día intentando quitarse el alquitrán de los ojos.

ONE GOOD DEED DESERVES ANOTHER

One summer evening a farmer and his wife finished their chores for the day. It was still light outside after supper, so they decided to go for a walk. They always enjoyed walks by the river, and they knew that soon winter would be upon them, making it too cold for a walk.

The family dog heard their footsteps and ran up to them, barking and wagging his tail. The wife petted the dog and said, "Do you want to go for a walk? Last time you went, you jumped in the river and got everything all dirty. Are you going to be good this time?" The dog wagged his tail in excitement.

The farmer looked at his wife and shook his head. "Do you really think that dog understands and will mind you? That dog has been worthless since the day we got him. We took him in as a stray dog. We've fed him. Given him a warm place to sleep. And how does he repay us? By being nothing but a bother."

The farmer's wife shot back, "Yes, he understands. You will some-day take those words back. Maybe even today."

Then all three—farmer, wife, and dog—went for a walk. As they came to the river, the wife noticed a snake trapped underneath a rock. "How did that poor snake get trapped under the rock?" the wife asked her husband.

"I don't know, but let's leave it there. Snakes are dangerous and we could get hurt."

The dog ran around the snake, but the snake hissed and scared the dog away. The farmer looked at his wife and wise-cracked, "Sure, some brave guard dog we have."

The wife pleaded with her husband, "We must do something. I can't stand the thought of that snake dying in such a cruel way."

The farmer went up to the snake. "All right, stand back. Hold the dog." He then kicked the rock off the snake. But the minute he kicked the rock, the snake reared up and trapped the farmer and his wife. They couldn't escape without running past the snake. The dog cowered by them with his tail between his legs. The snaked hissed and hissed, his red, forked tongue darting back and forth. He was ready to strike at any moment. His deadly gaze froze the farmer and his wife.

Snapping out of his fear, the man begged the snake, "Please let us go. I did you a favor by freeing you from the rock. Don't you think that one good deed deserves another?"

The snake answered, "In the snake world a favor is returned with a bad deed. That is the way of the animal world."

The wife now spoke up. "But you were going to die. We saved your life! I don't believe that the animal world is as you describe."

"Then we shall leave it to the animal world," the snake hissed. "We will let the next three animals that come by be the judge."

With no other choice, the farmer and his wife agreed to the plan.

Soon an old horse and an old ox came by. The snake asked them, "Do you think that good deeds are returned with bad deeds?"

Without hesitation the horse and ox answered, "Yes, we have seen it ourselves. When we were young we worked hard for our master. Now that we are old and no longer able to work, he has abandoned us. He has returned the favor of our good work for him with the bad deed of letting us go without food or a place to sleep."

As they went away the snaked hissed, "Two out of three. One more and you are mine."

Next a fox came by. The farmer asked the fox if he would help them escape from the snake. The fox, respected for his cleverness, said he had to talk to the snake first.

The fox asked the snake, "What is the good deed that the farmer and his wife did for you?" The snake told the fox about how they had freed him from beneath the rock.

The fox said, "I am uncertain as to just how this good deed was done. Without that knowledge I cannot say who is right in this argument."

The snake grew frustrated with the fox's questions. To hasten the discussion he writhed back under the rock so the fox could see how he was trapped and how the farmer had rescued him. As soon as the snake was back under the rock, the fox smashed the rock and killed the snake.

The farmer and his wife thanked the fox for helping them, but as they thanked him, they noticed that he was circling them with his fangs drawn back. They realized that now the fox was holding them prisoner.

The fox spoke to them in a low voice, "Yes, you see the snake was right. My own good deed now turns bad for you. Now it is my turn to eat you."

The farmer could not believe that his original good deed would continue to lead to such bad fortune.

Suddenly the farmer's dog growled and lunged at the fox. The fox, who had not noticed the dog at all, was so startled that he bolted away and left the farmer and his wife free at last.

The farmer looked at his wife, for he could not understand where his dog had suddenly gotten such a streak of courage. His wife assured him, "The dog has had it all along. He was just waiting for the opportunity to use it. Now he has repaid us for all the kindness we have shown him, for it is true, one good deed does deserve another."

THE FOOLISH COYOTE
(EL COYOTE LOCO)

One day Coyote was wandering through the fields looking for some food. It had been several days since he had eaten and he was starving. He tried to chase down several rabbits, but they were too fast. Just as he was about to give up for the day, he spotted a nest in a tree. Carefully he crept up to the tree and listened to hear if there were any baby birds in it. Sometimes a baby bird would fall out of a tree while trying to learn to fly, and Coyote would catch it and eat it. (See fig. 18.)

As he was listening, Coyote heard a mama pigeon talking to her baby pigeons. He yelled up in his loudest and fiercest voice, "Mama pigeon, throw down a baby pigeon, or I'll cut down the tree with my tail and eat all of your babies and you, too!"

The mama pigeon was afraid of Coyote, and to save most of her babies, she threw one down. As soon as the unfortunate baby pigeon fell to the ground, Coyote gobbled it up.

He then yelled up to the mama pigeon again, "Throw down another baby, or I'll cut down the tree with my tail and eat all of your babies and you, too."

The mama pigeon hated to do it, but to save the rest of her babies, she threw another baby pigeon down to Coyote.

After two baby pigeons, Coyote was full, so he wandered off to sleep in the field. He was confident that when he woke up it would be easy to get another baby pigeon to eat.

While Coyote was asleep in the field, another pigeon flew by and heard the mama pigeon crying and crying. He flew over to the nest and asked the mama pigeon, "Why are you crying? And where are your missing babies?"

Through sobs and tears she told him, "Coyote made me throw two of my babies down to him. He said he'd cut down the tree with his tail if I didn't throw my babies to him."

The other pigeon couldn't believe what he was hearing. He told the mama pigeon, "You poor, foolish pigeon. Coyote can't cut down the tree with his tail. He would need a sharp ax to cut down the tree. The next time he comes by, tell him what I've said." And with that good advice he flew off.

Coyote woke up and felt a little hunger pain in his stomach. He decided it was time for another baby pigeon. He went to the tree and yelled up, "Throw another baby down, or I'll cut down the tree with my tail and eat all of your babies and you, too."

This time the mama pigeon yelled back, "It'll take more than your tail to cut down this tree. You'll need a sharp ax. So go away, Coyote, and don't come back, because you're not getting any more of my babies!"

Coyote was furious. He had really enjoyed eating the baby pigeons, and now he knew that he would have to go hungry again.

He went down to the river to drink some water, and there he saw a pigeon drinking. The pigeon was laughing to himself about how silly Coyote was to tell the mama pigeon he could cut down the tree with his tail. Coyote overheard the pigeon and said to himself, "So this is who told the mama pigeon about the ax. Well, that's the last time this pigeon will interfere with my meals." And he pounced on the pigeon and caught him in his mouth.

The pigeon struggled and struggled, but it was no use. He was caught in the mouth of Coyote.

Coyote told him, "And now I'm going to eat you! Let's see if mama pigeon is going to help you now."

The pigeon immediately began talking to Coyote. He told him, "Coyote, you are so smart. You are even smarter than I am. Before you eat me you should go to the top of the hill and yell out to all the animals that you have caught me. That way they will know how smart you are."

Coyote thought that was a very good idea. He ran up to the top of the hill, still holding the pigeon in his mouth. He opened his mouth and yelled out loud for all the animals to hear, "I have caught this pigeon and I'm . . ."

As he opened his mouth, the pigeon flew out. As he flew away, he taunted Coyote by yelling back to him, "You are such a fool, Coyote!"

And you know what? Coyote *was* a fool!

EL COYOTE LOCO
(THE FOOLISH COYOTE)

Un día Coyote vagabundeaba por los campos buscando algo de comida. Habían pasado varios días desde que había comido y estaba muerto de hambre. Intentó cazar varios conejos, pero eran demasiado rápidos. Y precisamente cuando ya se iba a dar por vencido, vió un nido en un árbol. Se arrastró con cuidado hasta el lugar y escuchó con atención por si había algunos pajaritos. A veces Coyote atrapaba y se comía los pajaritos que caían de los árboles cuando intentaban aprender a volar.

Estando así, Coyote escuchó a una madre paloma hablando a sus pichoncitos. Con voz muy fuerte y feroz gritó, "Mamá paloma, echa para abajo un pichón, ó cortaré el árbol con mi rabo y me comeré a todos tus pichones y a ti también."

Mamá paloma tenía miedo de Coyote, y para salvar a la mayoría de sus pichoncitos, echó uno para abajo. Tan pronto como el desafortunado pichón cayó al suelo, Coyote se lo comió.

Entonces Coyote gritó a mamá paloma de nuevo, "Echa para abajo otro pichón, ó cortaré el árbol con mi rabo y me comeré a todos tus pichones y a ti también."

Mamá paloma no quería hacerlo, pero para salvar al resto de sus pichoncitos, dejó caer otro pichón.

Después de comerse dos pichones, Coyote estaba lleno, así que se fué por ahí a dormir en el campo. Estaba seguro de que cuando se despertara le sería fácil conseguir otro pichón para comérselo.

Mientras Coyote estaba durmiendo en el campo, un palomo pasó volando y escuchó a mamá paloma llorando y llorando. Voló hacia el nido y le preguntó, "¿Por qué estás llorando, mamá paloma? ¿Y dónde están los pichones que faltan?"

Entre sollozos y lágrimas le dijo, "Coyote me hizo arrojarle dos de mis pichones. Dijo que cortaría el árbol con su rabo si yo no se los echaba."

El palomo no podía creer lo que estaba escuchando, y dijo a mamá paloma, "Pobre paloma tonta. Coyote no puede cortar el árbol con su rabo. Necesitaría una hacha afilada para cortarlo. La próxima vez que venga por aquí, dile lo que te he dicho." Y con ese buen consejo el palomo se fué volando.

Coyote despertó y se sintió con hambre. Decidió que era hora para otro pichón. Se dirigió al árbol y gritó, "Echame otro pichón para abajo, ó cortaré el árbol con mi rabo y me comeré a todos tus pichones y a ti también."

Esta vez mamá paloma le contestó, "Hará falta más que tu rabo para cortar este árbol. Necesitarás una hacha afilada. Así que vete, Coyote, y no vuelvas, porque no vas a comerte ninguno más de mis pichones!"

Coyote estaba furioso. Verdaderamente había disfrutado comiéndose los pichones, y sabía que ahora iba a tener que pasar hambre otra vez.

Bajó al río a beber agua, y allí vió a un palomo bebiendo. El palomo estaba riéndose y hablando consigo mismo de lo tonto que había sido Coyote al contarle a mamá paloma que podía cortar el árbol con su rabo. Coyote escuchó al palomo y se dijo para sí, "Así que éste ha sido el que ha contado a mamá paloma lo de la hacha. Bueno, esta es la última vez que este palomo interfiere con mis comidas." Y se lanzó sobre el palomo cogiéndolo en su boca.

El palomo luchó y luchó, pero no sirvió de nada. Coyote lo tenía atrapado entre sus dientes.

Coyote le dijo, "¡Y ahora te voy a comer a ti! Vamos a ver si mamá paloma te va a ayudar ahora."

El palomo inmediatamente empezó a hablar a Coyote. Le dijo, "Coyote, eres tan listo. Eres aún más listo que yo. Antes de que me comas debes ir a la cima de la colina y gritar a todos los animales que me has atrapado. Así sabrán lo inteligente que eres."

Coyote pensó que esto era una idea muy buena. Corrió a la cima de la colina con el palomo en su boca todavía. Abrió la boca y gritó fuertemente para que lo escucharan todos los animales, "He atrapado a este palomo y voy a..."

En cuanto abrió la boca, el palomo escapó volando. Conforme se alejaba, se burló de Coyote gritándole, "¡Eres un gran tonto, Coyote!"

¿Y sabéis una cosa? ¡Coyote era tonto!

THE EAGLE AND THE LION

It was an especially hot day, and the eagle had worked very hard to catch some food. There had been very little food for the animals that year, and every animal was careful with whatever food it found.

Finally the eagle was lucky and caught a small rabbit. As the eagle sat eating the rabbit, a lion walked by and asked, "What are you doing with that small animal?"

The eagle replied, "It is a rabbit I caught. I'm eating it."

The lion asked, "You haven't been eating some meat I have buried over there, have you?"

"No," said the eagle. "I would never be so foolish as to take your food!"

But as soon as the lion left, the eagle said to himself, "But thank you for the invitation!" After making sure that the lion really had gone away, the eagle went searching and found where the lion had buried a deer. He dug up the deer and stole all of the meat. After he had finished eating, he went off and rested in a tree.

When the lion discovered what the eagle had done, he cried out, "Eagle, why did you steal my meat?"

The eagle answered, "You told me where the meat was, so I came and ate it. And if you don't like it, I'll grab you with my claws."

When he heard what the eagle said, the lion got angry. He roared, "Because you stole my meat I am going to have to fight with you. I'll meet you in the field tomorrow, and we will have our fight!"

The next day the eagle and the lion met in the field. Each was a fierce fighter, but by the end of the day neither was able to beat the other. Finally they gave up and agreed that the fight was a draw. Weary from the battle, they agreed not to fight any more and to make peace. They decided that each of them would rule over a certain part of the earth and in that way there would be no confusion that would lead to fights.

That is why to this day the lion is the king of the animals of the earth and the eagle is the king of the animals of the air. Together they are the kings of the animals, but each has its own kingdom.

3

Contemporary Cuentos

Stories by Modern Latino Storytellers

THE DUST DEVIL (EL DIABLO DE POLVO)

Original story by Angel Vigil

Once on a flat land under a tree sat a little girl. This little girl was crying. She wasn't crying like you cry when you cut your finger or lose a toy. She was crying from the bottom of her heart, like she hadn't a friend in the world.

Her papa came up to her and in a very concerned voice, said, "*Jita*, why are you crying like this? I've never seen you cry like this. Tell me what's wrong. Maybe I can fix it."

The little girl, weeping and wiping her tears, answered, "Papa, I'm lonely. I don't have any friends to play with."

Trying to console her, her papa said, "*Jita*, you know that we live on the farm out here by ourselves. There are no other children around."

Just then the cat came around the corner. That cat would come and wrap around your leg, curling its tail in the air, purring all the time. Then a bird came flying out of the sky. The bird would land on the shoulder of the little girl, and she was the only little girl in the whole world who could feed a bird on her shoulder. Over in the corral, gently swaying back and forth, was the cow. Every day the cow would let the little girl climb on its back and would take the little girl for a ride.

"See," said her papa, pointing to the little girl's animal friends. "You have good friends. There's the *gato*, the bird, and the cow. You have good friends right here on the farm."

The little girl screamed, "I want people friends!"

Her papa scolded her in an angry voice, "You have good friends! I have work to do in the fields. If you want to sit here and feel sorry for yourself, go ahead. Now you stay here and think about it." And her papa went to work in the fields, mad at the little girl for what she had said.

El Gato came up to the little girl and purred, "Little girl, what is wrong? Why are you crying?"

"*Gato*," sniffled the little girl, "I'm lonely. I want a friend to play with."

"Meooooow!" said the cat, swishing his tail quickly back and forth. "Come chase me like you do every day. We'll play hide-and-seek by the trees. Meooooow!"

"I want people friends!" the little girl said in a very harsh voice.

The *gato* walked away, dragging his tail, his heart broken because he thought that he was a friend of the little girl.

Just then the bird flew by and swooped down onto the little girl's shoulder. Out of breath she said, "Little girl, what's wrong? I've never seen you so sad."

Continuing to feel sorry for herself, the little girl looked the bird in the eye and whimpered, "I'm lonely, bird. I want a friend to play with."

"Oh, come fly with me like we do every day, little girl. We'll soar high above the earth and look down at the scurrying people and watch their busy ways." With that the bird quickly flew around the little girl, trying to cool her off with the beating of its colorful wings.

"I want people friends!" yelled the little girl.

The bird quietly flew away, her heart broken because she felt she was a friend of the little girl.

Next the cow moseyed up to the little girl. "Little girl," he mooed in his deep, slow voice, "What's wrong? Why are you crying?"

"Cow, I'm lonely. I want a friend to play with."

"Mooooo! Jump on my back and I'll give you a ride," offered the loving cow.

"I want people friends!" shouted the girl.

The cow walked away sadly because he thought he was a friend of the little girl.

Suddenly, without warning, a great whirlwind of dust came over the distant horizon. It was one of those whirlwinds that, if you walked into it on a hot summer day, would blow your hat high up into the sky. The whirlwind of dust came to a stop right by the little girl. When all that dust had settled from the top of the sky to the bottom of the earth, there stood a person. The little girl stared incredulously at the strange man standing before her. He was dressed in the finest clothes. It seemed impossible to the little girl that moments before he had been inside a whirlwind of dust. It seemed almost magical.

"Little girl," crooned the stranger, "I've come to be your special friend."

The little girl answered excitedly, "My special friend! Ooooooh! My own special friend!"

Suddenly the stranger's voice turned cold and menacing. "Yes, little girl. Why don't you come to my house?" He made a sudden, threatening move and tried to grab her by the arm.

From out of nowhere *El Gato* appeared. With great earnestness he pleaded with the little girl, "Little girl, don't go. It's the devil, *El Diablo*. If you go with *El Diablo*, we'll never see you again!"

That made *El Diablo* very mad. He kicked that *gato* so hard the *gato* went flying across the field.

Shocked by this mean kick, the little girl asked *El Diablo*, "Why did you kick my friend the cat? I don't like what you did to my friend the cat."

In his most soothing and false voice, *El Diablo* answered, "Oh, was that your friend the cat? Gee, I can't believe I made such a mistake. I thought it was a tumbleweed. I was just kicking that tumbleweed out of your way. In fact, at my house I have lots of cats. You'll love it at my house." Then, with his voice again turning mean and cold, he reached for the little girl. "Now why don't you come to my house!"

Just then the bird flew by and in a high, scared voice said, "Little girl, don't go. It's the devil, *El Diablo*. If you go with *El Diablo*, we'll never see you again!"

That made *El Diablo* really mad. As the bird tried to fly away, *El Diablo* threw a bolt of lightning. It struck the bird and fell to the ground with a mighty crash.

The little girl, once more speaking through tears, asked, "Why did you do that to my friend the bird? That was mean, what you did to my friend the bird."

Sweating just a little now, *El Diablo* reassured the little girl, "Wow! I can't believe I made two mistakes in one day. Why, I thought that was a snake dropping from the sky. I was just trying to knock that snake out of the way. I love birds. At my house I have lots of birds." Then his voice turned angry, and he spit out, "Why don't you come to my house, little girl!"

Moving faster than he ever had before, the cow came up to the little girl and said, "Little girl, don't go. It's *El Diablo*."

The devil finally lost his temper and kicked the cow so hard the cow went flying into the sky, right over the moon!

Lurching toward the little girl, *El Diablo* howled, "Yes, little girl, you're coming to my house!"

Just as he reached for the little girl, up jumped the cat. The cat dug his claws into the devil's face. With the cat scratching his face, *El Diablo* couldn't see a thing. Spinning around he made desperate lunges for the little girl. Just as *El Diablo* was about to grab her, the bird swooped in and dug her talons into his hand. Now *El Diablo* was really mad! He spun around twice and was just about to grab the little girl when, who was there — the cow!

With his head bowed, his horns pointing straight at *El Diablo*, the cow firmly said, "You're not about to get this little girl."

El Diablo started spinning and spinning. All the dust came back up around him from the bottom of the earth to the top of the sky. A giant whirlwind of dust again spun around *El Diablo*. This whirlwind of dust roared out of sight over a distant hill.

Later in the afternoon, the little girl's papa came back from the field and saw the little girl still under the tree. He came up to her and in a stern voice said, "Well, did you think about what I said? What happened today?"

Just then *El Gato* wrapped himself around the little girl's ankle, purring away. The bird landed on the girl's shoulder. And gently swaying back and forth in the corral, the cow mooed.

"Papa," said the little girl, "I may not have people friends, but the friends I have are the best friends a little girl could ever have!"

And that's the true story about why the cow jumped over the moon. And that's the true story why to this day some people, when they see a whirlwind of dust, call it a dust devil. Because they know that inside that dust devil is *El Diablo*, angry because he was not able to take another child home with him that day. But most of all that is the true story of how one little girl learned the true meaning of friendship.

EL DIABLO DE POLVO
(THE DUST DEVIL)

Erase una vez en una llanura una niña que se sentó bajo un árbol. Estaba llorando, pero no estaba llorando como se llora cuando uno se corta un dedo ó pierde un juguete. Estaba llorando de corazón, como si no tuviera ni un sólo amigo en todo el mundo.

Su papá se le acercó, y con voz preocupada le dijo, "Jita, ¿Por qué estás llorando así? Nunca te había visto llorando de este modo. Dime qué te pasa. Quizás yo pueda ayudarte."

La niña, llorando y limpiándose las lágrimas, contestó, "Papá, estoy sola. No tengo ningún amigo con quien jugar."

Intentando consolarla, su papá le dijo, "Jita, tú sabes que vivimos aquí en esta granja muy apartados. No hay niños cerca."

En ese momento, el gato apareció por allí. Aquel gato tenía la costumbre de acercarse y enrollarse alrededor de las piernas, enroscando su rabo en el aire y ronroneando todo el tiempo. También había un pájaro que venía volando y se posaba en el hombro de la niña, y ella era la única niña en todo el mundo que podía dar de comer a un pájaro en su hombro. Y en el corral, tranquilamente, estaba la vaca. Cada día la vaca dejaba que la niña se subiese a su lomo y la llevaba de paseo.

"Ves," dijo su papá, señalando a los amigos animales de la niña. "Tú tienes buenos amigos, el gato, el pájaro y la vaca. Tienes buenos amigos aquí mismo en la granja."

La niña gritó, "¡Quiero amigos personas!"

Su papá le regañó con voz seria, "¡Tienes buenos amigos! Tengo trabajo que hacer en los campos. Si quieres sentarte aquí lamentándote, hazlo. Quédate aquí y piensa en todo esto." Y el padre se fué a trabajar en los campos, molesto con su hija por lo que había dicho.

El gato se acercó a la niña y ronroneó, "Niña ,¿qué te pasa? ¿Por qué estás llorando?"

"Gato," gimió la niña, "Estoy sola. Quiero un amigo con quien jugar."

"¡Miau!" dijo el gato, meneando su rabo rápidamente de un lado a otro. "Ven, persígueme como haces todos los días. Jugaremos al escondite entre los árboles. ¡Miau!"

"¡Quiero amigos personas!" dijo la niña en una voz muy áspera.

El gato se alejó, arrastrando el rabo, con el corazón roto porque creía que era amigo de la niña.

Entonces el pájaro llegó volando y se posó en el hombro de la niña. Casi sin aliento, dijo, "Niña, ¿qué te pasa? Nunca te he visto tan triste."

Continuando con sus lamentos, la niña miró al pájaro a los ojos y dijo lloriqueando, "Estoy sola, Pájaro. Quiero un amigo con quien jugar."

"Oh, ven a volar conmigo como hacemos todos los días, Niña. Volaremos alto sobre la tierra y miraremos abajo a la gente corriendo por aquí y por allá, y observaremos sus ajetreadas vidas." Diciendo eso el pájaro voló rápido alrededor de la niña, intentando refrescarla con el batido de sus coloridas alas.

"¡Quiero amigos personas!" gritó la niña.

El pájaro se alejó volando en silencio, con el corazón roto porque se creía amigo de la niña.

Después se le acercó la vaca tranquilamente. "Niña, mugió" con voz profunda y lenta, "¿Qué te pasa? ¿Por qué estás llorando?"

"Vaca, estoy sola. Quiero un amigo con quien jugar."

"¡Muuuu! Sube a mi lomo y te daré un paseo," ofreció la cariñosa vaca.

"¡Quiero amigos personas!" gritó la niña.

La vaca se alejó tristemente porque creía que era amiga de la niña.

De repente, sin previo aviso, un remolino de polvo vino desde el horizonte distante. Era uno de esos remolinos, de los que, si te metes en ellos en un día caluroso de verano, se llevan tu sombrero hasta al cielo. El remolino de polvo vino a pararse justo al lado de la niña. Cuando todo el polvo desde lo alto del cielo al fondo de la tierra se asentó, allí había una persona. La niña miró incrédulamente al hombre tan extraño que se apareció delante de ella. Iba vestido con las ropas más finas. A la niña le parecía imposible que pocos momentos antes hubiera estado dentro del remolino de polvo. Le parecía casi mágico.

"Niña," le cantó el desconocido con voz suave, "He venido para ser tu amigo especial."

La niña le contestó con entusiasmo, "¡Mi amigo especial! ¡Ooooooh! ¡Mi propio amigo especial!"

De repente la voz del desconocido se tornó fría. "Sí, niña. ¿Por qué no vienes a mi casa?" Entonces hizo un movimiento repentino y amenazante, e intentó cogerla por el brazo.

De no se sabe dónde salió el gato. Muy seriamente suplicó a la niña, "Niña, no vayas. Ese es el diablo. Si te vas con él, ¡nunca más te volveremos a ver!"

Esto enfadó tanto al diablo, que dió una patada tan fuerte al gato que lo lanzó volando a través del campo.

Asombrada por la patada, la niña preguntó al diablo, "¿Por qué has dado una patada a mi amigo el gato? No me gusta lo que le hiciste."

Con voz falsa y consoladora, el diablo contestó, "Oh, ¿Era ese tu amigo el gato? Caramba, no puedo creer que me haya equivocado de esta manera. Pensé que era una mala hierba. Yo sólo quería apartarla de tu camino. De hecho, en mi casa tengo muchos gatos. Te encantaría venir a mi casa." Entonces, poniendo una voz fría y antipática otra vez, intentó agarrar a la niña. "¿Por qué no vienes conmigo a mi casa ahora?"

Justo entonces el pájaro voló cerca y con voz aguda y asustada dijo, "Niña, no vayas. Ese es el diablo. Si te vas con él, ¡nunca más te volveremos a ver!"

Esto sí que realmente enfadó al diablo. Cuando el pájaro intentó alejarse volando, el diablo lanzó un rayo. El rayo dió al pájaro y después cayó al suelo con un gran estallido.

La niña, hablando una vez más entre lágrimas, preguntó, "¿Por qué has hecho eso a mi amigo el pájaro? Lo que le hiciste estuvo mal."

Sudando ya un poco, el diablo tranquilizó a la niña, "¡Uau! No puedo creer que me haya equivocado dos veces en el mismo día. Pues, yo creí que eso era una serpiente cayendo del cielo. Sólo intentaba quitarla de en medio. A mi me encantan los pájaros. En mi casa tengo muchos." Entonces su voz se tornó enojada, y dijo de mala manera, "¿Por qué no vienes a mi casa, niña?"

Moviéndose más rápida que nunca, la vaca se aproximó a la niña y dijo, "Niña, no vayas. Ese es el diablo."

El diablo finalmente perdió su paciencia y dió una patada tan fuerte a la vaca, que ésta salió volando por el cielo hasta pasar por encima de la luna.

Precipitándose sobre la niña, el diablo aulló, "¡Sí, niña, tú te vienes conmigo a mi casa!"

Justo cuando iba a coger a la niña, el gato saltó e hincó sus uñas en la cara del diablo. Con el gato arañándole la cara, el diablo no podía ver nada. Dando vueltas hizo intentos desesperados por alcanzar a la niña. En el momento en que la iba a coger, llegó el pájaro y clavó sus garras en la mano del diablo. ¡Ahora sí que estaba enojado el diablo! Dió dos vueltas y estuvo a punto de agarrar a la niña cuando, ¿quién estaba allí?—¡la vaca!

Con la cabeza agachada y los cuernos apuntando directamente hacia el diablo, la vaca dijo firmemente, "No te vas a llevar a esta niña."

El diablo empezó a dar vueltas y más vueltas. Todo el polvo desde el fondo de la tierra hasta lo alto del cielo volvió a rodearle. Un remolino gigantesco de polvo giró de nuevo alrededor del diablo. Este remolino se alejó rugiendo hasta perderse de vista en una colina distante.

Esa tarde, el papá volvió del campo y vió a la niña todavía bajo el árbol. Se acercó a ella, y con voz seria le dijo, "Bueno, ¿has pensado en lo que te dije? ¿Qué ha pasado hoy?"

Entonces el gato se enrolló alrededor del tobillo de la niña, ronroneando. El pájaro se posó en su hombro. Y desde el corral la vaca mugió dulcemente.

"Papá," dijo la niña, "¡puede que no tenga amigos personas, pero los amigos que tengo son los mejores amigos que una niña podría nunca tener!"

Y esta es la historia cierta de por qué la vaca saltó por encima de la luna. Y esta es la historia cierta de por qué hasta hoy en día alguna gente, cuando ve un remolino de polvo lo llama diablo de polvo. Porque sabe que dentro del polvo está el diablo, furioso porque no pudo llevarse a otro niño con él aquel día. Pero, sobre todo, esta es la historia cierta de cómo una niña aprendió el significado verdadero de la amistad.

LA LLORONA'S FINAL CRY

Original story by Angel Vigil

For generations the people of the village had been telling their children the legend of *La Llorona*. Children would listen with wide eyes, breathless, as their parents described her cruel betrayal at the hands of the Spaniard and how, in a blind, mad rage, she had drowned her two children. Every night as the children went to sleep, they could hear *La Llorona*'s eternal cries as she walked by the banks of the river, calling for her lost children.

Two of these children, Mundo and Lupe, knew the stories of *La Llorona* especially well. Their *tio* had once seen *La Llorona* as he was walking home late at night. Out of the darkness a figure clothed in white had chased him until he collapsed in fear. He had fired a shot at her but missed. The next morning he described to them the horrible look on her face as she chased him.

Of course they had heard the stories from the nearby village, where a man had actually shot *La Llorona* before she escaped into the darkness. The next morning people found dried blood on a fencepost near the place where the man had shot her. This was the same village where two children who had disobeyed their parents were caught by *La Llorona*. According to the story Mundo and Lupe's parents told them, these disobedient children had never been seen again.

Their friends had often told them about the times when they were almost caught by *La Llorona*. At school they had heard the stories of last-second escapes from the grasp of *La Llorona*. Their friends' descriptions of *La Llorona*'s hot breath on their necks as they ran away from her always scared them the most.

Yes, these two children, Mundo and Lupe, brother and sister, knew the story of *La Llorona*. That is why the people of the village were so surprised the night she captured the two children.

The evening meal at Mundo and Lupe's house had ended as usual. The men had left the table to sit around the fire and swap *chistes*. The women stayed in the kitchen, cleaning up the dishes and putting away the food.

Mundo and Lupe had cleaned up their places and asked their mother, "Mama, can we go outside and play? It's too hot in the kitchen."

Their mother answered, "Yes, but only for a little while. Tomorrow is a school day, and I want you kids in bed early."

Mundo hated being treated like a child. Angrily he told his mother, "Mama, all the other kids get to stay up late. I'm not a baby anymore! Nothing will happen if we play outside until it gets dark."

His mother answered him in her usual impatient voice, "Mundo, you'll go to bed when I tell you to go to bed. Your sister can't stay out too late or she is impossible to get up in the morning. Now, you can play outside until I call you, or you'll just stay inside and help with these dishes."

Mundo had heard too much. He grabbed his sister's hand and rushed out the door. As he ran to play, he heard his mother cry out, "Don't disobey me! If you stay out too late, *La Llorona* will get you!"

Lupe looked at her brother and in a frightened voice asked him, "Will *La Llorona* really get us?"

"Of course not. Have you ever seen *La Llorona?*"

"Well, no. But you know La Sheri saw her last fall and *Tio* Alfonso almost got caught by her. What if we're next?"

Mundo couldn't help but laugh. In a teasing voice he yelled out to his sister, "Lupe, watch out! *La Llorona's* right behind you!"

Of course Lupe screamed and jumped around, only to hear her brother's laughter. She turned and yelled at him, "Sure, make a joke out of it. But I know that *La Llorona* probably wouldn't even take you, you're so mean!"

As they played the sun got lower and lower in the sky. The cool breeze from the river blew through the trees, and the rustling leaves made the whole earth seem playful. They ran after each other and played all the games they could think of: chase, hide-and-seek, and kick-the-can. Before they knew it, they were down by the river and the darkness of nighttime was all around them.

Birds, or maybe bats, swooped out of the sky. They could hear the fish splashing in the river. Or was it a beaver leaping into the water?

Lupe was sure she had seen a large snake go by. She cried out to Mundo, "Let's go home. It's already dark."

Stories by Modern Latino Storytellers

Mundo reassuringly answered her, "It's not too dark. We'll go home pretty soon. I just want to see the moon come up. Then we'll go home. Okay?"

"Okay, but what if . . ." Just as she spoke Lupe thought that she saw a figure pass between two trees by the river bank. She looked again, sure she had seen someone. She told Mundo, "Mundo, I saw someone. Over there. By the river. Let's go home!"

Mundo looked over where Lupe was pointing, but he didn't see anyone. But all of a sudden he was scared, too. Looking around he told Lupe, "Sure, if you're too scared to stay a little while longer, let's go home."

"You're scared, too! I can tell. Your voice always gets squeaky when you're scared."

"I'm not scared. I just think its time to go home. There are too many clouds to see the moon, anyway. Come on. Let's go."

Mundo and Lupe began to walk away from the river when they both heard a noise behind them. They looked around. They didn't see anything, but still they began running. Lupe held onto her brother's hand with all her might, and Mundo pulled her along as fast as they could go.

They were still by the river when they heard the woman's voice crying out, "*Aye, mis hijos.* Come to me. Come to me."

Mundo and Lupe froze in their tracks. It was *La Llorona* calling out to them! They turned around and looked over where the voice was coming from — and they saw a woman dressed in white coming after them! They knew that *La Llorona* wanted to catch them so they could take the place of her two lost children. They started running as fast as their little legs could carry them.

It was hard running because it was so dark and they kept tripping over things on the ground. They could hear *La Llorona* calling to them as they ran, "*Aye, mis hijos.* Come to me. Come to me."

All of a sudden they could feel the hot breath of *La Llorona* on their necks. Their little legs could run no faster, and then it happened. They each felt a cold and strong hand grab them. *La Llorona* had caught them!

La Llorona held them close, crying as she said, "Finally, after all this time, my children are returned to me. My prayers have been answered.

For all eternity I have walked along the river, crying for my children. They have finally heard me and come back to me from the land of the dead."

Mundo and Lupe struggled and struggled to escape, but *La Llorona's* hold on them was too tight. Lupe started to cry, and she reached out for her brother. Mundo was afraid to look at *La Llorona*, but as he grabbed Lupe's hand, he knew there was no hope.

Lupe pleaded, "What are you going to do to us? Please don't hurt us."

La Llorona looked at the two frightened children and said, "I won't hurt you. I will love you like my own two children. I have waited forever to get you, and now I'll never let you go. I'll love you forever."

Lupe cried out, "But we're not your children. I'm Lupe and that's Mundo. We're not your children. Please let us go."

La Llorona held Lupe tighter and told her, "Don't be afraid. I'll take care of you from now on."

Mundo and Lupe started crying so hard their little bodies shook. And then, through the darkness of the night, they heard another voice crying with an agony they had never heard before. It was their mother crying for them. As if carried to them by the wind, their mother's voice cried out, "*Aye, mis hijos*. They are lost in the night. Please bring my children back to me!"

Lupe looked at *La Llorona* and through her tears told her, "That's our mother. She is crying for us. Please let us go. Please!"

Through the still night air, the mother cried for her lost children. As she listened *La Llorona* heard the terrible pain of a mother's agony over her lost children. The more *La Llorona* listened, the more she recognized her own anguished cries in the voice of Mundo and Lupe's mother. Tears began to fall from her eyes. She could not bear to hear the cries of their mother.

Slowly she loosened her grip on Mundo and Lupe. With one final cry of her own she let go of the two frightened children. The two children were too frightened to move. Gently pushing them away, *La Llorona* told them, "Go. Go home. I can't bear to think of another woman suffering as I have over my own two lost children. Your mother's cries are too much for me to bear. My suffering is my own, and now I know that I will never be able to keep any children to take the place of my two beloved children. This is my eternal punishment for what I did. Now go. Go home. Your mother is calling you. Go home."

Mundo and Lupe took off for home without another word. As they reached the top of a small hill by the river, they finally knew they had escaped. They stopped to catch their breath and turned around to see if *La Llorona* was coming after them.

As they looked back at the river, they saw the strangest sight. Right where *La Llorona* had been standing was a pile of white cloth fallen shapelessly on the ground. It was as if *La Llorona* had disappeared right out of her clothes. Then they saw the light. They saw a white light going up into the clouds as if something were flying up into the sky, even into heaven, carried by the white light. The light was so bright, coming right out of the sky. And then it was gone.

Without stopping to look any more, they ran all the way home. When they got home their parents ran out, crying and hugging them as if they had come back from the dead. Their mother finally stopped crying enough to ask them, "Where have you been! We thought you had drowned by the river. We looked and looked for you by the river, but after we heard your cries we couldn't find you anywhere! Oh, don't ever scare us like that again!"

Lupe told her mother, "*La Llorona* caught us! She wouldn't let us go and . . ."

Before she could finish her mother said, "Don't make it worse by lying. Mundo, where were you and your sister?"

Mundo tried to tell her the same thing. "Really, mama, *La Llorona*."

Even though she was so happy to see them again, their mother was frustrated because she thought that Mundo and Lupe were not telling the truth. She told them, "That's enough. I thought you were dead, and for my broken heart and tears, all I get is this story. Both of you. Inside!"

"But mama!"

"Inside! We'll talk about this later. Mundo, I told you not to stay out in the dark, and look what happened. Both of you, go to bed."

Mundo and Lupe ran into the house. They were so glad to be home that they didn't care whether or not anyone believed their story.

The next day their father came back from the river with a dirty white garment he found. He asked Mundo and Lupe if they knew anything about it. As Mundo and Lupe told their parents the whole story of what had happened the night before, their parents began to realize the truth of the children's story.

Lupe asked her father what had happened to *La Llorona*.

Her father took his time as he tried to remember a story he had heard many years ago. Finally, in a slow voice he told them, "*La Llorona's* soul has been released from her misery. As punishment for what she did to her children she was doomed to walk the banks of the river for all eternity, crying for her children. Of course she would never find her children. That was her punishment. Her soul would not find eternal rest until she had suffered and made up for her terrible act against her children. Because she heard your mother's cries, she let you two go. This act of compassion was what she had to do to find peace. God has forgiven her, and now her soul knows eternal rest. All that is left of her in this world is her white garment. We must bury it to bring to an end the final cry of *La Llorona*."

Mundo and Lupe listened without saying a word. Somehow they knew that this was the best *cuento* they had ever heard.

From that day on the people of the village never heard the crying voice of *La Llorona* again. If the truth be told, they missed the voice. Parents could no longer tell their children to be good or *La Llorona* would get them. And children missed hearing about someone almost being caught by *La Llorona*.

But there were a few people in the village who still swore that they could hear the voice of *La Llorona* crying by the river. They said that the white garment was just a trick Mundo and Lupe made up to keep from getting in even more trouble. After a while even more people in the village began to say that they had heard *La Llorona* during the night. Some even claimed to have seen her.

And even though they knew the true story of *La Llorona's* final cry, when Mundo and Lupe grew up, they would still tell their children to be good or *La Llorona* would get them.

Original story by Geraldina Lawson

I want to tell you a story, one of the *cuentos* of Lupe La Loca. This happened a long, long time ago in Laredo, Texas. It was at the time when the Rio Grande was a source of water for the people living in Laredo.

Back during this time people didn't have any plumbing, and they needed a system to get the water from the river to their homes. So there was this system of the *Barrileros*. The *Barrileros* were men who would fill large, 50-gallon drums with water from the Rio Grande. After they had filled up their barrels, they would strap them on their *burros* and go through town calling out, "*Barrileros, Barrileros!*" And people would come out from their houses with 50 *centavos* to buy water from the *Barrileros*. (See fig. 22.)

This was hard labor, carrying the barrels in the hot sun, and 50 *centavos* was not much money. So it was only the poorest of the poor who did this job.

Now, there was one among them, a tall, lean, muscular, dark young man. When the people of Laredo saw him they whispered, "*Es Apache*," because he had no hair on his face or chest, and he would only occasionally grunt "*Sí*" or "*No.*" He wore an amulet of moonstone around his neck and carried a flute in his back pocket. (See fig. 23.)

It was also around this time that a family came from Piedras Negras and settled just outside of Laredo. The father built a splendid *hacienda* that was surrounded by a thick, high wall, a wall to protect his daughter.

She was a young woman whom people saw only at Mass on Sunday, wearing a beautiful white dress of ribbons and ruffles and lace. Her face was never seen, as it was always covered with a veil. But from the way she walked, so stately, and not seeing her face or hearing her voice, they thought she was "stuck up." So they called her *La Coqueta de Piedras Negras*.

Now it so happened that *El Apache* one day was carrying his water up to the *hacienda* of the family from Piedras Negras, and as he reached their home he called out *"Barrilero, El Barrilero."*

No one came out from behind that wall, so he went around behind the *hacienda*, and there a gate opened wide. He looked inside, and there on a swing was the young woman in her white dress of ribbons and ruffles and lace, a vision in white going up into the sky and down again. Up and down and up again.

This vision in white was singing in a most beautiful voice,

Palomita blanca, re blanca,
Donde esta tu nido, re nido?
En el pino verde, re verde,
Todo florecido, florido.

Little white dove, so very white,
Where is your nest, your very own nest?
In the green pine tree, so very green,
Everything with flowers, so very flowery.

And *El Apache* thought, "Yes, a *palomita*, a little dove!" And he pulled out his flute and he began to play along with her.

Now, the vision in white was not expecting company, and she was so startled she fell off the swing. *El Apache* immediately went over and picked her up. She looked at him, and they smiled at each other. Just a sweet and simple smile. He placed her back on the swing and gave her a little shove. A little push, and she'd go up into the sky again. Higher and higher as she did before. And again the music,

Palomita blanca, re blanca,
Donde esta tu nido, renido?
En el pino verde, re verde,
Todo florecido, florido.

Suddenly there was a loud sound. Her father came out and yelled *"Indio*, Apache! Get out of here! Filth!"

El Apache, frightened, pulled back and hid behind his barrel of water. He watched as the father dragged his crying daughter back into the *hacienda*.

No one saw *El Apache* after that. He was just an Apache, an *Indio*. They come and go.

And the young woman, she wasn't seen even at church on Sundays. It was like they had both disappeared, like clouds up into the sky, into nothing.

Then early one morning, when the sky was still a dull gray with streams of golden light, *El Apache* was seen with his burro with two barrels strapped to its side. He walked up to the *hacienda*, and as he reached it, he softly called out, "*Barrilero, El Barrilero.*"

The young woman came running out to meet him in her white dress of ribbons and ruffles and lace. When they met he took off his amulet of moonstone and placed it around her neck. As he did this he told her, "*Para tí palomita, para protejerte,*" ("For you, little dove, to protect you.")

He lifted her up into one of the empty barrels. As he placed her gently in the barrel, there again came a frightening sound.

This time it was the sound of a pistol. Bam! The father was coming after them.

El Apache quickly sealed up the barrel and led his burro away from there. The father kept close after them, again and again taking deadly aim. Bam! Bam! He was so close behind them.

El Apache knew that if they could make it to the Rio Grande they would be safe and free. With all his strength and all his speed, he pulled that burro down to the edge of the Rio Grande with its brown, muddy, rapidly churning waters.

Another shot, another deadly shot. Bam!

This bullet hit the barrel that held the young woman and set it loose. The barrel tumbled down toward the Rio Grande.

El Apache lunged after it. He tried to hold onto it.

Again another shot. Bam!

It hit *El Apache,* and they both tumbled down into the muddy, brown water. Gone.

Most of the people of Laredo just shrugged their shoulders. It was the only just end to a disobedient daughter and an arrogant *Indio*. It was the only just end. (See fig. 24.)

But there are a few others in that *pueblito* who, every once in a while, see an elderly Apache walking along the banks of the Rio Grande with a little *palomita* on his shoulder. As they listen carefully they can hear the *palomita* singing,

Palomita blanca, re blanca,
Donde esta tu nido, re nido?
En el pino verde, re verde,
Todo florecido, florido.

THE CORN WOMAN
(LA MUJER DEL MAÍZ)

Original story by Geraldina Lawson

I want to tell you another of the *cuentos* of Lupe La Loca. This is "The Corn Woman," the story of *La Señora* Maria Juana. (See fig. 21.)

Maria Juana was an older woman with gray hair, wrinkles, and a strong back. She lived all by herself on this little *ranchito*, where she had a field full of squash, chile, and especially corn.

Panfilo worked for *La Señora* Maria Juana. He was called *El Tontito del Pueblo*. He was just real slow. No one in the *pueblo* would hire him.

But *La Señora* Maria Juana hired him. She needed help working the farm. So everyday Panfilo would go out in the fields of the *ranchito* and help her take care of the corn.

Every single day that the sun came up over the hills, Maria Juana would take a handful of corn and stretch out her hand to the sun in a prayer. The breeze would blow some of the kernels of corn to all four directions, and the rest would fall down to the earth. It was a prayer *La Señora* made to the sun every day, and after the prayer *La Señora* and Panfilo would work in the field.

One day they pulled off so many ears of corn that they filled up all the corn bags. There was too much corn!

So *La Señora* Maria Juana told Panfilo, "This is too much corn for us. You take this sack of corn to the people in the *pueblo*." So Panfilo got the extra corn and headed out for the *pueblo*.

He went to the *cantina*, because that was where all the men gathered every day. He carried the sack of corn into the middle of the *cantina* and told the men, "*Señores*, this *elote*, this corn from *La Señora* Maria Juana is for you. She sent it to you. You can have it for whatever you want."

Then Panfilo went into a corner and sat down all by himself. There he drank his beer all by himself.

The men gathered around the corn and said, "This *elote*, it is fat, big, and firm. Look, you press it a little and the juice just comes out!"

So they went over to *El Capitán*. He wasn't really a captain. That's just what they called him.

They told him, "*Capitán*, look. *La Señora* Maria Juana, she sent this *elote*. How does she do it? So big, so fat, so juicy. And ours is so skinny."

El Capitán, smoothing out his mustache, said, "*Bueno muchachos, no sé*. I don't know. Maybe it's the water."

The men continued, "*Capitán*, we don't know what she uses. Her *elote*, it grows up to the sky, to the heavens."

"To the heavens, *muchachos*? What kind of *elote* can this be that grows up to the heavens? Where do its roots go?"

"Yes, *Capitán*, *las raíces*, the roots. They must go down, down, down to hell!"

"*Sí, muchachos*, those roots must go down to hell! Those are things of the devil. She must be a *bruja!*"

"*Sí, Capitán*, that's why the *elote* is so big. Her evil magic must make the *elote* grow so big."

El Capitán called the men together, and they talked about how they would get rid of the evil from the *pueblo*. They looked around and they saw Panfilo. Then they looked around and they saw Juanita — Juanita of the Swivel Hips.

They called her over to them. She was so excited because she really wanted to know what was going on. They laid out the plan for her.

"Tomorrow, Juanita, you go out and meet Panfilo on his way back to the *pueblo*. Bring him back to the *cantina*, and we'll give him enough *cervezas* that he'll tell us everything about this *elote*."

The next morning was like any other morning. The sun came up over the hills, and *La Señora* Maria Juana stretched out her hand filled with corn to the sun in a prayer, and a breeze came and blew the kernels of corn to the four directions and the remainder down to the earth.

La Señora and Panfilo spent all day working in the corn fields, hoeing and weeding. And once again, at the end of the day, there was too much corn. So *La Señora* had Panfilo fill up a sack with the extra corn and told him to take the corn to the people in the *pueblo* as he had the day before. So Panfilo filled up the sack and headed off to the *pueblo*.

And who comes along but Juanita. She comes right up to Panfilo and says, "Panfilo, you are so strong. Look at you. Your big shoulders. You carry that heavy sack so easily. Ay, Panfilo!"

Now, no woman had ever spoken to Panfilo, much less in this way. Panfilo didn't know what to say.

Juanita continued, "Panfilo, could I walk with you back to the *pueblo*? When we get there we could go to the *cantina*. You could buy me a *cerveza*."

The load on Panfilo's back got much lighter, as well as his feet. They made it back to the *pueblo* in no time.

As he strode into the *cantina* with Juanita by his side, he laid the corn on the floor. He told all the men there, "*Señores*, this sack of *elote* is sent to you from *La Señora* Maria Juana." When he had finished speaking, he went over to his spot in the corner and sat down with Juanita at his side.

The men came over and said to him, "Panfilo, how are you? How have you been?"

He replied to them, "*Bueno, señores.*"

"Panfilo, you want a *cerveza*? *Una cerveza para Panfilo!*"

They put down a beer in front of him. And one for Juanita. Then another beer came. And another one. The men thought, "Three or four beers. This ought to loosen his tongue!"

Then they asked Panfilo, "Panfilo, this *elote*, this corn that you bring us. How do you make it grow so big, so fat, so juicy? What does *La Señora* Maria Juana do to make it grow like that?"

Panfilo shrugged his shoulders. "*Señores*, we do the same thing that you do. The same water. The same soil. The same earth. The same sun."

Then Panfilo thought a minute. "The sun, the sun. *Señores*, there is something different."

The men gathered around Panfilo. "Yes, Panfilo. The sun? The sun?"

"Well, I don't know if I should tell you this. *La Señora* told me not to tell anyone. You know the *padre*, the priest, he might not like it so much, but *La Señora*, in the morning when the sun comes up, well, she holds up her hand like she's praying to the sun, and then a breeze comes, and the seeds fall to the ground. That's the only thing that's different."

"Ah, yes, Panfilo. It's the only thing that's different. Have another *cerveza*."

The men gathered around *El Capitán* and they said to him, "She prays to the sun! Not to Jesus Christ and *La Virgen*, as we've been taught."

El Capitán said, "Yes, this Maria Juana must be a *bruja*, praying to the sun."

"Yes, a *bruja!*"

Meanwhile, Panfilo was sitting away from the men, and he continued with his beers. Another one and another one until he passed out.

When Panfilo awoke he sat up and rubbed his eyes. Looking around he saw no one there. No Juanita. No men. He was all alone, all by himself in the *cantina*.

But he did see daylight coming through the windows, and he said to himself, "*Ay, Dios!* I have to get rid of this headache and get ready for work with *La Señora* Maria Juana."

As he came out of the *cantina*, he saw the men from the night before on their horses. They were speaking angrily, and he went closer to them to hear what they were saying.

They were talking about *La Señora* Maria Juana. They were talking about how they were going to get her. About how they were going to hurt her!

Panfilo got very frightened, and he ran all the way to the *ranchito*. When he got there he found *La Señora* with her hand stretched out to the sun in prayer, and the breeze came and blew the kernels of corn to the four directions, with the rest falling to the earth.

Panfilo ran up to *La Señora* and yelled at her, "*Señora*, hurry! Hurry! We have to go!"

La Señora looked at Panfilo and said, "*¿Panfilo, qué pasa?* Are you hung over? What's the matter with you?"

"*Señora*, the men are coming to get you! They think you're a *bruja*. We have to go. We have to hurry!"

La Señora didn't believe him until she heard what sounded like thunder, but it was the sound of men riding hard on horses. Riding fast. Then she believed him, and Panfilo took her hand, and they began to run up to the hills to hide.

But *La Señora* stopped him. She went back into her home. There she put her hand into a sack, and she put something into her pocket. *La Señora* then told Panfilo, "Now Panfilo, we can go."

They hurried up into the hills to hide behind some rocks as the men came into the *ranchito*. The men were on their horses, with their pistols drawn, calling out in front of her door, "Maria Juana! Maria Juana! Come out!"

But there was no one there to respond to them. There was nothing there but the silence.

The men got off of their horses, went up to the house and kicked down the door, storming their way into her home. They found nothing different, nothing that would be hiding secrets. The secrets of a *bruja*.

But they were not satisfied. They turned over the table. Nothing. They threw the chairs, her mattress, her bed. Nothing. Her pictures. Everything on her shelves came down. Crashing, breaking. Until there was nothing left. And still there were no secrets to be found.

In their anger and frustration, they went out to the field of corn. And standing before it *El Capitán* reached down and tore up a stalk of corn. Yelling to the men he said, "*Muchachos*, here is what we are looking for. The evil down in its roots!"

And the men in a frenzy pulled up every stalk. Every last one to its roots. Until that whole field, every stalk, lay flat against the earth.

The men looked back at the field, and they were satisfied that they had protected their families and their *pueblo* from such evil corn. Their work done, they returned to the safety of their homes.

La Señora Maria Juana and Panfilo came back down from the hills. They first came into her home, where they found it turned inside out. The floor was cluttered with the broken pieces of her furniture. She calmly went over and began picking up the pieces.

Panfilo, seeing *La Señora* close to tears, said, "*Señora*, I am strong. I can fix all this." And he picked up her mattress and turned over her bed on its right side.

They worked and worked to get her home back into some order. Then they went outside. And there outside, seeing the corn whose tassels once reached up to the sky now flat against the earth, destroyed, *La Señora* Maria Juana could no longer hold back her tears. She fell to her knees and cried out, "No, no, no. ¡*Ya No!*"

Panfilo came over, knelt down beside her, and very gently picked her up. He told her, "*Señora*, come. You must rest." He took her back inside the house and sat her down in her chair. "*Señora*, rest here. You must sleep. You must rest. I'll go out and take care of everything."

La Señora Maria Juana laid her head down and fell asleep, exhausted.

Panfilo went out into the field and gathered up the stalks of corn and set them up in piles and smoothed out the dirt and the land. Panfilo worked hard, very hard, all through the night.

When *La Señora* Maria Juana woke up and looked out the window, she saw the sun was already so bright that it must be high in the sky, so high that she had missed her prayer to the sun.

She ran outside, and there she saw Panfilo, with his hand filled with corn stretched out to the sun in prayer. Then the breeze came and blew the kernels of corn to the four directions, with the rest falling to the earth.

Quiero contar otro de los cuentos de Lupe La Loca. Este cuento se llama, "La mujer del maíz", y es la historia de la señora María Juana.

María Juana era una mujer mayor con el pelo canoso, arrugas, y una espalda fuerte. Vivía sola en un ranchito, donde tenía un campo lleno de calabazas, chiles, y sobre todo maíz.

Pánfilo trabajaba para la señora María Juana. Lo llamaban el Tontito del pueblo. Era sencillamente muy lento. Nadie en el pueblo le daba trabajo.

Pero la señora María Juana lo empleó. Necesitaba ayuda con las tareas del rancho. Así que todos los días Pánfilo iba a los campos y la ayudaba a cuidar del maíz.

Cada día cuando el sol salía por detrás de las colinas, María Juana cogía un manojo de maíz y alzaba la mano al sol en oración. La brisa se llevaba algunos granos de maíz hacia los cuatro puntos cardinales, y el resto caía a la tierra. Era un rezo que la señora hacía al sol todos los días, y después de rezar ella y Pánfilo trabajaban en el campo.

Un día recogieron tantas mazorcas de maíz que llenaron todos los sacos. ¡Había demasiado maíz!

Por eso, la señora María Juana dijo a Pánfilo, "Esto es demasiado maíz para nosotros. Llévate este saco para la gente del pueblo." Pánfilo cogió el maíz que sobraba y se dirigió hacia el pueblo.

Se fué a la cantina, porque allí era donde todos los hombres se reunían a diario. Dejó el saco de maíz en medio de la cantina y dijo, "Señores, este elote de la señora María Juana es para Uds. Ella se lo regala. Pueden hacer con ello lo que quieran."

Entonces Pánfilo se fué a un rincón y se sentó solo, y allí se bebió su cerveza.

Los hombres se reunieron alrededor del maíz y dijeron, "Este elote es gordo y grande. ¡Miren, se aprieta un poco y le sale jugo!"

Así que se fueron al Capitán, el cual no era capitán de verdad sino que lo llamaban así.

Le dijeron, "Capitán, mire. La señora María Juana nos envió este elote. ¿Cómo lo hace? Tan grande, tan gordo, tan jugoso. Y el nuestro es tan pequeño."

El Capitán, alisándose el bigote, dijo, "Bueno, muchachos, no sé. Quizás sea el agua."

Los hombres continuaron, "Capitán, no sabemos lo que hace. Su elote crece alto hasta los cielos."

"¿Hasta los cielos, muchachos? ¿Qué clase de elote puede ser ése que crece hasta los cielos? ¿Adónde van las raíces?"

"Sí, Capitán, las raíces. ¡Deben ir para abajo, para abajo, para abajo hasta el infierno!"

"Sí, muchachos, esas raíces deben ir para abajo hasta el infierno. Esas son cosas del diablo. ¡Esa mujer debe ser una bruja!"

"Sí, Capitán, por eso el elote es tan grande. Su magia negra debe hacer que crezca tanto."

El Capitán juntó a todos los hombres, y hablaron de cómo iban a librar al pueblo de aquella maldad. Miraron a su alrededor y vieron a Pánfilo. Entonces miraron otra vez y vieron a Juanita—Juanita la de las caderas ondulantes.

La llamaron para que viniera hasta ellos. Ella se puso muy contenta porque quería saber lo que estaba pasando. Le explicaron el plan que tenían para ella.

"Mañana, Juanita, ve a encontrarte con Pánfilo cuando regrese al pueblo. Tráelo a la cantina, y le daremos bastantes cervezas para que nos cuente todo acerca de ese elote."

La mañana siguiente fué como otra mañana cualquiera. El sol salió por detrás de las colinas, y la señora María Juana alzó su mano llena de maíz al sol en oración. Una brisa vino y se llevó los granos hacia los cuatro puntos cardinales y lo que quedó cayó a la tierra.

La señora y Pánfilo estuvieron todo el día trabajando en los campos de maíz, cavando y sacando las malas hierbas. Y una vez más, al final del día, había demasiado maíz. Por lo tanto, la señora hizo que Pánfilo llenara un saco con el maíz sobrante y le dijo que lo llevara al pueblo igual que había hecho el día anterior. Pánfilo llenó el saco y se encaminó hacia el pueblo.

Y quién aparece en este momento sino Juanita, la cual se acerca a Pánfilo y le dice, "Pánfilo, eres tan fuerte. Mírate. Tus hombros grandes. Llevas ese saco pesado con tanta facilidad. ¡Ay, Pánfilo!"

Ninguna mujer había jamás hablado a Pánfilo, y mucho menos de este modo. Pánfilo no sabía qué decir.

Juanita continuó, "Pánfilo, ¿podría ir contigo de vuelta al pueblo? Cuando lleguemos podríamos ir a la cantina. Y me podrías invitar a una cerveza."

La carga que llevaba Pánfilo a la espalda se hizo mucho menos pesada, igual que sus pies, y volvieron al pueblo en nada y menos.

Cuando entró en la cantina con Juanita a su lado, dejó el saco de maíz en el suelo. Dijo a todos los hombres que había allí, "Señores, este saco de elote se lo envía la señora María Juana." Cuando había terminado de hablar, se fué a su sitio en el rincón y se sentó con Juanita al lado.

Los hombres se acercaron y le dijeron, "Pánfilo, ¿cómo estás?"

El les contestó, "Bien, señores."

"Pánfilo, ¿quieres una cerveza? ¡Una cerveza para Pánfilo!"

Le pusieron delante una cerveza. Y una para Juanita también. Entonces le dieron otra cerveza. Y otra más. Los hombres pensaron, "Tres ó cuatro cervezas. ¡Esto debe aflojarle la lengua!"

Entonces le preguntaron, "Pánfilo, este elote que nos traes. ¿Cómo es que es tan grande, tan gordo, tan jugoso? ¿Qué hace la señora María Juana para que crezca así?"

Pánfilo se encogió de hombros. "Señores, hacemos lo mismo que Uds. La misma agua. La misma tierra. El mismo sol."

Entonces Pánfilo pensó durante un minuto. "El sol, el sol. Señores, hay algo diferente."

Los hombres se juntaron alrededor de Pánfilo. "Sí, Pánfilo. ¿El sol? ¿El sol?"

"Bueno, no sé si debería decírselo. La señora me dijo que no se lo dijera a nadie. Puede que al padre no le guste demasiado, pero la señora, por la mañana cuando sale el sol, pues, alza la mano como si estuviera rezando al sol, y entonces viene una brisa, y los granos caen al suelo. Esa es la única cosa que es diferente."

"Ah, sí, Pánfilo. Es la única cosa diferente. Toma otra cerveza."

Los hombres se reunieron en torno al Capitán y le dijeron, "¡Esa mujer reza al sol! No a Jesucristo y a la Virgen, como hemos sido enseñados."

El Capitán dijo, "Sí, esta María Juana debe ser una bruja, rezando al sol."

"¡Sí, una bruja!"

Mientras tanto, Pánfilo estaba sentado aparte de los hombres, y seguía con sus cervezas. Otra y otra hasta que perdió el sentido.

Cuando Pánfilo despertó, se incorporó y se frotó los ojos. Miró alrededor y no vió a nadie. Ni a Juanita. Ni a los hombres. Estaba completamente solo, a solas en la cantina.

Pero, sí vió la luz del día entrando por las ventanas, y se dijo a sí mismo. "¡Ay, Dios! Tengo que quitarme este dolor de cabeza y despabilarme para ir a trabajar con la señora María Juana."

Cuando salió de la cantina, vió a los hombres de la noche anterior montados en sus caballos. Estaban hablando exaltadamente, y Pánfilo se acercó para enterarse de lo que estaban diciendo.

Estaban hablando de la señora María Juana. Hablaban de cómo iban a ir a por ella. ¡De cómo le iban a hacer daño!

Pánfilo se asustó muchísimo, y corrió todo el camino hasta el ranchito. Cuando llegó, encontró a la señora María Juana con su mano alzada hacia el sol en oración, y vino la brisa y se llevó los granos de maíz hacia los cuatro puntos cardinales, y lo que quedó cayó a la tierra.

Pánfilo corrió hacia la señora y le gritó, "¡Señora, de prisa, de prisa! ¡Nos tenemos que ir!"

La señora miró a Pánfilo y dijo, "¿Pánfilo, qué pasa? ¿Estás con resaca? ¿Qué te pasa?"

"¡Señora, los hombres vienen a por Ud.! Piensan que es una bruja. Tenemos que irnos. ¡Nos tenemos que dar prisa!"

La señora no lo creyó hasta que escuchó lo que parecía un trueno, pero que era el sonido de los hombres cabalgando a galope. Cabalgando velozmente. Entonces, lo creyó, y Pánfilo cogió su mano, y empezaron a correr hacia las colinas para esconderse.

Pero la señora lo detuvo. Volvió a su casa. Allí metió su mano en un saco, y puso algo en su bosillo. La señora dijo entonces a Pánfilo, "Ahora, Pánfilo, podemos irnos."

Se apresuraron hacia las colinas para esconderse detrás de unas rocas al mismo tiempo que los hombres llegaban al ranchito. Los hombres estaban montados a caballo, con sus pistolas, y llamando a la puerta, "¡María Juana! ¡María Juana! ¡Venga afuera!"

Pero no había nadie para responder. No había nada sino el silencio.

Los hombres desmontaron, se fueron para la casa y echaron abajo la puerta a patadas, y así entraron por la fuerza. No encontraron nada raro, nada que guardara secretos. Los secretos de una bruja.

Pero no estaban satisfechos. Volcaron la mesa. Nada. Tiraron por el suelo y destrozaron las sillas, el colchón, la cama. Nada. Las fotos. Todo lo que había en las estanterías fué a parar al suelo, quebrándose, rompiéndose. Hasta que no quedó nada. Y por mucho que buscaran no había secretos que encontrar.

En su rabia y frustración, se dirigieron al campo de maíz. Y allí el Capitán arrancó una de las plantas. Gritando a los hombres, dijo, "Muchachos, aquí está lo que buscamos. ¡La maldad está abajo en las raíces!"

Los hombres arrancaron frenéticamente todas las plantas de maíz hasta las raíces. Hasta que el campo entero, todas las plantas, quedaron tiradas por el suelo.

Los hombres volvieron a mirar el campo, y quedaron satisfechos porque habían protegido a sus familias y a su pueblo de un maíz tan diabólico. Con el trabajo ya hecho, volvieron a la seguridad de sus hogares.

La señora María Juana y Pánfilo bajaron de las colinas. Primero, entraron en la casa, donde encontraron todo destrozado. El suelo estaba lleno de muebles rotos. Con calma la señora María Juana empezó a recoger los pedazos.

Pánfilo, viendo a la señora a punto de llorar, dijo, "Señora, soy fuerte. Yo puedo arreglar todo esto." Y recogió el colchón y puso la cama derecha.

Trabajaron y trabajaron para poner la casa en orden. Entonces salieron afuera. Y allí afuera, mirando al maíz cuyos penachos una vez habían llegado hasta el cielo, y ahora estaban tirados en la tierra, destrozados, la señora María Juana no pudo aguantar más las lágrimas. Cayó de rodillas y gritó, "No, no, no. ¡Ya no!"

Pánfilo se acercó, se arrodilló a su lado, y muy tiernamente la levantó en sus brazos. Le dijo, "Señora, venga. Debe descansar." La llevó dentro de la casa y la sentó en su silla. "Señora, descanse aquí. Debe dormir. Debe descansar. Yo me ocuparé de todo."

La señora María Juana echó su cabeza a un lado y se quedó dormida, exhausta.

Pánfilo se fué al campo y recogió todas las plantas de maíz y las apiló y rastrilló la tierra. Trabajó duro, muy duro, toda la noche.

Cuando la señora María Juana despertó y miró por la ventana, vió que el sol estaba tan brillante que debía estar alto en el cielo, tan alto que ella ya había perdido su rezo de cada mañana.

Corrió afuera, y allí vió a Pánfilo, con una mano llena de maíz alzada hacia el sol en oración. Entonces vino la brisa y se llevó los granos de maíz hacia los cuatro puntos cardinales, cayendo el resto a la tierra.

ANGELO THE STOWAWAY

By Abelardo Delgado

It was only recently that this story was told. It is the story of Angelo, the boy stowaway. Even though this story goes back to 1492, it was not until recently that we learned about it. In fact, it was during the Pope's visit to Santo Domingo that the story came to be known.

An old Indian woman, claiming to be the sixteenth descendant of another Indian woman, had kept the story to herself. Then she decided that, having no one else to pass the story to, she would make it public. By sharing it with the Pope she knew she would be sharing it with the world.

She had kept the story in an old wooden box. She knew it by heart, but it had been written long ago by the first Indian who had learned to write in Spanish. She got the attention of one of the Pope's guards and handed the box to him. He in turn gave it to the Pope. The box contained several old, wrinkled papers that were legible still. This is the story that was written on those wrinkled old papers.

ANGELO THE STOWAWAY

After Christopher Columbus had obtained money for his now-famous voyage to what he thought would be India, he went on to recruit his crew. He had to have enough men for each of the three *caravelas*, the *Pinta*, the *Niña*, and the *Santa María*.

History confirms what the ancient papers say about the trouble he had finding enough men to join him in this trip. The many men he talked to turned him down, saying he was crazy. They all feared that they would reach the end of the sea and fall off and die.

Angelo was an orphan boy of only 12 years at this time. He had heard about Colon, as Columbus is known in Spanish. He was interested in going with him.

As desperate as Colon was for a crew, he was not about to sign up a 12-year-old boy. He was desperate but not that desperate.

But Angelo insisted, "Please, Mr. Colon, let me go with you. I am young, I know, and I am not too tall, but I am very strong. I can already do a man's work. Please, sir, let me be part of your crew. I want to go with you, I must go with you."

Colon simply shook his head and sent Angelo away.

Angelo came back a few more times, but the answer from Colon was always the same. "You are too young. You cannot join my crew. Go away. Don't come and bother me again."

Colon began to make all kinds of promises to the potential recruits. Some men began to join his crew. Many of those who joined had very little going for them. They had very little to lose, even if they were to lose their lives. The idea of becoming part of a great adventure attracted others to join. Some dreamed of the riches that Colon said awaited them, and they ended up signing on. Colon also told them that by going with him they would become men of destiny. God wanted them to go West, and West they should go.

During the days leading to the departure, Colon had his crew bring plenty of water, food, and other supplies aboard. Angelo sat by the pier, watching the men load the provisions. He noticed they were loading some sacks full of grain. He knew that because he was small for his age, once on board he could fit into one of those sacks and hide.

Finally the day neared when Colon and his crew were to board the three *caravelas* and go into the unknown. Many well-wishers and the families of some of the crew members would come to bid them *adios*. Sails would be set to capture the wind, and off they would go.

The night before they departed, Angelo swam to the *Pinta* and climbed aboard. Angelo had made up his mind that he was going along even if Colon had denied him the opportunity of becoming a sailor like him.

Angelo had planned it well. He carried a sack with hard cheese and even harder bread. He also carried two large bottles of water, some dry meat, and some fruit. He had no idea how long the trip would take.

He did not know if the little food he had brought would last. He was even more worried about the water. He had heard it said that you can go a long time without food but not too long without water. Angelo was worried but determined to go. Angelo was young, but he was not dumb. He knew he had to ration the food and the water. He was going to take small portions, enough to keep himself alive. Angelo did not really know what to expect, but he was sure of one thing: He wanted to go on Colon's voyage.

Angelo had also thought about what would happen if he was discovered. Maybe they would kill him and throw him overboard. Thinking about all of that, his face and hands perspired and his eyes shed a few tears.

The night that he boarded the *Pinta* was a moonless night. The crew was celebrating the voyage by having a few drinks in the *cantina*. Others were kissing and blessing their loved ones. Some gave instructions to their older children as to what to do if they did not return.

A couple of the crew were aboard the ship. They stood guard. They were chosen from those who had no families. They did not expect a young boy to swim to the ship and sneak aboard.

Once Angelo had made his way onto the ship, making sure he was not seen or heard, he went right to the storage room below. Once below he took out a sack that looked like the others already in piles and got into it, making sure he could breathe. He made sure the sack was out of the way in the darkest corner. He made sure the crew would have to go through many sacks before they got to where he was. He went to sleep but not before saying some extra prayers. He knew the next day they would be at sea. He gave God a big smile, winked his eye, and said good night.

The days passed. Many of those days Angelo had a big problem that he had not anticipated. He got seasick. One particular time, when the sea got too turbulent, some crates fell and cut his head.

He survived those problems and many others. He adapted to the routine of the crew. He knew when they usually came down to get food supplies. He soon learned that he could add to the food he brought by using some of theirs. He only took a little bit to keep them from noticing it.

More days passed. Angelo had no way of knowing whether it was day or night at first. Later he discovered a tiny hole on the ceiling of the supply room. During the day a ray of sunshine entered through it. At nighttime when it was not cloudy, he could make out the moon or a couple of stars through the tiny hole.

To avoid getting bored Angelo imagined what kind of adventures awaited him once they found land. He imagined how the people and places would look. He even scared himself when he thought that there might be monsters or wild animals unimagined yet by him. Without knowing them he feared them.

One day he finally heard a big commotion up on deck. Land had been sighted! They had reached *la India*. Colon had been right all along. As usual, but a bit more excited, Angelo used the time he knew no one would be coming down to exercise.

When anchor was dropped and the crew boarded the small boats to go ashore, Angelo got ready to swim. Angelo was a good, strong swimmer. Angelo had thought of presenting himself to Colon once they were on land. Maybe Colon, having seen Angelo's determination to join the adventure, would make him a member of the crew. Maybe Colon would even be proud of him. At any rate it would soon be dark, and he could swim ashore.

Angelo never got to find out how Colon would react to having a stowaway. When Angelo reached the shore, Colon had already gone inland with some of his men. He had left a small group of his crew behind. They were to keep an eye on the ships and wait for his return.

Angelo saw that the people from the island had surrounded the men left behind and killed them all. Later, Angelo found out that the people from the island had become angry because Colon had taken 10 women and 6 children from the Indians who greeted him. Angelo became quite frightened. He was so afraid that they would also kill him. He was shaking and calling on his guardian angel, and his tears were freely flowing.

Angelo thought he was dead when he felt a hand touch his shoulder. He slowly turned to see who it was, fearing the worst. He saw that it was a boy about his age, one of the strange people.

The boy smiled and signaled for Angelo to follow him. Angelo followed right behind through small tracks among the bushes and trees. The boy kept smiling and signaling for Angelo to follow.

Angelo was afraid, but he had no other choice than to follow. It was very dark, but the boy knew his way. It seemed to Angelo that they had walked for hours before they reached a village with a few huts. He counted seven small huts. They seemed to be empty. Maybe the inhabitants were the same people who had killed Colon's men. Maybe they would soon return and kill him, too. Maybe the boy had made him his prisoner.

Finally they stopped. The boy spoke to Angelo, "Ixta, Ixta, Ixta." The boy pointed to himself as he said that.

Angelo imitated him, saying his own name, "Angelo, Angelo, Angelo." He finally said, *"Yo soy Angelo."*

They mispronounced each other's name, but eventually they got it well enough. The boy from the island said, "Anxelo." Angelo said, "Ista."

The boy offered Angelo a gourd filled with fresh water. Angelo drank. His fear had made him quite thirsty. He asked for more water. He was tired and he was still scared. The two boys could not communicate, so they stared at each other. They studied each other for a long while in silence.

The people from the village finally appeared. There was quite a commotion as they got to their huts.

Ixta grabbed Angelo's hand and pulled him over to where a man, a woman, and a small girl were standing. The girl appeared to be a few years younger than Angelo. They were startled to see the boy. Ixta talked to them in their own language. Later Angelo was to learn that language, which was Nahuatl. Other people came close to take a look at Angelo. He looked like the people they had just killed and like the others who had taken their children and women. They had anger in their eyes. Angelo sensed that his fate was the subject of so much discussion. Soon he could tell that Ixta was pleading for his life.

They took him over to some other people who were the leaders in the village. Angelo was sweating and shaking with new fear. Ixta's parents talked to the leaders. They signaled for Ixta to take Angelo inside the hut. The little girl went with them. Ixta introduced his sister to Angelo.

"Techintla," said the girl.

"Angelo," said Angelo.

After a while Ixta's parents came into the hut. They were smiling. Angelo relaxed. The people in the village had decided to keep Angelo and not to harm him. They thought that if they did this, the strange men who had taken their women and children would take good care of them.

They referred to Colon and his men as "those who had appeared in the sea monsters." They took the ships to be sea monsters.

It was not possible to tell Angelo all this because he did not understand them. It was enough to tell him the good news with gestures and smiles. Ixta took his arm in a sign of greeting. Techintla did the same. The grown-ups took Angelo outside, where the other people from the village were waiting. The leaders came close to greet him, and all of them shouted happily and raised their lances.

That night Angelo ate well. This made up for all those days he had eaten nothing but his own rations.

That night and many others passed. Angelo grew into a strong young man. He never referred to these people as Indians, since he had never heard the word. Later he learned they were of the Palitla tribe, and so was he.

Angelo thought of himself as a member of the Palitla tribe with much pride. He soon learned their ways and their language. In turn he had taught all of them the Spanish language. He helped build a hut for himself and for his friend Ixta. He thought about him as the brother he had never had.

He thought of Ixta's parents as his very own and he respected them very much. They were old and wise and among the leaders of the village. The village had actually very little need for leaders as all of them knew what to do and how to behave.

He even learned about their gods and rites without renouncing his own. He clung to his *Cristo*, the *Cristo* he had learned in catechism when he still had had a mother and father back in Europe.

Angelo did not only take but gave as well. He taught them all about Christ. This wasn't much—only what he remembered from catechism. The Palitla people listened to Angelo speak of Christ and thought the story to be curious, even funny, but they respected Angelo's God. They respected Angelo's *Cristo* so much that they incorporated the cross symbol into their own religious symbols.

Stories by Modern Latino Storytellers

Angelo liked his new life very much. He never expected his coming as a stowaway in one of Colon's ships would have turned out in this manner.

After the years passed his memory of Europe seemed so far away. His clothes had worn out and now he dressed like the other people from the Palitla tribe. Despite his lighter skin Angelo blended well since he was short like them. After a while not much fuss was made of the boy stowaway, Angelo.

The rest of the story goes the way of many stories. Colon never came back to the island of the Palitla people. Since he had not found any gold he did not think of returning. He had been angry when he learned part of his crew had been executed but he was too busy even for revenge. The Palitlas did have gold. It was to be found by a waterfall. They did not think of this mineral as important as having fruit and animals to eat.

Angelo soon came to admire Techintla, whose name meant "happy heart," very much. He fell in love with Techintla and they had an original Palitla wedding. Angelo and Techintla had many children. These children were among the first *mestizos* with one big difference. These *mestizos* had been the product of love.

Many of these children moved out of the village. They went on to have their own children. By this time the white men from Europe were all around them.

The Palitlas were among the lucky ones that were never invaded or bothered in any way. They went on to continue their own way of life for a long time.

The old Indian woman who had turned the box that contained this story over to the Pope was herself one of the descendants of Angelo and Techintla.

APOLONIO NEVAREZ JACKSON

By Abelardo Delgado

In the *World Book Encyclopedia* we find the following statement about Dr. Albert Einstein's work: "His famous equation $E=mc^2$ became the foundation stone in the development of nuclear energy. Einstein developed his theory through deep philosophical thought and complex mathematical reasoning."

In a recent visit to Garden City, Kansas, I found that not to be true. It wasn't Einstein but an old, half-Chicano, half-Navajo cook who made the greatest contribution to Dr. Einstein's theory. The place for that great contribution was Chilili, New Mexico.

I was visiting Don Cosme Panyagua in the barrio of Las Nalgas in Garden City. It was around noon, so Don Cosme and his wife Elvira asked me to share the noon meal with them. I accepted.

A couple of their grandchildren came in, rolled a *tortilla* with *sopa de fideo,* grabbed two Pepsis from the refrigerator, and dashed back to the yard to continue their Star Wars battle. Two dead tree trunks were their spaceships.

Don Cosme was no longer fit to work out in the sugar-beet fields near Garden City, so the migrant Head Start had hired him to go every Friday and tell stories to the children. He liked his new job very much. I had gone to see him because I was evaluating the legal services in that area. He and his wife had been recent clients.

As we ate he began to tell the story of Apolonio Nevarez Jackson and Dr. Einstein. I was glad I had accepted the invitation to lunch because the food was delicious and I was hungry. Don Cosme and I ate our *sopa* and *caldo con tuetano* along with some freshly made *tortillas de harina*. He drank *canela caliente*. I had a Diet Pepsi. He paused as if to arrange in his mind the tale he was about to unload on me.

He referred to Dr. Einstein as Don Alberto, as if they had been old drinking buddies. I could just picture Dr. Einstein as a farm worker hoeing beets a *surco* away from Don Cosme.

Don Cosme began his tale by telling me he had been born in Dixon, New Mexico. He went on to tell me in a matter-of-fact tone that Dr. Einstein, the famous German-Swiss-American mathematician and physicist was rather fond of Mexican food. Dr. Einstein was especially fond of red chile from New Mexico. It was not uncommon for him to make special trips to small, out-of-the-way restaurants that specialized in *chile colorado* dishes.

"That's how I met Don Alberto," Don Cosme told me as he went on with the story in the same charming manner he used with the children on Fridays. The *chamaquitos* from the Head Start center loved him.

Don Cosme continued his story, "It was *un domingo*, and I had stopped for coffee at Chole's."

Chole, the owner, was a pleasantly plump woman. Her restaurant was in El Rito. Chole's cafe consisted of three small tables with two chairs each.

"When I got there five *Americanos* were already eating. One of them was the famous Don Alberto. I ordered coffee and two *sopaipillas*."

I had been in a hurry to visit other families that day. I felt like cutting him off and excusing myself, but by now I was hooked. I wanted to know how the *cuento* of Don Alberto turned out.

Don Cosme continued, "Chole knew Don Alberto. She made the introductions. We shook hands. I was surprised to hear him speak in Spanish. His Spanish was a bit *mocho,* but he was understandable."

Don Cosme laughed as he got to this part. He displayed a good set of very fine teeth. It could be due to the fluoride in the water in the region where he had grown up in New Mexico.

After learning that Don Alberto liked *chile colorado,* Don Cosme recommended the restaurant in Chilili. Apolonio Nevarez Jackson was the owner, cook, waiter, dishwasher, and bouncer. The latter was seldom needed, only when a *borracho* would come in and try to bother the customers. Apolonio would gently but forcefully throw him out. His restaurant had a big name for such a tiny place. It was known as *La Rosa Abierta de Dia y de Noche*. The Open Rose of Day and Night consisted of a long counter with four stools. Apolonio had bought all this in the army surplus store in Albuquerque.

Some of this story is documented history. Everyone in Chilili knows it. I think the story is preserved in vinegar. It has stayed pretty much the same throughout the years. No one dares to add or subtract anything from it.

The two grandchildren ran in. Each one stopped to give Don Cosme a big kiss and big hug. They ran out shouting, "The force be with you, grandpa." Hearing them, I thought how easy it is for Chicano children to jump in and out of their two cultures.

Don Cosme continued, "It wasn't until the following year that Don Alberto got around to eating at *La Rosa Abierta de Dia y de Noche*. I have that date carved in my memory." Upon saying this Don Cosme touched his forehead. *"Grabado en la memoria."*

He paused. He was trying to arrange in his mind what part of the story to say next. He softly said, "July 7."

He did not give the year. That struck me as odd. I wanted to ask him for the year. He had already started with his *cuento* on a new route. I did not dare interrupt him or fall behind.

Apolonio doubled as a *curandero*. He had some herbs in the back of the restaurant. He also had an adobe hut in the back. He lived there. Apolonio was one of the champion *dicho* sayers in the whole state of New Mexico. He liked to discuss philosophy and religion with his customers. He was very knowledgeable in these subjects. It looked like he had spent the better part of his life in a seminary studying to become a Jesuit priest.

His English was flawless, and so was his Spanish. Usually, of course, he spoke Navajo. He used to listen to the Navajo radio station while he prepared the orders. Some said he was a member of the peyote Indian church. Others said he was a devout Catholic who went to Mass every day. Yet many swore he was an atheist who believed in nothing. All of these were possible, but all were rumors. The truth is that he did spend many hours reading all kinds of books. He liked to drink tequila and read. He said the drink helped him to concentrate better.

His true art was cooking. He liked to experiment with all kinds of food combinations. His specialty was *chile colorado*. He had a different chile dish each Sunday. Sometimes he went too far, like the time he put applesauce and raisins in his *chile colorado*.

Don Cosme went on, "The old problem that Don Alberto was having with his theories about time and matter was the dogma that matter cannot be either created or destroyed. In our way of thinking, it simply meant that if you added a pound of *frijoles* to a pound of rice you would end up with two pounds of food, right?"

I nodded, fully captured by his words.

"Wrong!" Don Cosme cut me off. "Let me go on with the story. Not all the credit should be given to Apolonio. Don Alberto was by then on the verge of arriving at the same idea. It was Apolonio who had the problem solved in the two-burner gas stove on which he cooked."

I continued to listen to the rest of the story, which Don Cosme unveiled at his own pace. The grandchildren interrupted once again. One had fallen off the spaceship and had scraped his elbow. The other was giggling about it. This made the other one cry even louder.

I had my third cup of hot cinnamon tea sweetened with brown sugar. Don Cosme joined me with a cup of his own as he got ready to finish the *cuento* of Apolonio Nevarez Jackson.

"The punch line of the story is that Apolonio had prepared a tasty *chile con carne* dish with various spices. He had added equal portions of rice and beans. Apolonio had known for a long time that when you cook rice and beans together, the finished dish weighs more than if you had cooked the same amount of rice and beans separately. Apolonio knew that this increase was known to millions of poor Mexicans who often had nothing but rice and beans to feed an entire family. It was as if God made the food *rendir*.

The food did indeed grow to feed the entire family. Mixing beans and rice always produced something extra. More taste, more protein, and actually more food was produced by mixing them together. Mixing a pound of rice with a pound of beans always gave you two pounds and some extra ounces.

When Apolonio served Don Alberto a plate of his *chile con carne* and explained all this to him, Don Alberto wanted to know why that happened. Don Alberto had never thought this could happen. His white hair stood up more than usual. His thick eyebrows, like rows of sugar beets with weeds, raised almost to meet the hair on his head when he realized that what Apolonio was saying negated the idea that matter cannot be either created or destroyed. *Arroz* and *frijoles* mixed together disproved the law that science had held up to that point. To add to Dr. Einstein's amazement, Apolonio added that any Indian and Mexican wife knew that.

The story goes on to say that Don Alberto ran out of *La Rosa Abierta de Dia y de Noche* as if death herself was chasing him. He went out like one of those rockets they were to invent much later. He did not even stop to pay for his *chile con carne*. All he had in his mind as he ran out was the miracle, the scientific miracle of *frijoles con arroz*.

If Apolonio had only been able to look inside Dr. Einstein's mind, he would have seen a right-side computer and a left-side computer operating at full capacity. At that very moment Dr. Einstein was formulating the theories that would become the foundation for experiments in atomic energy.

It wasn't too long after this that the first atomic bomb was tested in Los Alamos and others were dropped on Hiroshima and Nagasaki. Apolonio is not credited with the mass killings and destruction. No atomic submarine has been named after him, nor have workers from nuclear electrical plants thanked him for his contribution.

Apolonio Nevarez Jackson, Chicano and Navajo, will not be found in any page of the *World Book Encyclopedia*. Today it is even hard to find his ill-kept tomb in Chilili. Don Cosme tried once to have Anglo newspaper reporters write this story in the local papers. One had actually written it, but the editor decided not to run it.

I left Don Cosme's house. I thanked him and his wife for the meal, the hot *canela*, and the story. I asked Don Cosme if he would mind if I wrote the story just as he had told it to me. I wanted to share it with as many people as possible.

He answered, "What are stories for if not for sharing?"

I agreed, and here it is.

PANO AND LA GUADALUPANA: ALTAR ADVENTURES OF CHOLO, VATO, PANO, AND MAMA CHICA

By Dr. George Rivera

Pano's aunt, *Tia* Maria, came over in the morning as she did every day to take care of him. Pano was especially excited because his aunt had brought over Pamela, his older cousin. Cholo and Vato, his two dogs, were running around in circles because *Tia* had even brought their mother, Mama Chica.

"Today we're going to Our Lady of Guadalupe Church to clean the altar because it is December and the Feast of Guadalupe will soon begin," said *Tia* Maria. "Pano, you know that your *Tia* Guadalupana does this every year."

"And I will take care of you and the dogs while Mama works," Pamela said.

Cholo, Vato, Pano, and Mama Chica were so excited about going that they ran around in circles.

"A feast is what kings have. So is she a queen, *Tia*?" asked Pano.

"Our Lady of Guadalupe is very special. She is the Queen of the Americas and is the mother of us all," Pano's aunt said in a serious voice.

Mama Chica nudged Cholo and Vato with her nose so that they would pay attention instead of playing.

"We know, we know," barked Cholo and Vato, "Queen of the Americas and us."

When they got to the church, Pano's aunt made them walk very quietly when the priest came to meet them. (See fig. 25.)

"I am glad to see my favorite Guadalupana coming to help. And who are all these little ones? How can you tell these dogs apart?" asked Father Hidalgo.

"Cholo is dark brown, Vato is light brown, and Mama Chica is silver," answered Pano's aunt. "Is it okay to have them here?" she asked.

"I am sure that our Lady of Guadalupe would love these little dogs," said the priest.

Pano, Cholo, Vato, and Mama Chica just looked at each other because they had never seen this special lady.

"Look there on the altar," *Tia* Maria told them. "Do you see her?"

"Where, *Tia*?" asked Pano.

"There on the back wall of the altar," Pamela said, pointing to the back of the church.

Cholo started to bark, but Mama Chica ran up to him and nudged him so that he would be quiet.

"But I see her, I see her!" said Cholo.

There she was, bigger than any lady they had ever seen. *Tia* and Pamela made the sign of the cross. Pano kneeled down, and all of the dogs bowed their heads for a little while.

"All of you stay here while I clean the altar," *Tia* told them. "Take care of them, Pamela. Don't let them run and knock down any candles."

"Who is that man kneeling with all the roses?" asked Pano.

"That is Juan Diego, who saw *La Virgen* at Tepeyac. He was an Aztec Indian," answered Pamela.

"If you are so smart, when did this man see her?" asked Pano, trying to ask his cousin a very hard question.

"It was a long time ago, in the year 1531," answered Pamela. "Each year we honor her with a feast on December 12 because she is the mother of all who need her."

"How do you know all of this?" asked Pano.

"I know it because your *Tia* taught me everything about our Lady of Guadalupe," replied Pamela.

"Is she the Queen of all the Indians?" asked Pano.

"She is the Mother of Jesus, but she has a special place in her heart for all the people of Mexico and Latin America. She loved us so much that she even left her picture on Juan Diego's poncho. She looked just like that picture," said Pamela.

"Will we ever get to see her?" asked Pano.

"One day we will all see her, because we are all God's children," said Father Hidalgo as he overheard Pano asking so many questions.

"But what about Cholo, Vato, and Mama Chica? They are not children. They are little dogs. So what about them?" asked Pano.

"Yes, yes, what about us?" asked a concerned Mama Chica.

"To make sure that even your dogs will be with her someday, I will bless them," said Father Hidalgo.

Cholo, Vato, and Mama Chica were so happy that they ran around in circles by the altar. Pano hugged Cholo, Vato, and Mama Chica because he loved them and never wanted them to be away from him for even one day.

"Father blessed Cholo, Vato, and Mama Chica!" Pano told *Tia* Maria.

"That was very nice of Father Hidalgo. Did they thank him?" asked Pano's aunt.

"They did," laughed Pamela. "They all licked his hand."

When they got home, Pano's mother and father had just arrived from work.

"Did you have fun today, *mijo?*" asked Pano's father.

"Oh, yes, they did," said Pano's aunt as she packed her things to leave.

"They even saw Our Lady of Guadalupe on the altar and got a special blessing," Pamela added.

"Cholo, Vato, and Mama Chica got blessed!" exclaimed Pano.

"How wonderful, *mi jito,*" said Pano's mother as she hugged all of them.

"Come on, it's time to go," called *Tia* to Pamela and Mama Chica.

As she walked out the door, Mama Chica turned and barked at Cholo and Vato to remind them to be good because they had been blessed.

For the rest of the evening, they were very good. When Pano's mother put him to bed with Cholo and Vato beside him, she could hear Pano praying.

"Guadalupe, take care of my mama and papa, *Tia*, Cousin Pamela, Cholo, Vato, and Mama Chica, too," he said in a low voice.

After a long and wonderful day, they curled against each other and finally fell asleep.

THE FLOOD

By Patrick Mendoza

She had the distinct feeling that someone or something was watching her. Though she wasn't frightened, Amparo Salinas knew that whoever or whatever it was stood just outside her bedroom door in the long, drafty hallway on the second floor of her parents' house near the Cimmaron River. But when she looked, there was nothing there except that old wool coat and slouch hat hanging from the coat tree. With each breath of the mountain wind that came through the corridor, the coat seemed to beckon her with its armless sleeves, and Amparo could have sworn she heard it whisper her name.

"Aaaampaaarooo, Aaaampaaarooo."

When she told her mother of these things, her mother laughed at her and said, "Amparo, don't be silly. Most eight-year-olds hear and imagine that same kind of thing. There is nothing to worry about. The *padres* in church always say, 'When you hear voices that aren't there, you are either very old or it is *la voz de Dios* (the voice of God) calling to children.' Amparo, since you are not old, then it must be God. So watch what you do and be good."

This was not the first time Amparo had heard this speech, for she had gone to her mother before during these last two weeks of August 1934. Yet with each day's passing, the feeling of being watched overwhelmed Amparo. During the early evening, while doing her schoolwork in her room, the voice and feeling returned. She wasn't frightened, but she was concerned, so concerned that during the day at school she found it hard to concentrate in her third-grade class.

She knew something was going to happen either to her, to her family, or to the Moreno Valley, hidden away in the mountains of northern New Mexico. But what could happen to a valley? Had not the old ones said that the valley was not only protected by God but by all of his angels? It is how they said their small town of Angel Fire got its name.

Los viejos, the old ones, told the story of so long ago when the Ute Indians roamed this valley. In the early autumn and winter mornings, they saw dancing, colored lights above Agua Fria Peak. They believed that the lights, which were created by the sun's rays hitting the crystallization of the early morning air, were in fact the fires of the gods.

Because of that the Utes made the valley a sacred resting place for all warriors. When the black-robed *padres*, who came with the first *conquistadores* into the valley, tried to Christianize the Utes, the *padres* told the Utes that there was only one God. But to appease the Utes they added, "Maybe those lights are those of God's helpers, the ones called angels." And so it came to pass that those lights above Agua Fria Peak were called *El Fuego de Los Angeles*, the fire of the angels, or angel fire.

The thought of this story eased Amparo's mind, but she could not shake the feeling that she was being watched. That old wool coat still seemed at times to beckon her, and no matter how many times her mother comforted her, Amparo knew that something was going to happen. And then it did.

August is the rainy season, and on this particular day Amparo felt as if the heavens had opened up and dumped all of their reservoirs onto the valley. It was not unusual for the majestic blue of the mountain skies to darken with clouds in the afternoon and to drop rain almost daily, but today was different. The rains had started early that morning and had not let up. After a while it seemed that with each passing hour the intensity of the storm increased. And the dry land that was her parents' front yard soon became a river.

Close to nightfall this new river finally aroused her father's concern. He must get his family to higher ground before dark or face certain death from the flood that was getting closer to their door.

"Amparo," Carlos Salinas yelled to his daughter. "Get ready to leave. Your mother and I will take your little brother Felipe across the water first, then I will come back for you. Dress warmly and put on your raincoat. We may be out all night in this rain if we cannot get the car up high enough."

From her window on the second floor, Amparo could see her parents struggling to get Felipe across the ever-growing river in their yard. Afraid but ready, Amparo turned toward her bedroom door to go downstairs when she noticed the coat tree was empty. Her father, she thought, must have taken that wool coat and slouch hat for some protection against the raging weather outside.

But soon her thoughts were not of old coats and hats but of survival — hers and her family's. By now the weather had gotten worse, and it was raining so hard Amparo could barely see more than three yards in front of her. And though the sun would not set for another hour, the sky was already so black it looked like night.

Amparo's father finally returned to take her across the yard. She grabbed his hand firmly and started out into the blinding rain. As they crossed the increasing flood in their yard, Amparo was caught in a torrent of water, a flash flood caused by the Cimmaron River. Not tall enough to stand above this wave of water and not strong enough to withstand its onslaught, Amparo was swept away from her father's grasp. Weighted down by her many layers of clothing, the water took her down and turned her helpless body around and around in its swirling waters.

Just as she felt herself drowning and she could breathe no more, Amparo felt a strong arm reach down through the waters and grab her. As the arm grabbed her small body, she clawed at the sleeves of the jacket and held onto the arm with all of her remaining strength. And as that arm pulled her above the water's surface, Amparo's nostrils were filled with the smell of wet wool. She knew it was her father. Through the blinding rain she could barely make out the image of a man in a slouch hat, pulling her out of danger.

When Amparo was through coughing up the water she had swallowed and could see more clearly, there kneeling over her were her father and mother. She immediately reached up and hugged her father, crying, "Pa Pa, if it hadn't been for you, I surely would have drowned today. But when I felt you grab me, I hung onto your wool coat with all of my might. It was all that was there that I could feel and smell. Oh Pa Pa, I love you so much. And as I came out of the water all I could see was your image in that hat and you watching over me. Yes, truly, I would have died today. Hold me Pa Pa, just hold me."

As he held his precious daughter, Carlos Salinas was truly puzzled. He owned no wool coat or slouch hat, and though he had tried to save Amparo, he had failed. When he had finally caught up to where the water had taken her, he had found her safely on the shore. He did not understand what had happened, but it was not he who had saved Amparo.

From that day on Amparo and her family had no idea who or what had saved her on that terrible night, but they knew someone had been watching over her. Maybe it was *la voz de Dios* Amparo had heard, or maybe it was the voice of one of his helpers, for this was the town of Angel Fire. And from that day on, Amparo Salinas never again saw that wool coat or slouch hat hanging on that old coat tree just outside her bedroom door.

4

Finale

Glossary of Spanish Words

acequia—irrigation ditches held in common by community organizations of all landowners owning property on the ditch line. This system of communal water rights is one of the most important aspects of life in the Southwest. The annual cleaning of the acequia is a major event. *See* mayordomo.

adiós—good-bye

adivinanzas—riddles

agua—water

aguila—eagle

alabados—religious songs or mournful hymns often associated with members of the fraternity of Penitentes

amigo—friend

arroz—rice

barrilero—barrelman

borracho—drunkard

brujas—witches. The belief in witches is part of a complex legend system in Latino culture.

bueno—good, well

burro—donkey

caldo con tuetano—bone-marrow soup

caliente—hot

canela—cinnamon

cantina—tavern

caravela—Spanish galleon, a large ship common in the fifteenth and sixteenth centuries carreta de la muerte—a hand-carved wooden cart; the death cart of Doña Sebastiana

centavos—cents

cerveza—beer

chamaquitos—young children

chile colorado—red chile

chile con carne—chile with meat

chistes—short anecdotal stories, usually with a comic twist at the end

Christo—Jesus Christ

compadre—technically, the godparent of one's child; more commonly, a very close friend

con—with

coqueta—coquette, flirt

cuentista—storyteller

cuento—story

curandero—healer, a person who has the knowledge of the healing powers of plants and natural substances

dichos—proverbs

Dios—God

Domingo—Sunday

duendes—mischievous wandering spirits or dwarfs. The legend of the *duendes* is that after the Lord and the devil had their arguments at the beginning of time, some of the angels stayed with the Lord and some went with the devil. When the Lord closed the doors to heaven and the devil closed the doors to hell, many angels were caught between heaven and hell with no place to go. These angels came to earth and became the *duendes*. The *duendes* spend their time causing mischief in human affairs.

El Diablo—the devil

elote—corn

El Santo Niño—the Holy Child, Jesus Christ

entrega de novios—the delivery of the newlyweds. A part of the Hispanic wedding ceremony in which the newly wedded couple is presented to their families and they receive the blessing and advice of their families. The ceremony features verses sung and accompanied by violin and guitar.

frijoles—beans

gato—cat

grabado—recorded, engraved

hacienda—house

harina—flour

hija—daughter

hijo—son

Indio—Indian

Indio-Hispano—Indian-Hispanic; a term recognizing the mixed nature of a culture containing both Indian and Hispanic influences

jita—daughter, a term of great affection from a parent to a child

jito—son, a term of great affection from a parent to a child.

La Gloria—heaven

La Llorona—the Weeping Woman

león—lion

loco—crazy

Los Ancianos—the old ones. *The Old Ones of New Mexico,* by Robert Coles, is a wonderful book about the elders of Hispanic culture; it is highly recommended.

mayordomo—the ditch boss of the acequia, a position of much authority and prestige

memoria—memory

mijo—my son, a term of great affection from a parent to a child

mocho—chopped, cut up

muchachos—boys

muralistas—muralists

muy justo es.—It is very just.

nosotros—we

oso—bear

Padre—Father, priest

palomita—little dove

perro—dog

piñon—a pine tree that provides the edible piñon nut, a regional favorite

porque quisimos—because we wanted

primo—cousin

pueblo—village

raíces—roots

ranchito—a little ranch

rendir—produce

santeros—sculptors who carve small wooden statues of religious figures. *See* santos.

santos—small wooden carvings of Catholic saints and religious figures

Señor—mister, sir

Señora—married woman or an elder woman

Señorita—unmarried woman or a young woman

sopa—soup

sopa de fideo—soup with noodles

surco—row

tia—aunt

tilma—cloak

tio—uncle

tontito—fool, simpleton

una—one

viejita—little old lady

viejito—little old man

viejos—elderly people

voz—voice

Bibliography

Aranda, Charles. *Dichos: Proverbs and Sayings from the Spanish.* Santa Fe, N.M.: Sunstone Press, 1977.

Beatty, Judith, and Edward Garcia Kraul, eds. *The Weeping Woman, Encounters with La Llarona.* Santa Fe: The Word Process, 1988.

Boss, Gayle, and Cheryl Hellner. *Santo Making in New Mexico: Way of Sorrow, Way of Light.* Washington, D.C.: Potters House Press, 1991.

Brose, David A. *Do Not Pass Me By: A Celebration of Colorado Folklife.* Vols. 1 and 2. Available on cassette from Colorado Council on the Arts, Colorado Folk Arts Program, 750 Pennsylvania, Denver, CO 80203.

Brown, Lorin W. *Hispano Folklife of New Mexico.* Edited by Charles L. Briggs and Marta Weigle. Albuquerque: University of New Mexico Press, 1978.

Campa, Arthur L. *Hispanic Culture in the Southwest.* Norman: University of Oklahoma Press, 1979.

———. *Sayings and Riddles in New Mexico.* The University of New Mexico Bulletin, Language series, vol. 6, no. 2; whole no. 313. Albuquerque: University of New Mexico Press, 1937.

Caso, Alfonso. *The Aztecs: People of the Sun.* Norman: University of Oklahoma Press, 1958.

Chavez, Fray Angelico. *My Penitente Land.* Albuquerque: University of New Mexico Press, 1974.

Cobos, Rubén. *Refranés: Southwestern Spanish Proverbs.* Santa Fe: Museum of New Mexico Press, 1985.

Coles, Robert. *The Old Ones of New Mexico.* Albuquerque: University of New Mexico Press, 1973.

Cortes, Carlos E., ed. *Hispano Culture of New Mexico.* New York: Arno Press, 1976.

Dickey, Roland F. *New Mexico Village Arts.* Albuquerque: University of New Mexico Press, 1990.

Duran, Gloria. *Malince, Slave Princess of Cortez*. Hamden, Conn.: Linnet Books, 1993.

Espinosa, Aurelio. *The Folklore of Spain in the American Southwest: Traditional Spanish Folk Literature in Northern New Mexico and Southern Colorado*. Edited by J. Manuel Espinosa. Norman: University of Oklahoma Press, 1985.

Espinosa, José Manuel. *Spanish Folktales from New Mexico*. New York: American Folklore Society, 1937.

Everts, Dana L. *Tradiciones del Valle, Folklore Collected in the San Luis Valley*. Edited by Mark V. Dalpiaz and Dana L. Everts. Alamosa, Colo.: Rio Grande Arts Center, 1986.

Frank, Larry. *New Kingdom of the Saints, Religious Art of Northern New Mexico, 1780-1907*. Santa Fe, N.M.: Red Crane Books, 1992.

Glazer, Mark, ed. *A Dictionary of Mexican American Proverbs*. New York: Greenwood Press, 1987.

Paredes, Américo. *Folktales of Mexico*. Chicago: University of Chicago Press, 1970.

Payne, R. B. *Recuerdos del Pasado, Recollections of the Past*. Available from Exceptional Student Training Institute, Box 134, San Luis, CO 81152.

Rael, Juan B. *Cuentos Españoles de Colorado y Nuevo Méjico*. New York: Arno Press, 1977.

Robe, Stanley L., ed. *Hispanic Folktales from New Mexico: Narratives from the R. D. Jameson Collection*. Folklore Studies, 30. Berkeley, Los Angeles, London: University of California Press, 1977.

———. *Hispanic Legends from New Mexico: Narratives from the R. D. Jameson Collection*. Folklore & Mythology Studies, 31. Berkeley, Los Angeles, London: University of California Press, 1980.

Steele, Thomas J. "The Death Cart: Its Place among the Santos of New Mexico," *Colorado Magazine* 55 (1978):1-14.

Thompson, Stith. *The Folktale*. New York: Holt, Reinhart & Winston, 1946.

Weigle, Marta, and Peter White. *The Lore of New Mexico*. Albuquerque: University of New Mexico Press, 1988.

Yolen, Jane, ed. *Favorite Folktales from Around the World*. New York: Pantheon Books, 1986.

About the Author and Biographies of Contributing Latino Storytellers

Angel Vigil

Angel Vigil is Chairman of the Fine and Performing Arts Department and Director of Drama at Colorado Academy in Denver, Colorado. He is an accomplished performer, stage director, and teacher. As an arts administrator he has developed many innovative educational arts programs for schools and art centers.

Angel is an award-winning storyteller. His awards include the Governor's Award for Excellence in Education, a Master Artist Award for storytelling from the Colorado Council on the Arts, and an Individual Artist Fellowship from the Denver Commission on Cultural Affairs.

Angel also cowrote *Cuentos*, a play for schools based on the traditional stories of the Hispanic Southwest. He is a featured storyteller on *Do Not Pass Me By: A Celebration of Colorado Folklife*, a folk arts collection produced by the Colorado Council on the Arts.

Abelardo Delgado

Abelardo B. Delgado was born in Mexico and came to the United States in 1943 not knowing a word of English. He has a bachelor of science degree in Spanish and a secondary education degree from the University of Texas at El Paso. He is a nationally known consultant on migrant workers, culture and folklore, and undocumented worker programs. He is one of the pioneers in creating and promoting Chicano literature, and he is one of the most anthologized Chicano poets. His novel, *Letters to Louise*, won the first prize in literature from Tonatiuh, Quinto Sol, Berkeley, California.

Geraldina Lawson

Geraldina Lawson grew up Chicana in the border town of Laredo, Texas. She has developed a *cuento* series based on a character from her childhood, *Lupe La Loca*.

She has been telling *cuentos* professionally since 1989, taking her stories to schools, professional groups, festivals, and art galleries. She is the owner of *Artes del Pueblo* art gallery in Denver, Colorado. In 1990 the Colorado Council of the Arts awarded her a master/apprentice folk arts grant. She not only tells the traditional *cuentos*, but she is especially active in creating new *cuentos*.

Patrick Mendoza

For 17 years Patrick Mendoza has made his living as a professional storyteller. He has toured the United States as well as England, Ireland, Scotland, Canada, and Mexico with his tales and songs of Americana. His most recent original work is a folk opera, *Song of the Plains*, based on the story of the Cheyenne Native Americans and the Sand Creek tragedy.

Dr. George Rivera

Dr. George Rivera is a faculty member in the Department of Sociology at the University of Colorado at Boulder. He has published two books about the effect of AIDS on youth: *HIV/AIDS: Images of Hispanic Youth* and *Latinos: Youth Living With HIV/AIDS in the Family*. He is presently working with illustrator Tony Ortega on a series of children's books featuring the further adventures of Cholo, Vato, and Pano.

Juan Francisco Marín and Jennifer Audrey Lowell (Translators)

Juan, born in Spain, has a degree in history and geography from the University of Sevilla. Jennifer earned her B.A. in Spanish at the University of Colorado in Boulder.

Jennifer and Juan teach languages and translate. They have collaborated on everything from bilingual, culturally-focused, suggestopeadic curricula and children's curricula and children's literature, to a television program that teaches English as a second language to children. They are married, have two children and divide their time between Colorado and Spain.